Praise for *The Bodies Keep Coming*

"In the mode of Atul Gawande and other doctors of color, Brian H. Williams tells riveting stories about the traumas inherent in our country, while laying out how racism infects and weakens our healthcare systems. This is a page-turner!"

—**Mary Karr**, *New York Times*–bestselling author of *The Liar's Club*, *Cherry*, and *Lit* (Liar's Club series)

"An engrossing account of Dr. Brian H. Williams's quintessentially American journey from military brat to Air Force Academy graduate to nationally recognized trauma surgeon, set against the backdrop of a nation still struggling to reconcile its democratic ideals with its racist origins. Bold and incisive, *The Bodies Keep Coming* examines how this contradiction manifests in hospitals throughout America and offers a pointed analysis for a better future."

—**Dr. Damon Tweedy**, *New York Times*–bestselling author of *Black Man in a White Coat: A Doctor's Reflections on Race and Medicine*

"An insider's view of the families, healthcare workers, and forces—structural racism, an epidemic of gun violence, rampant health inequity—within our broken health system and America's broken promise. Gripping, candid, and indelible, Dr. Williams's memoir is an urgent call to arms, and an evidence-based blueprint for meaningful healing."

—**Dr. Lucy Kalanithi**, clinical associate professor of medicine, Stanford School of Medicine

"Profound and powerful, *The Bodies Keep Coming* takes us on an extraordinary journey into the high-stakes world of trauma surgery. In this deeply affecting book, Dr. Brian H. Williams takes us along as he works, often as the only Black surgeon in the ER, to save hundreds of gunshot victims in some of America's busiest urban hospitals. This is a must-read for anyone interested in questions of race, violence, and medicine. It's the rare case of an introvert cracking himself open to let us step inside his world. The trip left me spellbound."

—**Jamie Thompson**, journalist and author of *Standoff: Race, Policing, and a Deadly Assault That Gripped a Nation*

"A powerful and necessary read, *The Bodies Keep Coming* offers extraordinary insights into America's epidemic of violence and a Black surgeon's experience on the front lines."

—**Dr. Seema Yasmin**, author of *Viral BS: Medical Myths and Why We Fall for Them* and *What the Fact?! Finding the Truth in All the Noise*

"The hallmark of a great surgeon lies beyond the ability to perform surgery. Those who transform medicine, make us question medical and societal establishments, and are brave enough to put racial equity front and center are the real heroes. Dr. Brian H. Williams is one of those extraordinary physicians. In *The Bodies Keep Coming*, he shares frontline stories through his eyes as a trauma surgeon. Dr. Williams is a masterful storyteller, and you can hear and feel his authenticity on every page. Empathy, anger, humor, and, ultimately, hope accompany you as he takes you on this literary ride."

—**Dr. Nancy Snyderman**, surgeon and former medical editor for NBC News

"In this beautifully written memoir, Dr. Brian H. Williams reveals through jarring personal remembrances the destruction of violence in the American medical system and our society. Although he could have simply offered up a narrative devoid of hope, Williams leaves readers hopeful that healing exists for us all through love."

—**Dr. Deirdre Cooper Owens**, author of *Medical Bondage: Race, Gender, and the Origins of American Gynecology*

"Dr. Brian H. Williams's stunning book is simultaneously an inspiring testament to the skill and dedication of the people working on the medical front lines of America's enduring tragedy of gun violence, and a searing indictment of the pervasive institutional racism that brought us that tragedy in the first place and continues to sustain it. It is not a comfortable read, but it is an essential one."

—**Dr. Elliott Currie**, author of *New York Times* Notable Book of 2020 *A Peculiar Indifference: The Neglected Toll of Violence on Black America*

"With an urgency born of decades on the front lines of America's busiest emergency rooms, Dr. Brian H. Williams offers a keen diagnosis of the painful traumas ailing us at the intersection of race and violence. Honest and bold, heartbreaking and brilliant, and ultimately healing and beautiful, *The Bodies Keep Coming* is a must-read for all seeking a recovery plan for our nation's deepest wounds."

—**Rev. Dr. Michael Waters**, author of *Something in the Water: A 21st Century Civil Rights Odyssey*

"*The Bodies Keep Coming* is a powerful, captivating, and thought-provoking exposé of how racism is threatening healthcare within the United States. This book can change the paradigm in healthcare if we are serious about changing the sequelae of discriminatory and outright racist policies, government action and inaction in regard to a select few populations, and their contributions to the detriment of our health. This is a must-read for anyone interested in repairing the past on this long-standing, unnerving public health crisis sweeping America and achieving health equity and social justice once and for all."

—**Daniel Dawes**, author of *The Political Determinants of Health*

"Absent sentimentality or euphemisms, *The Bodies Keep Coming* forces us to peer into history, ourselves, and the world around us to construct a calculated assessment of society's trauma, gun violence, and healthcare inequities. Propelled by anger on a path toward justice, Dr. Brian H. Williams's deeply introspective and beautifully written work of nonfiction illuminates a long-awaited escape route forward from our bloody tunnel of hell into the healing light of tomorrow."

—**Dr. Wes Ely**, author of *Every Deep-Drawn Breath*

"With hard-earned insights gleaned from operating tables, Dr. Brian H. Williams reframes the conversation around America's unequal health outcomes by showing, layer by layer, how the status quo didn't evolve by chance. Coming at a pivotal moment when our society is reevaluating its most basic assumptions about health, wealth, and race, this landmark book could not be more timely. *The Bodies Keep Coming* forces an important conversation that we can no longer afford to ignore."

—**David Chrisinger**, executive director of the Writing Workshop at the University of Chicago's Harris School of Public Policy and author of *Stories Are What Save Us* and other books

"Our nation's unprecedented epidemic of gun violence finally receives a firsthand voice in this relentless and brilliant narrative. Dr. Brian H. Williams gives readers an opportunity to stand in his shoes as a Black trauma surgeon at the epicenter of bloodshed and death by firearms. Feel the intimate rage and frustration he endures day after day. How do we bring change? Williams cracks open raw conversations about generational racism embedded within healthcare and in our entire culture. Within these pages, our future is challenged and ultimately given hope."

—**Angela Ricketts**, author of *No Man's War: Irreverent Confessions of an Infantry Wife*

"In *The Bodies Keep Coming*, Dr. Brian H. Williams masterfully explores his struggles with being a Black man, a military officer, an American, a public figure, and an accomplished trauma surgeon. This book belongs in the library of anyone interested in gun violence, human rights, and race. It is a powerful contribution to the body of literature exploring the profound issues of our generation. Dr. Williams defines many of the problems America is struggling with, and he offers insightful solutions by using his own journey to illustrate the lessons he wants us to learn in order to embrace a better future. This is a must-read for anyone wanting to understand contemporary America."

—**Bryan Mark Rigg**, author of *Hitler's Jewish Soldiers* and *The Rabbi Saved by Hitler's Soldiers*

"As Dr. Brian H. Williams reveals the layers of his experience as a trauma surgeon, we learn about his own traumas. He witnesses repeatedly the cost of racism and gun violence in America and searches for ways to heal a wound that has scarred his community and his own soul. Everyone needs to read his powerful testament of passionate devotion to truth and healing."

—**Linda Joy Myers,** president of the National Association of Memoir Writers

The Bodies Keep Coming

THE
BODIES
KEEP
COMING

**DISPATCHES FROM A BLACK TRAUMA SURGEON
ON RACISM, VIOLENCE, AND HOW WE HEAL**

BRIAN H. WILLIAMS

Broadleaf Books
Minneapolis

THE BODIES KEEP COMING
Dispatches from a Black Trauma Surgeon on Racism, Violence, and How We Heal

Copyright © 2023 by Brian H. Williams. Published by Broadleaf Books, an imprint of 1517 Media. All rights reserved. Except for brief quotations in critical articles or reviews, no part of this book may be reproduced in any manner without prior written permission from the publisher. Email copyright@1517.media or write to Permissions, Broadleaf Books, PO Box 1209, Minneapolis, MN 55440-1209.

Library of Congress Control Number 2023004872

Cover design: Faceout Studios
Cover image: Surgeon: shutterstock_2155302075, RF

Print ISBN: 978-1-5064-8312-2
eBook ISBN: 978-1-5064-8313-9

Printed in China

To Kathianne—for love, strength, and nudging me into the arena,
and
Abeni—for being the light that brightens each of my days

This is a work of nonfiction. I use actual names for members of my family and most individuals identified in the media. To protect the privacy of others, especially patients, I use pseudonyms and, in a few cases, composite characters. I am grateful to the survivors of the Dallas police officers, who have agreed to have their loved ones' stories told in these pages. All errors or omissions are mine and mine alone.

CONTENTS

CONTENTS

The price one pays for pursuing any profession or calling is an intimate knowledge of its ugly side.

—James Baldwin

PART I

Unconscious

We have to do with the past only as we can make it useful to the present and the future.

—Frederick Douglass

1 | TAGGED AND BAGGED

Within these four walls I have wrecked the lives of far too many Black mothers. The family room is a windowless, white-walled cell in the hospital, with hazy fluorescent lighting, hard-bottomed plastic chairs, and a worn end table with a box of tissues. Four of us have filed into this cramped space, tucked away from the emergency department's main hallway, twisting our torsos to let the door exhale shut behind us.

A public safety officer stands sentry in one corner. He is Black. Beside me, in an opposing corner, is the chaplain. She is Black. Sitting beside the two family members is the violence recovery specialist. She is Black. I am also Black: too Black for some, not Black enough for others. But still Black enough for this story to be meaningless were I anything but.

Outside it is well past midnight but not yet dawn—the resting pulse of the city before it awakens. Inside the emergency department it's the nonstop energy of a Vegas casino. Cleaning staff shuffle from one examination room to the next, changing linens, removing trash, and mopping floors. Doctors tap computer keyboards, zoned on their screens like college kids pulling all-nighters. Nurses push stretchers with patients lying on their backs in various states of distress. Some moan. One bays like a wolf separated from his pack. Another patient wrestles two nurses and the medical student trying to restrain him. Most lie ummoving, watching the alien activity around them like they are background extras in a science fiction movie. Our routine work is routinely disrupted by a patient arriving, on the verge of death.

As a trauma surgeon, I have worked at some of the most stressful and difficult hospitals in the country: Tampa, Boston, Atlanta, Dallas, Chicago. Working to save patients from life-threatening acts of violence brings me tremendous job satisfaction. When the trauma pager goes off with notification of a mortally wounded patient, I feel like a child on Christmas morning. And the bloodier the better.

My wife says this makes me sound like a psycho and that I should keep this to myself. I don't usually admit to the gallows humor we trauma surgeons share, understood only by those who make a steady living off the tragedies of strangers. Admitting to the adrenaline high that fuels us in this work, the drama of trauma, can indeed make one sound a bit unhinged, so I usually stay mum.

Comfortable wearing her own roller-coaster emotions on her sleeve, Kathianne usually encourages me to be less closed off. She is underwhelmed by my resume: Air Force Academy graduate, aeronautical engineer, decorated military officer, medical school, and Harvard-trained surgeon. These may give me instant credibility with people who know nothing about me, but to my wife, I'm just the guy who is not so handy around the house. A running joke between us is that I repair people, not cabinets. She exists on a higher plane of self-awareness to which I still aspire, and for years she has pressed me to "deal with your shit." She talks about family of origin and unresolved childhood trauma. "It's about letting down your walls," she says. "Being authentic. Intimacy means *into me you see.*" Relentless, she probes with questions like "How does that make you feel?" and "What does that say about your values?" The answers are not always apparent to me.

Easier to answer is the question to which I've responded countless times over my quarter century in medicine: Why did you choose to become a trauma surgeon? Most times I keep it simple and say, "I didn't choose trauma surgery. Trauma surgery chose me." Or, like my adolescent daughter tells it, "My daddy likes fixing hurt people." If it were only so simple. Maybe I focus on fixing strangers, so I do not have to focus on fixing myself.

Seated across the family room, two women stare at me, their fingers intertwined in a knuckle-whitening grip. In the silence, my pristine, knee-length white coat speaks with authority before any words come out of my mouth. Louder than the phlegmatic wheeze of the older woman I feel surveilling me. Louder than the sniffling of the younger woman in her grasp. Louder than the soft scrape of metal legs on tear-stained tile as I position my chair across from them. I sweep the backside of my coat to prevent it from wrinkling as I sit to be at eye level with the two women.

The older one, who appears close to my age of fifty-one, is a Black mother desperate for good news. She has skin darker than mine, with hair styled in rows of salt and pepper locs peeking from beneath a kente cloth headscarf. She reminds me of a younger version of my mother. The younger one is college-aged and wears faded blue jeans and a black hoodie with an image of Erykah Badu. Delivering devastating news is part of my job, and a light dims within me every time I speak the words. Shifting in my seat, I try to let my face reveal nothing, which, of course, reveals everything.

"I'm Dr. Brian Williams," I say with somber formality. "I'm the trauma surgeon working tonight."

Showing deference to the elder of the two women, I confirm her relation to my patient. Yes, she is indeed the mother. I'm sure the presence of the hospital chaplain must reveal something. She has only one reason to stand solemnly beside me, which the mother may have already deduced. Why else would the chaplain bring them to this private room, away from the mayhem of the emergency department?

I've been a trauma surgeon long enough to become hyper-aware of my own mortality. I see danger everywhere. To me, seemingly inconsequential activities like driving through an intersection, walking across the street, and riding a bike are life-threatening actions worthy of the utmost vigilance. All deserve self-protective behaviors that, for better or worse, I have instilled in my wife and daughter as well. I know I can kiss them goodbye after breakfast and by lunch my wife could receive a phone call asking her to come to the hospital and identify my body. I know because it is a phone call I've made to countless families.

"I'll walk you through what happened with Malik after he arrived at the hospital," I continue. "You can stop me at any time if you have any questions." I always use the first names of their injured loved ones, the wounded and dead who cannot speak for themselves.

The mother's eyes enlarge, focusing on my every move like heat-seeking missiles, as if scared I might attack her. But I wonder if *she* might attack *me* when she hears what I have to say. It has happened before. In the past, grief-stricken family members have called me incompetent, a liar, and even a murderer. Once, a brother of a deceased gunshot victim pinned me to the wall and sprayed me with spittle and obscenities until he was breathless and choking back tears. Intense emotions can short-circuit the brain's executive functioning, causing rational people to commit irrational and sometimes violent acts. Thankfully, those violent encounters have been rare for me. Still, I empathize with those family members because I've experienced that uncontrollable state of mind myself. Sometimes I envy these strangers who are free to vent their anger; working to suppress mine can be exhausting.

Speaking in a measured monotone, I don't use confusing medical terms, and I enunciate each word for clarity. There must be no misunderstanding of what I have to say. "Malik sustained several gunshot wounds and arrived in critical condition," I tell them. "The paramedics were already doing CPR in the ambulance when they brought him to us. When he arrived, his heart was not beating, and he wasn't breathing."

At this point, I'm never sure which is less traumatic: to fast-forward to what they already know, or to take my time, to allow them to brace for the emotional tsunami barreling toward them. I usually choose the latter, and having prepared her the best I can, I say the words no parent should ever have to hear.

"I'm sorry. We did everything we could, but despite our best efforts, your son Malik died from his injuries."

I always say it like this—"He died," "She died"—with no Hollywood drama. Direct. Succinct. Clear. No euphemisms like "He passed," or "She didn't make it," or "He transitioned." *I'm sorry. He died from his injuries*: it's a phrase I have said hundreds of times, and it sounds hollower each time I say it. I've had to ensure the scores of family members I met before this woman—and those yet to come— understand they will never see their loved one alive again. I want to avoid adding trauma on top of trauma, and I strive to do it right every time.

The mother ratchets open her fingers, freeing her daughter's hand. Her head drops into her ashen palms, which smother her face now slick with tears. Shaking her head and rocking back and forth, she leans into her daughter, who rubs her back with soothing maternal strokes. "No, no, no, no, no," she moans without end. She shakes. She rocks. Faster. Harder. With increasing ferocity until she plunges to the floor, landing in a heap and dragging her daughter with her.

"He gone! He gone! He gone! I can't believe he fucking gone!" She slaps the floor and kicks at some unseen assailant.

There are invisible chains binding mothers of dead children, ones only they know and bear. A rusted weight grinding flesh and bone unlike any pain I have experienced. Watching her flail, I do not flinch. I must remain composed. Nothing she does will surprise me because I have been here before, performed this scene and delivered this line numerous times, each time with a different mother in the lead role.

Like most, this mother is devastated beyond our ability to provide solace. She wails and flails, her screams and limbs shredding the air, adding her tears to the community of past tears on the tiled floor. She reaches skyward, like an inconsolable infant reaching for her own mother, except she is now the mother, one who has outlived the infant she nurtured into a teenage boy.

I rise from my chair to give her more space, reflexively smooth my white coat, and bow my head to avoid intruding on her grief. I stand silent. Stoic. Statuesque. What more can I can do? The public safety officer also stands silent. Stoic. Statuesque. He is present to serve and to protect. The chaplain and violence recovery specialist also remain silent. In some small way, we four strangers must provide some measure of consolation during her moment of grief. Right now, that looks like waiting, and we do not interrupt.

The daughter finally speaks. "Are you sure it's him?" It's a rhetorical question. She knows it's her brother but is hoping for a miracle. She had answered the midnight call summoning them to the hospital. She had confirmed her brother's identity by photos of the tattoos on his body, which is now a bloodied corpse lying steps away in the trauma bay where nurses prepare him for transport to the medical examiner.

Before we entered the family room, I first met in a secluded corner with the chaplain, the homicide detective, and the violence recovery specialist. All confirmed my patient's identity. Notifying next of kin is a conversation I have nearly every time I am on trauma call, and I have to ensure I give life-altering news to the correct people. "It's all over Facebook," said the violence recovery specialist. "And Instagram." Many violence recovery specialists are former gang members or gun violence survivors themselves, working to mediate neighborhood violence and assist with post-injury recovery and repatriation. They become trusted messengers and go-betweens. The one working with me tonight has a network of connections she can call upon to help defuse any potential escalation in violence and provide psychosocial support to the family.

Outside the emergency department, friends and family gather by the dozens. Flashing black-and-white cruisers encircle the area, and even more police officers secure the perimeter. The potential for retaliatory violence outside the entrance to our emergency department is real. When I'm done speaking with the mother and daughter, I will play my small role to defuse tensions by joining the violence recovery specialist and another doctor—he's from the South Side and a hero to many gathered here—to speak to the crowd, one of whom will be shot dead weeks after Malik. Unlike Malik, he is a rising hip-hop artist whose death will become headline news.

Apparently, news of the shooting circulated at viral speed before I even pronounced Malik's official time of death, discarded my bloodied scrubs, and wiped his blood from my clogs. I change into clean scrubs as soon as possible after a trauma. What message would I send to continue working in such a bloodied state—walking the hospital halls, seeing patients, speaking to families? Scrubs might seem a small worry on a life-and-death night in the ED, but as a Black doctor, I can't afford any imperfection in appearance, skill, or temperament. Perceptions become reality and, just as I repair a stab wound to the heart, I have no margin for error.

Black men in medicine represent less than 3 percent of doctors, and I know future Black men attempting to cross the threshold into the profession are depending on Black doctors like me. Patients have told me to get their "real" doctor, leave the room, remove their tray of half-eaten food, or empty the trash bin. Some have ignored me and others have spat at me. Some have prayed for me and others have wished me dead. I have been called a racist and a healer, a nigger and a sellout, a hypocrite and a hero. No matter our social status, from gang members to doctors, Black men still serve as a mirror for people's fears. A screen on which to project one's anxiety—and disgust. An endangered species navigating a world both hostile to and dependent upon our existence.

The mother of my patient lives in a neighborhood within walking distance from one of the premier medical centers in the nation, and yet she is trapped in a web of disenfranchisement and death. Despite our hospital's noble mission, our neighbors' proximity to first-class healthcare does not guarantee access to routine, preventative care. And without access, health equity is nothing more than an empty slogan devoid of any tangible transformation for suffering communities.

Shot in the head, chest, and arms, Malik arrived at the hospital with his left upper arm bent at a nauseating angle from a bullet-induced fracture, a bloodied t-shirt with multiple bullet holes, and brain matter creeping over skull fragments dangling from his sticky, short-cut afro. Despite the fact that he was dead on arrival, our team attempted to revive him. Fewer than 10 percent of victims with gunshot wounds to the head survive, and, if they do, they usually live in a persistent vegetative state, requiring around-the-clock medical care that may be inaccessible to families without health insurance who survive on low-wage salaries.

Conventional wisdom in trauma surgery is that gun violence is worse from Memorial Day to Labor Day. In the gallows humor that bonds trauma surgeons, "Shooters polish their guns for the summer, and lock 'em up for the winter." It is a trope I've heard countless times, one I've often repeated. But with over two decades in medicine, I've learned the lethality of bullets is not seasonal. Black people are gunned down year-round.

In treating these patients, I see myself. In comforting their families, I see mine. A few years from now, my cousin will be shot and killed in front of her three young children. For me, working to end the epidemic of gun violence is more than an academic pursuit or my vocation. It is personal.

"Doctor, please take me to see my boy." The mother is grasping fistfuls of my white coat. On her knees, she pleads with me, then the heavens, back to me, back to the heavens. She releases her grip, leaving wrinkled, dusty handprints. "I lost my oldest last year; now this. Lord, why you do this to me?" It is less a question and more a tortured reproach. I want to take her to see her son, but I can't. His body is a crime scene, evidence to be preserved for his post-mortem examination, the autopsy.

The chaplain eases beside me. "Thank you, Dr. Williams. I'll take it from here." Her timing is perfect, for there is nothing more I can do. My expertise is medical, not spiritual.

"Again, I'm so sorry for your loss," I say. "Here's my card. I'm here all night if you think of any questions."

Few mothers ever call me. Like I do on every trauma shift, I move on. The trauma team moves on. The hospital moves on. I must be ready for another victim, arriving by lights and sirens. I file away this mother's son's death in the emotional lockbox straining to contain the feelings of injustice for the countless others like him. In these moments I reckon with the role I play as a Black doctor in a society that devalues Black lives. I wrestle with the futile feeling that the nobility of my work does not have a sustainable impact. The essence of my job is plugging bullet holes in young Black men and women, at least the ones I can save—and then sending them back to an environment where they remain at high risk of reinjury and death.

What is it about these neighborhoods where I have worked that endemic violence persists in tandem with health inequity? What does it say about our nation's values that we allow it to persist? Looking at Malik's sister now, I can't help but think that the histories and policies designed to quarantine Black people from mainstream American society have somehow managed to reach across generations and help kill her brother.

Nationwide, young Black men aged fifteen to thirty-four represent 2 percent of the population but 37 percent of gun homicides. Some people call my patients victims of "Black-on-Black" violence, but I remind them: interpersonal violence is a byproduct of proximity and we live in a mostly segregated country. Since we have sorted ourselves into homogenous racial and ethnic neighborhoods, a result is that "white-on-white violence" occurs at the same rate, according to the US Department of Justice. I also remind them Black men are fatally shot by police at more than twice the rate of white people, even though white men are more likely to be armed in the same scenario. And each year, more people are shot and killed by police than in all the mass shootings combined. The extremes to which America contorts its values to minimize all these deaths are untenable.

Malik, like hundreds of others, is merely another statistic for our hospital death registry. The national news will not cover his death. The local news might. If the mother does call me with questions, the most truthful answer I can give—the one internalized yet never verbalized during my twenty-plus years in medicine—would be: *Ma'am, your child is nothing more than another Black body that came to be tagged and bagged. Nobody gives a damn.*

I wrote this book so lives like Malik's are not ignored. I wrote it to show you the world of a Black trauma surgeon, in a profession lacking role models, who routinely deals with the human toll from the epidemic of gun violence. I wrote it to remind us all that if Black lives actually mattered to policymakers in the United States, they would take action that mattered. Weaving together memoir, medicine, historical records, and scientific research, we will explore various dimensions of health-care inequity. There are three main threads in this story: a narrative account of my experiences inside the hospital, my personal story, and a critical look at healthcare inequity. You will learn as I learn, experience events as I did, and eavesdrop on my interpretation of the world. Together we will ask questions about racism, violence, healthcare, and how we heal.

I wrote this book to help us acknowledge the intergenerational impact of policies and inequalities rooted in our nation's choices. In a study by the Trace, nearly 50 percent of mass shootings occurred in majority-Black census tracts. When less than 10 percent of US census tracts have majority-Black populations, why do shootings like these predominantly occur in majority-Black neighborhoods? Why does a nation with the wealth, resources, and ingenuity such as ours allow the human toll of gun violence to persist? I wrote this book to connect issues we often assume are separate—to lay racism beside violence beside healthcare inequity and to see what rises to the surface.

I also wrote it because a tragic loss of life occurred on my watch. On July 7, 2016, a Black sniper ambushed fourteen police officers providing security for a demonstration in downtown Dallas, Texas. It began as a peaceful rally protesting the killings of unarmed Black men by police, most recently Alton Sterling in Baton Rouge, Louisiana, on July 5 and Philando Castile in Falcon Heights, Minnesota, on July 6.

As the leader of the trauma team at a Dallas hospital that evening, I became the only surgeon in history to operate on multiple on-duty police officers victimized in a mass shooting. The shooting became the worst loss of life for US law enforcement since 9/11 and shattered all my attempts to keep my head down and focus only on the body in front of me. Soon, my comfortable life of anonymity disintegrated, forcing me to navigate a new reality as a public figure—a life I did not seek, did not want, and for which I was ill-prepared.

The shooting, and its aftermath, taught me the many ways America hungers for soothing stories of heroism and unity in the face of tragedy, how we discard hard truths about racism and violence, and how our healthcare system profits from both. It forced me to look up from the body on the gurney in front of me and see all the ways in which, as Carol Anderson writes, "Racism lies around like a loaded weapon."

Tonight, completing the home stretch of this twenty-four-hour shift, I am prepared for more gunshot victims who are likely to come. I exit the family room to let Malik's mother and sister grieve in private. I avert my gaze from the elderly woman sitting outside the door, awaiting a nurse to take her vital signs. In an unavoidable invasion of privacy, I'm certain she overheard the cries and deduced what I did to that mother. I smooth the collar of my white coat and confirm the top three buttons are buttoned. Not two buttons. Not four. Definitely not zero. It is always three. Attention to detail. Professionalism at all times.

I walk with a purpose, like I am back at the Air Force Academy marching in formation: head high, spine erect, shoulders back, and eyes straight ahead. Past the workstation where nurses and doctors and trainees answer phones and tap computer keyboards and talk to patients. Robotically, I reply to one nurse's "Hey, Dr. Williams," and another nurse's "How ya doin', Doc?"

Inside the emergency department is a specialized area called the trauma bay. There are six rectangular areas, three on each side, marked by thick red lines on the floor. Within a sprawling health system, with thousands of employees and nearly five thousand trauma activations each year, this is where I spend most of my time. My home away from home. With a stretcher, crash cart, overhead surgical lights, and more equipment to save the critically injured, we can resuscitate multiple gunshot victims at the same time. Sometimes we treat victims from opposing sides of a shootout. Fortunately, we can draw heavy-duty curtains when needed to divide the bay into six individual "rooms." Yet, in matters of life and death, privacy and modesty are not guaranteed.

In one of these rooms, three nurses surround Malik, preparing to place him in a white body bag. Ms. Mona, a Black woman on the cleaning staff (they are almost always Black), works around them. Ms. Mona and I are friendly, having had many brief and cordial late-night conversations in the halls she cleans. Our conversations usually go something like: "How you doin', Dr. Williams?"

"I'm good, Ms. Mona," I say. I always say I'm good, even when I'm not. "How are you?"

"I'm blessed, Doc. I'm blessed."

"That's good to hear, Ms. Mona."

"That white coat suits you, Doc. Your kinfolk must be proud."

"No doubt." I usually manage a weak smile. Ms. Mona has a way of touching that guarded part of me that still looks over its shoulder even when allowed to roam free.

"Well, I'm proud of you too," she nods with a smile that deepens the wrinkled valleys on her face. "You make us all look good."

She speaks as if Black people are part of a collective unit. Low-wage workers, invisible to many and no kinship to me, take as much pride in my success as my own family. "You're the first Black doctor I've ever seen in my whole life," one Black mother had said to me a few years earlier when I worked in Atlanta: "Hallelujah! Thank God you was here for my boy."

Tonight, though, Ms. Mona and I do not speak. Tonight, she is focused on the bloodied floor, pushing and pulling her mop. The slurping strands sweep the crimson pool to streaks of pink and then to a clear sheen. The worlds of two women, strangers, intersect in death. One lost her sole surviving son to violence, and another makes minimum wage to wash the floor of his blood.

I help the nurses lift Malik into the body bag, leave the team to their post-mortem routine, and finish my trek to the overnight call room—another windowless cell but with a bed, computer, television, and a full-sized bathroom. I drape my white coat on the door hook, slump into the desk chair, and call the medical examiner to report another apparent homicide.

My chest tightens: empathy for another mother who outlived her child. Sorrow for another life lost to gun violence. Helplessness knowing that no matter what I do, more Black bodies will follow.

Soon these emotions are body-slammed by the loyal companion that has been with me for years: rage.

2 | DEMONS

I did not plan to become a doctor. It did not occur to me that I, the loner with an intense stare and a disheveled afro, could become a doctor like the elderly white male doctors who cared for me. As a youth, I saw no one who looked like me dressed in a long white coat adorned with a stethoscope.

One of my earliest childhood memories is the feeling of impending death from lack of oxygen. "You'll be all right, Brian," my mother consoled, eyeing me in the rearview mirror. Wheezing like a tortured seal, I bobbled my head in acknowledgment, unable to move enough air through my lungs to speak. My father, a career Air Force noncommissioned officer, was deployed to some unknown locale, so my mother piloted this run to the hospital on her own. "You're gonna be okay. We'll be there soon."

I hungered for air, and seconds seemed like hours, but I knew she'd get me there. She always did. Living on an Air Force base, we didn't have far to go, and minutes after burning rubber from home, we scurried into the emergency room. After the usual routine—a breathing treatment to loosen the vice grip on my lungs, height, weight, vitals—I sat hunched in an exam room, feet dangling two feet from the floor, as the doctor gently pressed here and felt there along my shirtless torso. Like all the doctors I visited as a child, he was an elderly, white man who resembled Marcus Welby, MD, from the famous 1970s television series. And like all those doctors, he inspired my awe.

As a military kid I always had access to healthcare, and I assumed that was true for everyone. To be sick and unable to see a doctor? I could not fathom it. Because of my childhood asthma—a condition afflicting, hospitalizing, and killing Black children at a much higher rate than white children—I made many breathless trips to the emergency room. For many Black children, environmental injustice is an ever-present companion in neighborhoods located near municipal dumps, factories, and highways resulting in increased exposure to respiratory toxins. My situation differed; my sister and I were trapped in a house with parents who smoked. I wonder if the white doctor judged my parents for that reason. Or because we were Black. Or both.

"Open up and say *ahhh*." I coughed as the doctor gagged me with a popsicle stick and gasped when he placed an ice cube masquerading as a stethoscope to my back.

"Cold, huh? Sorry about that."

My mother hovered, not saying a word as the man with the soothing voice in the long white coat poked and prodded while asking me about sports and school. Despite my asthma and scrawny physique, I still did relatively well in team sports, thanks to a combination of medication and tenacity. I made the all-star teams for football, where I played running back, and baseball, where I played catcher. One season the football coaches awarded me the "Unsung Hero" award. When presenting the trophy, my coach said, "Brian is not flashy, but he gets the job done." Motivated to achieve group goals, not individual accolades, I internalized what I believed to be true: stay humble, do the job, and be rewarded. The naivete of youth.

"Well, we're done," the doctor said, smiling again. He gave my mother instructions about when to return to the hospital, said something to her about smoking, wished me luck in my upcoming game, and disappeared like an apparition. Alone with my mother, I grabbed my shirt.

"Mom, can I axe you something?"

"Brian, it's *ask*, not *axe*," she admonished. "Say it correctly." My mother, forever conscious of speech and presentation, corrected our grammar daily. In the era of a single landline serving the entire family, she policed my friends as well. If one called our house and asked, "Is Brian there?" she'd respond "Yes"—and hang up. I quickly learned when calling my friends to say, "May I please speak to so-and-so?" In later years, she taught me word processing on a Radio Shack desktop computer (which doubled as an escape portal for my interactive space exploration video games), gave me a Roget's Thesaurus the size of a microwave (as if the Webster's Dictionary weren't enough), and would point to the encyclopedias lining our living room wall if I had the audacity to ask her a question I could investigate myself.

Once I complained to my mother about my Black friends mocking how I talked. "They keep calling me an Oreo," I told her. I have since heard many versions of this pejorative term: Coconut. Banana. Pick a race or ethnicity, and there is sure to be a food to describe why the interior is more appealing than the shell.

"Ignore them," she said. "Remember: all skinfolk ain't kinfolk. People will say a lot of things about you, but nobody who matters will criticize how you speak."

Discipline flowed in our home mainly from my mother. My sister and I feigned fear on those rare occasions she said, "Wait until your father gets home." We'd slink away in relief, knowing we had already survived the worst. A stream of priceless maxims also flowed from my mother like: *Stay in your lane. You own the car, but the white man owns the highway. Still waters run deep.* When boldness compelled me to highlight times she violated her own rules of impeccable grammar, she'd bump me back into my lane with a terse "Do as I say, not as I do." She knew impressions mattered in the spaces my sister and I navigated, and she ensured our speech, an easy target, left zero room for criticism. Our family, with its deep Southern roots, had flourished in a few generations, and she expected my younger sister and me to go even higher. Today, when people share what they intend to be compliments—such as "Brian, you don't sound Black"—I say, "Blame my mother." I still tease her sometimes. "Hey Mom, let me axe you somethin'," I say, just to rile her up.

Squirming into my shirt, I self-correct. "Ask," I said. "Are there any Black doctors?" A decade before Bill Cosby reigned as America's favorite television dad, Dr. Heathcliff Huxtable—and decades before it became known that he was drugging and sexually assaulting women— my mother smiled like any parent deflecting an uncomfortable truth. A truth I could not yet articulate but felt just the same.

To me, the smiling man in the long white coat with the fancy degrees and plaques and awards broadcasting greatness from his office walls was a god. And like the Eurocentric religious ideals force-fed to me in Sunday school, his profession of medicine did not seem like somewhere I belonged. From that early age, I knew an unspoken truth. No matter how smart, articulate, or well-behaved I would become, there were always places Black boys would not be welcome.

Like many prepubescent boys, I dreamt of a career in professional sports and aspired to play wide receiver for my favorite football team: the back-to-back Super Bowl champion Miami Dolphins. Along with football and baseball, I played basketball. Poorly. If the stereotype of innate basketball skills defined Blackness, I rode the bench for an ice hockey team.

My athletic deficiency was on glaring display within my crew of friends: The Demons. But we were far from the neighborhood menace our name implied. The Demons were a group of fifth-grade military brats passing the time in the late 1970s at Kadena Air Force Base in Okinawa, Japan. As the children of parents from all branches of the military, we lived on the main southernmost island of the Japanese archipelago. The US existed as a far-off land we called "The States." We bonded over our shared obsession with Dungeons and Dragons and skateboards, and we spent hours nearly every weekend mainlining quarters into arcade games. We spent so much time together at school, at sports, and at play we decided we needed a name. Days passed as we debated the pros and cons of calling ourselves The Wizards, The Zombies, or The Knights, inspired by our fantasy role-playing games—until one afternoon Walter screamed toward us on his skateboard, stopping with a deft flick of his foot to launch the board into his hand. He reached into his backpack and produced a brown paper bag with his prize purchase: a packet of reflective stickers with various demons in menacing poses. Delighted, we each grabbed a few and slapped them on our skateboards and BMX bikes.

The Demons were a model of horizontal leadership. Nobody ruled. We settled disagreements by majority vote or, in those rare cases of a tie, by a coin toss. Walter, Corey, Kelly, and I made up the group. Two white kids, Walter and Corey; one Asian American, Kelly; and me. All three could beat me in a foot race, and the sun rarely set before Kelly relished aloud the distorted racial athletic stereotypes. Barely winded, Kelly would savor his undefeated record with an ear-to-ear grin and a shove on my shoulder: "I thought you're s'posed to be fast!" Breathing heavily after another loss, I'd try to exert my dominance. "Shut up, butthole," I'd gasp, the best I could do without collapsing unconscious. It unfolded the same way every time, never getting old. We'd laugh and shove and move on to the next adventure.

Growing up, I was an average athlete but a superb scholar. A straight-A student, I excelled in what we now call STEM: science, technology, engineering, and math. Although I was a loner, I don't recall feeling lonely. I felt most at home with my vinyl records, library books, and my own thoughts. As I grew in age but not speed, music consumed increasing portions of my life, and I traded my cleats for drumsticks. I had actually started playing drums before I could walk, and during adolescence this passing hobby morphed into a time-consuming obsession. I worshiped the rock and metal greats. I liked it hard. I liked it fast. I liked it loud.

In junior high school, I funded my obsession by mowing lawns for $10 each (I didn't have the entrepreneurial sense to adjust my rate based on acreage) and delivering newspapers from a canvas shoulder bag, pedaling my BMX bicycle through the neighborhood. In high school, determined to continue working two jobs and maintain straight As, I stopped mowing lawns but continued to deliver papers while also working at a record store. This allowed me to buy even more records with my employee discount. I'd plug my space-helmet-sized headphones into a rickety hand-me-down stereo from my father, turn the dial to ear-bleeding volume, and pound my bed and pillows to vinyl beats and eight-track fills. Moving to my kit, I'd beat the crap out of my drums, almost as if I were trying to break them (I did).

The world in my headphones was the antithesis of how I presented myself to the world in which I lived: quiet. I still do not speak much—which, I've been told, unnerves people. "You're an enigma," a senior trauma surgeon once told me. "Very hard to read. It makes people wonder: What's your agenda?" I quietly savored what I, at the time, considered a victory. Why should I have to explain I had no agenda other than to be of service? I assumed my work spoke for itself.

Every three years my family would pack up and start another adventure in some new locale. Perpetually in motion and never quite settled, I gave little thought to my peripatetic life and how it informed my view of the world. Travel helped me develop the skills to move freely among many spaces: Black, white, and otherwise. My family—a father, mother, two kids, and a series of dogs, each replacing their deceased predecessor—lived as a globetrotting unit bound by the location of my father's latest Air Force orders. Before I graduated from high school, I had lived in five states—Massachusetts, Florida, New Mexico, Hawaii, and Virginia—and also Japan.

Mark Twain said, "Travel is fatal to prejudice, bigotry, and narrow-mindedness," but in our insular community on a military base, rank trumped race. I took for granted my unique experience, socializing with kids from all over the country who lived in the same nomadic manner as we did. My parents had a multiracial social circle. House parties with a potpourri of noncommissioned families, friends, food, and music from around the world were the norm. Thanksgiving included turkey, ham, lasagna, collards, pierogies, and stir fry. Soul food, Polish cuisine, Italian, and Asian standards mixed for an annual feast with my parents' closest friends.

The Demons were an important part of my rich experience of diversity. But they were also there—silent, inscrutable, complicit—when I experienced what sociologist Elijah Anderson described as my "nigger moment."At some point in their lives, Anderson writes, every Black American "is powerfully reminded of his or her putative place as a Black person." Mine happened at eight years of age.

That afternoon after school I ran home as fast as my legs would propel me, retrieved my baseball cap, mitt, and Louisville slugger for our regular pickup baseball game. Ours was a dirt field with barely enough grass and too many shards of glass—a beautifully dangerous oasis, the center of our universe. But on that day, everything imploded when an unknown white kid walked over to me and said, "We ain't lettin' any niggers on the team today."

My eyes darted between the dozen faces in a haphazard arc before me, searching for an ally. I found none. I knew most of the boys and thought of them as my friends. We attended the same school and played baseball together all the time, but some joined the attack, laughing and pointing and taunting. Even the Demons, who were present, stood silently.

The scratchy lump in my throat left me mute. *Nigger?* It was a new word to me, and I knew it was meant only for me.

Nigger is the tactical nuke decimating any Black person within earshot and sparing bystanders the fallout. *Nigger* derives from niger, the Latin word for "black," and did not start its life as a racial slur. Harvard law professor Randall Kennedy writes: "No one knows precisely when or how niger turned derisively into nigger and attained a pejorative meaning. We do know, however, that by the end of the first third of the nineteenth century, nigger had already become a familiar and influential insult." He goes on to describe *nigger* as "dangerous, vital, evocative, volatile, unsettling, chameleonlike. Notorious the world over, it occupies a singular niche. No word comes close to generating the amount of controversy that *nigger* provokes."

Of course, none of this etymology appeared in my third-grade public school curriculum. But I knew its purpose was to degrade, dominate, and dehumanize. And I longed to use my bare hands to rip that kid's life out by the throat—or get my butt kicked trying.

"Not today, Nigger," he sneered, as if I hadn't heard him the first time, as he stepped toward me. He hadn't laid a hand on me, but it felt as if he had spat in my face, punched me in the gut, and kicked me in the gonads. My rage morphed into reason as I computed my numerical disadvantage. Even with the Demons present, who did nothing, I was alone.

I shuffled away, serenaded by a giddy chorus of "Bye, Nigger," and "Go back to Africa, Darkie." I mounted my bike, pedaled home, and immediately clawed the Demon stickers off my bike and skateboard. I'm not sure what angered me more: the barrage of racial slurs or the silence of the Demons. I sensed that true allies would stand up for what is right. If even your crew remains silent when you need them most, whom could you ever trust?

3 | MY COMFORT AND MY PAIN

Nigger may have been new to me, but it wasn't to my father. My dad knows firsthand what it means to come of age during state-sanctioned segregation. He was a few months shy of his eighteenth birthday when President Johnson signed the Civil Rights Act of 1964, which makes me the first person in my family born with all the inalienable rights professed by the framers in the Constitution.

Bill Henry Williams was both a superb scholar and athlete. A gifted high school basketball player and student nicknamed "The Professor." Raised first in South Carolina, and later in Florida, he doesn't talk much about his childhood. Visiting his South Carolina farm as a preschooler, I chased chickens that clucked and ran and flapped. I slurped cheekfuls of fresh watermelon, still warm from the field. Today my cousins still work the land, growing soybeans.

After the Emancipation Proclamation, the plantation owner had ceded the land to my formerly enslaved great-great-great-grandfather. I don't know if he did it because of a crisis of conscience or to comply with directives from the Freedmen's Bureau, which reallocated lands to the stolen Africans who had been enslaved for hundreds of years. A mission of the Freedmen's Bureau was to help formerly enslaved people become self-sufficient. Unfortunately, the abolition of the Bureau in 1872 and the end of Reconstruction in 1877 opened the door for the era of Jim Crow and domestic racialized terrorism.

To this day, I still learn interesting facts about my father in some passing discussion with family—a surprising anecdote from my mother or a jaw-dropping story from my younger sister. She can always get him to open up in ways I never could. One of those stories involved his mother's death when my father became a teenager, literally.

Late in the afternoon of my father's thirteenth birthday, his mother had a severe asthma attack and her family called for an ambulance. The driver refused to enter the Black neighborhood to take her to the hospital where she could have received life-saving care. She died later that day. My dad still blames himself for my grandmother's death. He had offered to refill her asthma medication, but my grandmother had given him a reprieve to enjoy his birthday celebration. I don't blame my father. I blame a healthcare system that then, like now, devalues the lives of Black people and decided sending an emergency transport to save my grandmother's life was not worth it.

Across the country, Black people dying because of lack of emergency medical services continued until 1967, when unemployed Black men in my wife's home state of Pennsylvania collaborated with an Austrian doctor, a medical resident, and two ambulance drivers to create the Freedom House Ambulance Service. It served as the model for the modern emergency medical transport services we take for granted today. In matters of health equity, when Black people benefit, everybody wins.

Weeks after my grandmother's death, my father and his three younger sisters were divided among the households of several relatives. Most were shipped off to the Bronx, New York, but my father landed in Jacksonville, Florida, where he later met my mom, fell in love, and tied the knot. A few months after their second anniversary, they had me. My father became a career Air Force noncommissioned officer who served twenty-three years. In fact, my family has served continuously in the Armed Forces going back to the Revolutionary War.

I am descended from people who took oaths to fight in foreign countries to guarantee the rights of life, liberty, and happiness denied in their home country. I am also descended from enslaved people who know, better than anyone, the value of those rights when denied.

For generations, escaping the Allendale farm was a wartime ritual for the Williams men. The twentieth-century military lineage begins with my great-grandfather, who left the farm to serve in World War I. A generation later, his son volunteered to serve in a segregated US Army unit during World War II. Both risked their lives fighting in the name of patriotism. World War II historian Stephen Ambrose noted the irony that "the world's greatest democracy fought the world's greatest racist with a segregated army." Highly decorated and mission-critical units such as the Tuskegee Airmen, the 761st Tank Battalion known as "Patton's Panthers," and the Red Ball Express truck convoy that resupplied allied forces pushing inland during D-Day. Both my great-grandfather and grandfather were part of this legacy. Both returned to state-sanctioned racism. Denied the financial support for education and housing loans the federal government extended to millions of WWII veterans, they continued to labor on the farm.

The Servicemen's Readjustment Act of 1944, better known as the GI Bill, provided college tuition and low-cost home loans to many returning veterans. It elevated a tremendous number to a new level of economic prosperity. But the benefits were denied to nearly one million Black veterans who had served with honor and distinction. Racial discrimination was easy to perpetuate, especially in the South, since the federal government relegated administration of the program to the states. Two decades later, a similar strategy proved devastating for Black Americans, when the states were given authority to administer Medicaid. The racial health gap still persists more than a half century later.

White veterans enjoyed benefits allowing them to get college degrees and purchase homes, while Black veterans were denied the same assistance. This contributed to another gap: wealth. In 2019, the typical white family had eight times the wealth of a typical Black family. Home ownership is the primary means of transferring inter-generational wealth, and as home values have increased over the decades, Black veterans and their descendants were denied the wealth accumulated by white veterans—most of whom were Irish, Italian, Polish, Jewish, and other working-class European immigrants—in the postwar years. "The GI Bill did not explicitly exclude the 1.8 million Black Americans who fought in World War II and Korea," writes a former assistant secretary of the US Department of Commerce and a former president of the NAACP in a commentary in the *Boston Globe.* "But in practice, the bill's benefits were almost entirely restricted to whites, making it one of the worst racial injustices of the 20th century."

My father joined the US Air Force during the Vietnam War and never looked back. By all accounts the military changed the trajectory of my father's life, and thanks to his service, I never had to decide about life on the family farm. I traveled the world and never worried about food insecurity, affordable housing, or access to healthcare. I'm still not sure what my father did during his early years of military service. He never said much except to give vague answers—short sentences illuminating little about those difficult times. When people say to me, "You don't speak much," I respond, "Blame my father." To this day he is thrifty with his words.

Watching him don his Air Force uniform each day, I learned about sacrifice, patriotism, and service. And as imperfect as I knew our country to be, I still believed in the ideals of liberty and justice for all. To this day, the national anthem evokes an almost Pavlovian response in me. I stand and face the music, and every Memorial Day, Fourth of July, and Veterans Day, I shamelessly dress head to toe in red, white, and blue. If hard work and military service are the benchmarks for patriotism, my family should appear on the recruitment poster.

My father was the engine of our family, but my mother was the fuel that kept it humming. Her influence, as a working mother of two who maintained a steady presence with exacting standards, extends as far back as I can remember. Born in 1949, Gwendolyn Swanigan Williams was the third of four children raised in low-income shotgun houses in Jacksonville, Florida. My younger sister and I were enraptured with her stories of growing up. Although she had grown up poor and Black during Jim Crow, she managed to end most of her tales about her childhood with a full-throated, belly-busting laugh. Raised by a single mother, she spent her summers launching herself limb-to-limb in pecan trees and still has the battle-scarred legs from some ill-timed leaps.

As a teenager, my mother channeled her fearlessness into marching for civil rights. She tried to "rile up the white folks," in her words, by doing lunch counter sit-ins at Woolworth's and risking jail and worse by crossing the "Boulevard," the road separating the Black neighborhood on the west side of Jacksonville from the white neighborhood on the east. Once in the white section of town, she and her friends had the audacity to walk on the *sidewalk* instead of the middle of the street, as expected of Black people. And of course, she would happily take a sip from the "Whites Only" water fountain if it suited her. "I did little things just to prove to them that I could do it," she'd say. "We'd just keep on doing it until the police came."

Although she was the third of four siblings, my mother assumed the responsibility of raising her youngest sister, who had an intellectual disability. In her later years, my aunt had a complicated medication regimen challenging even to me, with a medical degree and board certifications in two surgical specialties. "Mom, that is too complicated for her," I said, when she listed all the medications her sister had to take and the schedule on which she had to take them. "Didn't they know about her developmental delay?" Like so many Black people today, my aunt was too poor to pay for better medications with simplified dosages and schedules and too poor to get a medical advocate. Inequity in healthcare access and affordability inflicts death on Black Americans at a rate 24 percent higher than white people.

Well into my practice as a trauma surgeon, my mother called and told me my aunt died of heart failure. Even having a doctor in the family couldn't save her from a healthcare system that, in many ways, values profits over people.

During high school, before she met my father, my mother worked to upgrade her professional prospects and applied for a competitive program for senior students called Diversified Commercial Training. She and several classmates spent the first half of the day in school and the latter half working in professional settings at sponsoring companies. The goal of the program was to train Black students with skills to find professional jobs beyond the expected low-wage service sector jobs like hairdressing or housecleaning. The training program placed my mother at a local bank, where she started in the basement, working the customer service lines as the only Black person on a team of seven. She spent her afternoons answering phone calls, confirming account balances, and resolving disputes.

One day a long-standing client, a highly influential member of the community, had a problem she could not resolve over the phone. Long before video calls, of course, my mother used the only option in her toolbox. She asked the client to come in for a face-to-face. But when the customer arrived, she became apoplectic, refusing to work with "this little nigga gal who knows way too much about my finances."

After verbally abusing my mom, the client threatened to close her account. The white bank manager directed my mother to gather the client's information and obliged the woman on the spot. He closed her account and, inviting her to take her business elsewhere, he escorted her out of the building. In the 1960s, a white man standing up for a Black woman and turning away a wealthy and powerful client? I'm sure it happened more often than we know, but it's still shocking to hear my mother tell it.

My mother parlayed her experience into a career in banking, working her way out of the basement, up the ranks to teller and finally management in American Express. My father's military orders, dispensed at the whim of Uncle Sam, could have derailed my mother's career progression, as it does for many military spouses. Fortunately, she had a mobile skill set with a multinational company and always had a job waiting for her wherever we moved.

The Demons eventually disbanded, although we remained a unit even after the baseball incident. While the world fixated on detainees at the American embassy in Iran during the waning months of the Carter administration, our fathers received Permanent Change of Station orders—"PCS orders" in military parlance. Our families left Okinawa one by one over the course of eighteen months, relocating back to the States.

My family moved to Hawaii, a perpetual tropical paradise with two seasons: hurricane season and the rest of the year. Most of our time in Hawaii remained peaceful, but I started to get into fights when I felt insulted. In the years following the baseball incident in Okinawa, fueled more by anger than good sense, I scrapped with this kid or that one—anyone who called me "nigger" or "monkey" or "darkie." If I didn't beat some kid for insulting me, I fought because they'd crossed my younger sister. Smile at her wrong and I would punch you in the face out of familial obligation.

I don't recall being victorious as often as my mother recounts. I was on the skinny side of average, usually over-matched, and my pugilistic pursuits tapered as I entered middle school. But on one otherwise postcard-perfect afternoon, I was the Category 5 hurricane.

"Brian Henry! Get off him!" My mother yelled as she hurried across the pavement. She was closing the distance, and I knew I had little time.

"Call me nigger again," I growled from atop my prey. Pinning him on his back, I straddled the dark-haired boy, his torso between my knees as my fists connected in a syncopated rhythm on his face. Squirming beneath me, he cupped his hands, protecting his face and muffling his cries for mercy. Crimson streamed from his nostrils, and his lips swelled purple.

"Brian Henry! STOP!"

Hearing "Brian Henry" from my mom usually stopped me dead in my tracks, except this time my mother's ear-splitting commands did not register. Years later, in medical school, I would learn how the limbic system, part of the primitive brain, controls emotions and can hijack rational thoughts and actions. Once that happens, there is no reasoning with someone. I grabbed two fistfuls of hair, repeatedly slammed his head into the ground, trying to split his skull like a ripe coconut.

"BRIAN! HENRY! WILLIAMS!" The trifecta. I had crossed the red line into egregious preteen conduct. With her supermom strength, she lifted me from my prey. "Have you lost your mind?" I squirmed from her grasp and stomped home, widening the distance between us. I raged at her. I raged at the kid. I raged at the world—this white world where I wasted so much time trying to assimilate.

In an instant I had also validated some of the worst stereotypes about Black youth, and could not unring that bell. Hours later, our doorbell rang. The kid and his father stood at the door. "Look what your boy did," the man said to my father, waving at his son's swollen lip and black eye.

My father could communicate a lifetime's worth of displeasure with the slightest shift in his gaze. I felt the heat of his glare.

"Dad, he called me a nigger!" What more did I have to say? With the baseball incident in Okinawa, I had said nothing and done nothing. But a lot changed in the intervening years, and being called nigger meant fight's on!

My dad turned to the boy's father and said nothing. I now understand that he knew I told the truth. He glared impassively at the man whose son protested his innocence.

"Nuh-uh, Dad," he begged; "I just called him a fool." He was a comically bad liar.

The two dads locked in a stare, a showdown without guns. The silence, too much for me, compelled me to again launch into my oral defense. My father, with all the speed of a turtle racing through molasses, turned to me, placed his hand on my shoulder, and absorbed all the tension and angst and fury consuming me. He said not one word to me, but his message resonated loud and clear: *Don't worry, Son. I've got you.* Then he glared at the other father again. Long. Hard. Sustained.

After a seeming eternity, the other dad blinked. Holstering his pride, he mumbled, "Let's go," and guided his son away by the shoulder. My dad closed the door, and we didn't talk about it again.

It was the last time I threw a punch at another human being.

But it was not my last fight. I have been fighting myself ever since, never freed from my pent-up rage. The violence faded away, but the anger remains. Anger is my strength and my weakness. It is my comfort and my pain.

As I matured, no matter how angry I became, I mastered the art of showing nothing, saying nothing, and doing nothing. "Watch out for Brian," my mother says to this day. "He doesn't say much, but still waters run deep." Being an angry Black man is not a pathway to career success. To lose control even once, at work or in life, is never an option.

Nearing the end of my sophomore year of high school we moved again, leaving Hawaii for Langley Air Force Base in Hampton, Virginia. For the first time, my parents bought a house, planted roots, and have been in that same home since Ronald Reagan was president. I didn't remain in Hampton for long. Two years later, I followed my father's example and joined the military.

Initially en route to study aeronautical engineering at the Massachusetts Institute of Technology on an Air Force ROTC scholarship, I changed course when I had earned a congressional appointment to the United States Air Force Academy. On track to become the first college graduate and first military officer in my family, I felt both proud and burdened by the weight of familial expectations. Within weeks of graduating, I joined more than one thousand teenage recruits on the picturesque, eighteen thousand-acre campus of the United States Air Force Academy in Colorado Springs. It was the perfect place to get lost in the crowd. And to find myself.

4 | THE LONG BLUE LINE

"Basics! Uh-tench-hut!" To say the squad leader barked his orders was an insult. He detonated his commands like bunker-busting bombs, as we shell-shocked recruits snapped to attention.

"You are now at 7,258 feet above sea level. That is far, *far* above that of West Point or Annapolis. The air is thin up here. Precious. And we will not waste any of it on the likes of you."

Cadet Kenneth L. Jackson paced in front of our novice formation. His crew-cut sandy blonde hair stood at attention beneath his impeccably perched blue service cap, its gleaming bald eagle emblem glaring at us. He owned all of us without saying a word. The creases pressed into his uniform were sharp enough to draw blood, and skin-tight gloves bleached whiter than white molded to his fingers. Metal taps on his heels struck the pavement with an ominous click, click, click, showing not only us, but the earth beneath his feet he was in command. Ramrod perfect posture—always. It would not surprise me if he ironed his socks and underwear. Over the ensuing six weeks of basic training, I'd learn the man had standards from which he never deviated.

His cocksure cadre—senior cadets responsible for our training—snaked through our formation, hissing into the ear of one cadet to "pull some more chins," and to another to "get your shoulders back and down," and to another to "keep your eyes caged straight ahead."

To the west, the Rocky Mountains posed for a postcard-worthy photo, and one thousand feet below, Colorado Springs sprawled to the east.

It might as well have been on another planet.

While most of my high school classmates enjoyed their last summer before college, I stood in formation at the United States Air Force Academy with dozens of strangers, on day one of Basic Cadet Training—also known as Beast. An apt nickname considering what the following six weeks entailed: an organized regimen of physical training, sleep deprivation, and patriotic indoctrination gift-wrapped with incessant gaslighting. One moment we were "the very best America had to offer," and the next we were "useless vermin" taking a spot from a more deserving candidate. The cadre never accepted our best as good enough, and failure to do our best was unforgivable.

"Do not speak unless spoken to," Cadet Jackson said. "If you get the privilege to have one of my cadre address you, you will reply with one, and only one, of your seven basic responses."

Cadet Jackson parked himself in front of me, turned, and inched his finger toward my chin. My heart stopped.

"Do not dirty my glove with your chin, Basic," he sneered. His finger came within a whisper of my face but never made contact. "Back. Baaaaaack. Let me see you pull some chins."

I knew his finger could do no harm, but as it crept closer, it seemed like a searing dagger. I ratcheted my head back like a rooster ready to crow. "Now get your shoulders back and down," he whispered in a commanding monotone, enunciating each word for clarity. He spoke with calm condescension. In complete control, he had no need for bombast or threats. Why would he? Unlike me, he had the rank, experience, and a deadly finger ready to pierce my mandible.

I stood with arms pinned to my sides, working to bring my shoulder blades together like palms in prayer. My chest jutted forward as I contracted muscles I didn't know existed. "Good job, Basic. Hold that position and don't move." He scanned me from head to toe. Cocking his head, he hissed, "What's your name?"

"Brian Williams." I grunted.

What a mistake. He exploded, peppering the space between us with a flamethrower of spittle. "IS THAT ONE OF YOUR SEVEN BASIC RESPONSES?!"

I had exited the bus five minutes earlier, with no idea what a basic response was, and now I paid the price. Nowhere did my acceptance packet mention seven responses or pulling chins or a sadistic cadre. It said bring nothing, not even a toothbrush. Uncle Sam would issue everything.

I soon learned we trainees were allowed only seven phrases when addressing the cadre:

Yes, sir (or ma'am).
No, sir.
No excuse, sir.
Sir, may I make a statement?
Sir, may I ask a question?
Sir, I do not understand.
Sir, I do not know.

Cadet Jackson's dismissive glare scorched the skin on my face as he dialed down the heat to simmer. "Basic Cadet Willie. You're just taking up space at my Academy," he snarled. Standing nose-to-nose, he misstated my name with a nasally drawl. Mocking me. Daring me to correct him. Disgusted by my presence. He enumerated my exhaustive list of failings—physical, mental, familial, and otherwise—which he apparently ascertained within thirty seconds of making my acquaintance.

"You understand me, Willie?"

"Yes, sir."

"That was weak. SOUND OFF!"

"YES, SIR!"

I would learn many acronyms throughout training. SAMI for Saturday morning inspection, SERE for survival, evasion, resistance, and escape, and SMACK for soldier minus aptitude, coordination, and knowledge. At the moment I stood frozen straight, as Uncle Sam's proxy issued a military-grade ass kicking, and learned about BOHICA: bend over, here it comes again.

Thus began my journey to internalize the ethos of Duty, Honor, Country as consecrated by the Air Force. We were 1,362 basic cadets facing a future of sacrifice in service of the greater good, and I welcomed it. The pending adventure was a mystery, but I was determined to finish it. The Academy made the thirteen years I later spent in medical school, surgical residency, and trauma fellowship feel like a tea party. Or to put it another way: if medical training is like taking a long sip of water from a fire hose, the Academy is like taking a sip after being hit and backed over again and again by the fire truck.

Cadet Jackson marched away while continuing his anti-motivational oratory, exuding command presence with every clickity step. Over the following years, I came to respect how much he cared about his subordinates and his uncompromising standards in service of the mission. Put simply, he had our backs. All of us, from the superstars to the stragglers, endured a trial by fire that initiated our transformation. He began deconstructing the individuals and rebuilding future leaders: those who accepted that the whole was always greater than the sum of its parts. The mission came first, then came your classmates, and then came you.

Some of Cadet Jackson's words remain seared in my memory to this day: "You will become a collective unit of high speed, low drag basic cadets, or you will go home. There are no individuals here. Never leave a classmate behind. Understand this: you succeed together and you fail together."

Within minutes of stepping onto the Academy grounds, I appreciated the importance of standards, mission, and unity. To arrive early was to be on time, to arrive on time was to be late, and to arrive late—well, that was never an option. If one of us arrived late, all of us were late, and the consequences—for everyone—were severe, motivating us to police ourselves.

On his command, we marched onto the Academy grounds in lockstep. For six weeks we made no phone calls, had no access to news, and didn't leave the Academy grounds (except a brief reprieve for Parents Weekend midway through training). Standards were the same for everyone. Race, class, legacy: these were no basis for special treatment. We all lived by the same standards and had to earn privileges as a collective unit. The message was clear: we are better together, so leave no person behind.

Before the sun vanished behind the craggy vista of the Rocky Mountains that first evening, we had learned a critical lesson. None of us could get through Beast, never mind the four years at the Academy, alone. To sell out one of our classmates was never an option. Nobody had to tell us we would succeed together or fail together. That enduring truth was obvious before Taps played, signaling lights out. As many grads say, "The Academy is not always a great place to be, but it is a great place to be from." That is what it means to be part of the Long Blue Line.

A few weeks into Beast, I lay on my belly on the warm concrete, working to relax my body as I peered through the sight on my M-16. I drew in deeply through my nostrils, paused, then slowly released the breath. Caressing the barrel with one hand, I focused on the target with concentric circles 100 yards downrange. The forefinger of my other hand remained outstretched, away from the trigger so as not to shoot prematurely in my exuberance.

"Basics. Clear your safety." Cadet Buckley, the cadre in charge of our weapons training, surveyed our line of trainees aiming downrange. Dressed in our drab, olive green fatigues, we looked like a row of lethal pickles. In fact, we called them our "pickle suits," the uniforms we'd wear until we received the camouflaged battle dress uniforms the following year.

Having completed our small arms training with a 9mm, we were now learning about the M-16, the standard-issue military assault weapon. The civilian counterpart of the M-16, the AR-15, has been used in the most lethal mass shootings in the United States. Columbine, Sandy Hook, Aurora, Sandy Springs, Uvalde: the AR-15 was the weapon of choice in the shootings that catapulted these places from obscurity and into the national gun debate. The AR-15 attracts the attention of the media in a way handguns, used in most urban violence, do not.

My mother forbade me from playing with toy guns of all kinds. Forty years before a police officer gunned down twelve-year-old Tamir Rice playing with a toy gun in a Cleveland park, less than two seconds after opening his cruiser door at the scene, my mother protected me from a deadly menace I was too young to comprehend. A southern girl raised in the era of Jim Crow, she understood the dangers I faced. As a teen, marching during the Civil Rights movement, she knew about Black boys and guns, police and violence, racism and death—and she committed to protecting me from it all.

"Ready," Cadet Buckley barked. A hulking figure two heads taller than me and built like a linebacker, if he stood downrange, the bullets would bounce off his chest and fall like raindrops from an umbrella. Based on his accent, I figured he was from the Midwest and probably learned as a youth to hunt and shoot from his father. His childhood, as I imagined it, was likely the antithesis of mine.

"Aim!"

My finger kissed the trigger.

"Fire!"

Exhaling, I squeezed the trigger, along with two dozen shooters, and the Rocky Mountain air echoed like Fourth of July fireworks. It was my first time firing an assault weapon, and I was eager to do it again. I felt powerful. I felt important. I felt alive.

As I cradled my weapon, hoping to score high enough to earn a marksmanship badge, I did not fully understand the racialized arc of gun history. Nor did I foresee how this history would intersect with my own path, how I would someday walk into emergency departments and operating rooms to work on bodies riddled with bullets. Squeezing the trigger, I knew only the blast of my supersonic bullet tearing through the air toward its target downrange.

Twenty years earlier, on May 2, 1967, thirty members of the Black Panther Party, twenty-four men and six women, exercised their legal right to carry firearms openly as they entered the statehouse in Sacramento, California. They strolled past security, entered the legislative chamber, and silently protested the unchecked police brutality in their Oakland neighborhoods. The tipping point had occurred when Oakland police shot and killed unarmed teenager Denzil Dowell and left him to die without calling an ambulance (Dowell was accused of robbing a liquor store). The Black Panthers had already organized legally armed patrols to protect their neighborhoods from police violence, but the California assembly, with the backing of the National Rifle Association (NRA), had different ideas.

The image of two dozen armed Black people "invading" the state Capitol came to define the Black Panthers. They broke no laws and left peacefully, but they were considered a menace nonetheless. Although there were no threats, altercations, or deaths, almost all were arrested. Stereotyped as violent extremists, the Black Panthers, in the words of one author, "committed to defending Black people—with weapons, but also with education and with services designed to raise families out of abject poverty."

Still, the media christened the Black Panther protest the "Sacramento Invasion," and it engendered a swift reaction. With the backing of the NRA, Governor Ronald Reagan stated that he saw "no reason why on the street today a citizen should be carrying loaded weapons," and called guns a "ridiculous way to solve problems that have to be solved among people of good will." Republicans who controlled the California Assembly passed legislation to expand gun control within the state, effectively disarming the Black Panthers. Reagan signed the Mulford Act into law on July 28, 1967, validating cynics who proclaimed that the surest way to enact gun control was to see Black Americans purchase firearms en masse.

By intent, the Mulford Act aimed to disarm the Black Panthers, and in doing so, removed the ability of Black Oakland residents to defend themselves from the police violence that was tacitly sanctioned by the state. It was one of the strictest gun control laws of its era. Don't miss the irony of this: the NRA, longtime opponents of limiting gun rights, supported the measure. Yes: the largest, most powerful, and most effective gun-rights lobby in the history of this nation sided *against* the rights of Black people to carry guns.

As an eighteen-year-old cadet in basic training, I gave little thought to gun violence or gun policy in the United States. I remained blind to the history threading its way from my firearms training to the violence ravaging Black neighborhoods, and the efforts America made to keep guns from people who looked like me. My family did not own firearms, and I believed guns, beyond the military and law enforcement, were the purview of two separate worlds: hunting enthusiasts and criminals. My binary vision remained fixed for decades. Media portrayal of firearms influenced my perception. The visual entertainment often depicted Black men glorifying AK-47s and Uzis in music, movies, and hip-hop videos. And in the 1990s, journalists, academics, and politicians peddled the myth of "superpredators": young Black men who purportedly prowled city streets, plotting to rape, murder, and pillage. The implicit message being amplified was that Black people—especially young Black men like me—were an existential threat to the American way of life.

The superpredator theory turned out to be built on false assumptions and racist tropes, and crime statistics simply didn't support it. But if a Black man like me could swallow that twisted narrative about gun violence, I'm sure it was a gluttonous meal upon which many Americans gorged.

That afternoon in basic training, I focused most on earning enough points for a marksmanship badge. I finished the day without reaching my goal. Still, in one afternoon, I spent more time learning about gun safety than most states now require as a condition of owning a gun.

As an eighteen-year-old, I had yet to learn one of the unspoken realities of American life: who possesses the gun matters. White men with guns are considered patriots, cops are protectors, and Black men are criminals. And even though I wore a uniform and served my country as an Air Force officer, in some circles I would always fit that last description.

Over four years our physical, academic, and military training continued. Room inspections, uniform inspections, physical fitness tests, sleep deprivation, hunger, and some unsanctioned hazing: through it all, I internalized values about attention to detail, teamwork, and service above self. These timeless values still serve me today.

Those years tested me in ways I did not predict. I awoke thinking about mission, service, camaraderie, and I slept dreaming about integrity, loyalty, and respect. I knew when I strayed from those ideals, I could always course correct and achieve greater heights. I learned that some failures are beyond my control but that I could integrate those lessons into my life to recover and ascend.

Weeks before graduation, my classmates and I gathered in the common room to watch a bystander's video of four Los Angeles police officers beating Black motorist Rodney King. They struck him more than fifty times with nightsticks and kicked him over and over again as he cowered on the pavement. Public outrage ensued. Then the narrative predictably morphed: from police brutally beating a defenseless Black man, pummeling him with a swarm of batons as he lay prostrate on the ground, to attempts to discredit King.

Our cadet lives continued uninterrupted. Operation Desert Storm, the first US war in Iraq, ended one hundred days after the initial bombs dropped on Baghdad. Thus, the geopolitical temperature had cooled by the time I graduated, pinned on my gold 2nd Lieutenant bars, and moved to Williams Air Force Base on the outskirts of Phoenix, Arizona, to start undergraduate pilot training. The success of the war should have made the path to a second term as president for George Herbert Walker Bush, our commencement speaker, a cakewalk. It was not. A bad economy and a third-party run by billionaire and fellow Texan Ross Perot helped propel a scandal-ridden Bill Clinton to eight years in the White House.

Months before election night, as those three men campaigned to become leader of the free world, a majority-white jury acquitted the officers who had brutalized Rodney King. Protests erupted, setting Los Angeles ablaze for six days. On TV we watched buildings burn, shops being ransacked, and a group of Black men pull a white man from his truck and batter him with a brick to the head. The financial devastation exceeded $1 billion with more than 50 deaths, 2,300 injuries, 12,000 arrests, and more than 1,000 buildings set ablaze.

It sickened me—not just the vandalism but the brick to the head of a bystander. *Why do that?* I thought; that's exactly what they will use to morally convict all of us. And as the apparent spokesperson for all Black people within my circle of white friends, I found myself trying to answer their questions. "Why would they do that to their neighbor-hood?" a white friend and fellow officer said to me as we turned off the TV after watching the news. "It's an expression of anger at systemic oppression," I said—even though I only had a basic understanding of what the words meant. I tried to channel Martin Luther King Jr. who, responding to the protests of the 1960s over police brutality, said, "A riot is a language of the unheard."

"Look, Willie," he rebutted, looking me straight in the eye. "There are niggers, and then there are people like you. *Those* people? They're niggers."

Every now and then, someone close surprises us by saying the quiet part out loud. I had considered this fellow officer a friend and even an ally. Do people slip and drop that bomb only once? Or do they slip because they use the word all the time? Nevertheless, I said nothing. Offended, indignant, and insulted? Yes. And silent.

My deep shame now is admitting that, on some level, I agreed with him. I, too, put myself in a different category from other Black people—the ones I felt chose to spend their time in the streets instead of in the books. Those who prepared to go to jail instead of going to college. I was nothing like them; I was better. And once that belief took root in my psyche, it grew, and it informed what I felt about who I was, what I represented, and my purpose in the world.

I didn't admit to anyone—even myself—that I, too, felt angry and destructive. How I sometimes wanted to scream, curse, break, and scorch the earth. It would take several more years before I began to see myself in the Black men burning LA—and to see them in me.

One afternoon a few years after graduation, I sat in my jet-black Porsche, barely a half mile outside the main gate of Eglin Air Force Base, a flight test center tucked away in the Florida panhandle. My hands were at 10 and 2 on my steering wheel and my eyes were glued to the rearview mirror, watching the driver's side door open on the police cruiser parked behind me. Out stepped a police officer, who sauntered to my side of the car. I had already opened the tinted window to give him a clear view of the interior.

"Do you know why I pulled you over?" he asked.

"No, Officer," I said, in an even monotone.

Nothing moved except the beading sweat slithering down my shaved head. My heart pounded to escape from my chest, echoing in my head. A disobedient bead of sweat snaked by my nose, leaving an itchy trail I desperately wanted to scratch but dared not. I didn't move my hands. I didn't turn my head to address him, frozen as I was, like I was in formation at the Academy. No movement. Eyes front. Speak only when spoken to. Answer with a modified version of the seven basic responses.

"Is this your car?"

"Yes, Officer." He peered into the car as I answered.

"Where are you headed?" I wore my blue uniform with shiny officer's rank on my shoulders and medals on my chest, and there were military stickers on my windshield permitting access to the base, which was less than one mile ahead. Where else would I be heading?

"Back to work, Officer."

"License and registration, please." He was cordial and professional. But none of that quelled the surge of adrenaline igniting my fight or flight response, the evolutionary thread connecting us to our ancestors' desire to survive in a hostile environment. Images of Rodney King's bent, brutalized body on the pavement looped through my brain.

"It's in the glove compartment," I said. My left hand remained at 10, while my right retrieved the documents.

"Step out of the car, please."

"What?" I spoke, before catching myself.

"I said: step out of the car." He went from cordial to commanding in a flash. I kept one hand visible while I opened the door, placed one spit-shined shoe on the pavement, then the other. I held my hands at a height high enough to not be a threat, low enough to not appear guilty—except I had no control over whether I appeared guilty to this cop or not.

"Turn around and put your hands on the hood," he ordered.

This son of a bitch, I thought. I did as I was told, my fear curdling into a rage that I knew I had to control. On the main road to the base, car after car of officers, noncommissioned officers, and their families rubbernecked at this spectacle: a uniformed man spread-eagle, with his hands on the hood in the middle of a weekday.

The officer finally informed me I'd been doing 36 miles per hour in a 30 mph zone. I drove off, shaken and furious. Later, some of my coworkers who had passed by and recognized me asked, "What was that all about?"

"Just a speeding ticket," I demurred. But I have always felt that traffic stop had less to do with my driving six miles over the speed limit and more to do with driving an expensive car while Black.

America always manages to remind people with skin like mine that no matter how many professional successes, medals, and awards we earn, we should never forget our place. I don't know what that officer truly thought, and I'll never know. Maybe the stop was routine, not racial profiling. Maybe the cop was doing his job and not on some power trip. Maybe, I tell myself, I should stop being so paranoid.

But that's the issue. The loop of remembering and analyzing and interpreting and wondering that Black people in America are expected to do so others may feel comfortable: those are the perpetual mental gymnastics of wondering if we'd be treated differently if we weren't Black. Like my mother said, we own the car, not the highway.

All I know is none of my white friends have been stopped as many times as I have, or ordered out of their cars, or made to stand spread-eagle with their hands on the hood for going six miles an hour over the speed limit. And I doubt any of them wonders if a routine traffic stop will mean a ticket or death.

One evening during college football season, fellow Academy grad Lt. Casey Gordon and I were at a hole-in-the-wall bar celebrating the Air Force Falcons' victory when we began discussing our career plans. We were both due for transfers within the year, and although the final decision belonged to Uncle Sam, we could make our desires known.

"What are you doing next, Casey?" I asked.

"Med school," he replied.

He said out loud what I had been thinking for nearly one year. What I believed was no longer possible. Like me, Casey was an Air Force Academy graduate working as an aeronautical engineer at Eglin Air Force Base. We ordered another round as he laid out the path—the one I thought closed a decade prior when I majored in aeronautical engineering instead of pre-med. "All those extra classes they made us take at the Academy cover the core requirements for med school," he said. "Bio, Physics, Chemistry: pass those and you can get a degree in anything and still apply to med school."

Nursing my last beer amid screeching guitars and pounding drums, I contemplated what I would do. Could I become a doctor? Should I become a doctor?

Like it did to my father's life, the Air Force changed the trajectory of mine. After four years at the Academy, I spent an additional six years on active duty, promoted to 1st Lieutenant in year two and to captain in year four. By year six, I cruised on an enviable trajectory, certain to continue rising to higher positions of leadership. Still, another career beckoned. No longer constrained by my childhood beliefs that Black people weren't doctors, I wanted to become one myself. For that to become a reality, I had to make a drastic course correction. So I did what no sensible adult should do while semi-inebriated: I made a major life decision. Savoring a long pull of my beer, I set the empty bottle on the bar top, turned to Casey, and bailed from my engineering career.

"Well, if that's all it takes to become a doctor, then I'm going to med school too."

5 | A NEW CALLING

The man was basically dead on arrival, but the trauma fellow, the most senior trainee on the team, cracked his chest anyway. It was the summer of 1999, and I was a third-year medical student, standing wide-eyed and speechless about five feet from the foot of the bed. Beside the red crash cart, which held all the lifesaving medications and supplies, I stood close enough to see the action but not too close to be a nuisance.

The swarm of doctors and nurses trying to revive the limp body before us enthralled me. They cut off his clothes, poked his arms with intravenous catheters, and calmly spoke rapid fire in what sounded like a foreign language I would only later master.

"Still no pulse."

"He's in PEA."

"Give a round of epi."

"I don't hear breath sounds on the right," said the junior resident, a stethoscope snaking from her ears to the patient's bare chest. No breath sounds meant his lung, pierced by a bullet, was deflated, and his chest cavity likely filled with blood.

"Let's place a right chest tube," said the trauma fellow, who supervised the junior resident performing the procedure. In a blink, a red geyser ejected from a two-inch incision between two ribs, painting the stretcher, resident, and floor. The patient continued to hose red into a plastic tube inserted through the incision. Blood should have pumped in a circuit—away from his heart, through his arteries, back through his veins, and return to his heart—but instead it drained through a tube speared into his chest into the pleuravac: a clear, closed-system canister on the floor. The average human blood volume is five liters. Over one-third of his pooled in the canister and continued rising, like a bucket filling with water.

It was my first night on a call with the trauma team at Tampa General Hospital. To a neophyte like me, a medical student at the University of South Florida, it all appeared to be utter chaos when this gunshot victim arrived in traumatic arrest. But I didn't have to understand a word the team spoke to know this patient was in critical condition.

"Set up for a thoracotomy," the fellow said to a nearby nurse. Like magic, a tray of surgical tools materialized. The following sequence of events happened at lightning speed. One second the fellow, guided by the gray-haired attending physician who sauntered in and now bent over beside him, held the scalpel against the patient's left chest; then blood was cascading onto the tile floor. The trauma fellow cranked open the rib spreaders, and his arm disappeared up to his elbow, snaking into the chest cavity as he grasped the aorta of the dying patient. He continued to bark one-word commands: *Cross-clamp. Knife. Scissors. Paddles.*

Soon, however, the commands ceased. The attending, the most senior doctor in the room, the one in charge of everybody and guiding the fellow through the procedure, said, "Enough. I'm gonna call it. Time of death: 2:07 a.m." With two fistfuls of blue fabric, he yanked off his tearaway gown, peeled off his gloves, and tossed the bloody heap in the red biohazard bin. "Thank you, everyone," were his departing words as he strolled out of the room with zero fanfare, recognition, or drama.

As the energy in the trauma bay slowed and those around us began to clean up, the fellow called me over, his energy skyrocketing. "Come here, Williams," he said, directing me to his side with an ear-to-ear grin. "Get a closer look at this."

I crept across the blood-splattered floor and peered into the open chest cavity. "Slide your hand here—and be careful not to catch yourself on a rib," he said. "They'll shred that glove and cut you. Assume every patient has AIDS or hepatitis or some other shit I guarantee you don't want to catch."

Sound medical advice. Truthful and direct, and also a bit insensitive, I thought. The fellow guided my hand around the splintered rib edges and into the thoracic cavity, where the lungs and heart lay. "Put your finger there. You feel that hole?" I pushed gently, and my finger popped through a narrow space under a dense mass of tissue. But I couldn't see the space, and I wasn't sure what it meant.

"That's a hole in the posterior wall of the left ventricle," the fellow said, with a hint of joy. "This banger never had a chance."

My brain didn't register his choice of words. Before us lay a beautiful, bloody mess. Sure, I thought, it was sad this procedure didn't end well. But the idea you could know so much about the human body that you could, in seconds, make decisions and incisions that could save a life? I thought the fellow who did it was a badass. A god.

I had just seen my first emergency department thoracotomy: the final hope for reviving an injured patient dying from massive internal bleeding, requiring a foot-long incision between two ribs allowing access to the left chest cavity. It's a last-ditch, Hail Mary procedure.

And that was the moment I decided to become a trauma surgeon. My transformation had begun. The ideals of serving humanity— ideals that had dominated my career in the military and drew me to a career in medicine—were beginning to ebb. The desire for adrenaline-fueled glory began to replace them. Honestly, what could be more awesome than pulling patients back from the brink? As my wife once told me, "Being a trauma surgeon is pretty damn sexy."

Trauma surgery was my first clinical rotation after two years of lectures, gross anatomy, labs, shadowing, and passing the first two parts of the three-part United States Medical Licensing Exam. I still had more than eleven months of required rotations on internal medicine, obstetrics and gynecology, family practice, pediatrics, and psychiatry, and another year of electives. That meant I had plenty of time to change my mind about the specialty to which I'd devote decades of my life, maybe choose a less stressful one. Still time to choose a specialty not requiring work on nights, weekends, and holidays. A specialty less taxing on any future marriage and family. One where violence and death would be the exception, not the rule. But trauma surgery became my paramour. Surgery became my first thought in the mornings when I awoke, and what I last studied at night before I slept.

After six years on active duty, I had entered medical school with the sure notion that I wanted to be a doctor but only a vague idea of what kind. I had no concept of what it meant to be a trauma surgeon or how to become one. But within days of taking trauma call every other night, twenty-four hours on followed by twenty-four hours off (in reality, it was more like thirty-six on, twelve off), I could see that trauma surgeons were the real badasses in the hospital. When the proverbial shit hit the fan, they were the ones called to clean the mess. Saving lives every day and bringing calm to chaos wherever they appeared: these were my people.

Like I said, the fact that my fellow had called a dead Black boy—some grieving mother's son—a "banger" didn't register. Frankly, if it had, it wouldn't have made a bit of difference to me. I had said it myself many times before, and I would say it many times after.

"If he was DOA," I asked the fellow, "then why do a thoracotomy?" Even then, in awe of the drama I had witnessed, I couldn't dismiss the ethical quandary. The survival rate for patients who undergo an ED thoracotomy is very low, and those who do survive frequently have permanent, severe neurological damage. Why perform a disfiguring procedure on someone you can't save?

The trauma fellow patted me on the shoulder in a paternal manner that left me confused. Was he impressed by my inquisitiveness or amused by my ignorance? "MRB, my friend. MRB," he said with a radiant smile. MRB, which stands for "maximum resident benefit," refers to procedures that help residents gain experience and sharpen their procedural skills. The challenge is balancing resident autonomy with patient safety, which would become an organizational crisis at one of my future institutions. "Williams, you should always be looking for procedures that provide maximum resident benefit," he told me. "Central lines, chest tubes, intubations, and especially an ED thoracotomy: never let a DOA stop you from getting to practice a procedure."

I accepted his explanation, which made some sense. Only later would I realize the extent to which a young, Black, male gunshot victim could be treated as less than a life to be saved and more as a warm human specimen on which to practice. As I advanced in my career, from student to resident to fellow to attending, I began to see how the first death I saw as a medical student put all that was wrong with medicine on bloody display: how ostensibly acting in service of the "greater good" can actually inflict unbearable harm on those least able to advocate for themselves. How we justify our actions by saying some patients have nowhere else to go or that we offer their only hope. How easy it is to rationalize committing acts against people who look nothing like us, and how simple it is to segregate their reality from our own. How many patients and families suffered on my watch because I ignored this truth while ascending the medical hierarchy?

The quintessential rite of passage in medical school is gross anatomy, in which you dissect human cadavers. Working in four-person teams of first-year medical students, we'd spend one evening studying textbook anatomy, the following morning in lecture, and the afternoon methodically dissecting the cadaver from head to toe. Over the course of a semester, we meticulously worked our way from the superficial layers of skin deep to the internal organs. We'd peel back layers of skin, identify muscles, bones, and ligaments, remove the heart, liver, and other organs, and even take a buzzsaw to the skull to remove the brain for examination.

Today it is common for people to donate their bodies to medical science after their death, whether it be for dissection, tissue harvesting, or medical experimentation. But this has not always been the case. A few years before I started medical school, nearly ten thousand bones were found buried beneath the Medical College of Georgia. Some 75 percent of those bones came from Black bodies. In the nineteenth century, during the earliest years of formalized medical education, medical students stole the corpses of recently deceased Black people to use in dissection courses. It was expected, accepted, and encouraged. Black and white people could not be buried together, so obtaining remains merely required students to sneak, in the dead of night, to the segregated burial grounds on the edge of town and abscond with the corpses. And the remains rarely received a dignified return to the grave; some were disposed of in the city streets, sewers, or incinerators.

This practice never ended; it merely evolved. Today there is a for-profit and unregulated industry supplying cadavers to medical schools in which corporate interests often trump ethical concerns. Indeed, the modern equivalent of midnight nineteenth-century graverobbers is the twenty-first-century body broker who often preys on individuals with low medical literacy or financial stability. Body brokers are formally known as non-transplant tissue banks and are different from the organ and tissue transplant industry, which is closely regulated by the US government. They promise to cover the costs of a dignified burial in exchange for indviduals, or their families, donating their bodies for science after death. Frequently, the brokers provide neither, instead harvesting tissue and organs in what an investigative report by the Associated Press described as an industry where bodies are "traded as raw material in a largely unregulated national market."

Biochemistry, histopathology, pharmacology, physiology, and basic clinical skills, such as how to use an otoscope to examine a patient's eardrum: I learned a lot in medical school. There's no denying that. Yet it's what I didn't learn that astounds me. This history, and much more, did not appear in my medical school curriculum. Like the human body, which is much more intricate than the surface might suggest, medical education itself deserves our attention. Racism, violence, and inequality are written into the DNA of professions like medicine, far beneath the surface of skin we see.

Buried deep in the history of medical education is the Flexner Report. Published in 1910, it was a landmark study commissioned by the Carnegie Foundation with advocacy from leadership at the American Medical Association (AMA). The AMA lamented that the unregulated medical education system of the time produced poorly trained and unqualified doctors, and Abraham Flexner was an educator chosen to conduct a nationwide survey. Their concerns about the quality of medical education did have merit, but the recommendations affecting Black medical schools, future doctors, and patients reverberates to this day.

The report succeeded in providing much needed standardization to medical education; more than half of the medical schools in the United States and Canada closed. With those newer standards, however, came higher education fees, which narrowed the potential pool of applicants to those with the resources to pay. It's not hard to identify the immediate disadvantage for racial and ethnic minorities, women, and the poor. It also helped solidify the power of the AMA, which now controlled the pipeline of who could become doctors. In short, fewer doctors with less diversity in race, class, and gender meant less competition and higher earnings. The era of the wealthy, white, male physician was born.

More importantly, the Flexner Report explicitly discriminated against Black medical schools and doctor-candidates. Abraham

Flexner wrote that Black doctors should train in "hygiene rather than surgery" and should primarily serve as "sanitarians," to prevent the spread of infectious diseases. Flexner also reported that medical facilities should remain segregated, and white doctors should treat Black patients as a means of protecting white people from "a potential source of infection and contagion." He concluded by recommending closure of five of the seven Black medical schools, leaving only Howard in Washington, DC, and Meharry in Nashville, Tennessee.

The impact of the Flexner Report is evident today in the perpetual underrepresentation of Black people in the medical profession. Fewer Black men entered medical school in 2016, the final year of office of our first Black president, than in the 1970s, when I asked my mother if there were any Black doctors.

Then, in May 2001, I became one myself and left Tampa to continue my medical odyssey in Boston.

In the summer of 2001, I was a high-speed, low-drag surgery intern flying through the halls of the world-renowned Brigham and Women's Hospital in Boston. One morning the chief resident, Dr. Lee, a physically unimposing Asian-American man a few inches shorter than me, approached. Like Cadet Jackson from my days at the Air Force Academy, his size belied his command presence.

"Williams," he said in a soothing yet directive baritone.

"Yes, sir," I said. Years of Air Force military protocol still flowed in my veins.

"There are two types of interns: those who forget and those who write it down."

"Yes, sir."

As I marched alongside Dr. Lee, nurses, patients, and staff scurrying in the hallway parted for him like the Red Sea. He continued to speak in his signature militaristic cadence. "Which type of intern are you?"

I paused before answering, the silence expanding and engulfing us both. I had spent four years at the Air Force Academy memorizing a universe of facts and quotes and airplane silhouettes, then four years in medical school memorizing more facts and formulas and diseases. I almost turned a straightforward question with only one answer into a trick question with options. "The kind who . . . writes it down?" I finally answered. My voice trailed upward an octave.

"That's right," he grinned, pleased with my answer. He was pleased to have an intern hanging on his every word. But most of all, he was pleased with himself. Pleased because he was a chief resident at one of the premier surgery residency programs in the country, and he was one of the most important people in the hospital. Dr. Lee was arguably more important than the surgical attendings, to whom we both answered. It was he who remained in the hospital at all hours of the day and night, directing the team, making the day-to-day medical decisions for dozens of patients, and handling emergencies. He had earned his rarefied position, and he knew it. So why should he pretend otherwise?

Brigham and Women's Hospital, one of the main teaching hospitals of Harvard Medical School and known as "The Brigham," has a storied history in academic surgery. During my residency, larger-than-life portraits of surgeon-icons adorned our main surgery conference room. Dr. Eliot Cutler served in the Army Medical Corps during World War I and was lauded for his work in valvular heart surgery. Dr. Francis Moore became a pioneer in transplant surgery. Dr. Harvey Cushing was a renowned neurosurgeon, confidante of Franklin D. Roosevelt, and vocal opponent to government-sponsored health insurance. The Brigham is home to Nobel Laureates, surgical innovators, and leaders who transformed healthcare.

After four years of medical school, I began my fifth year of training, the first with MD behind my name. As a chief resident in the summer of 2001, Dr. Lee was six years ahead of me, having already finished four years of clinical training and a two-year research sabbatical. He continued to flip more pearls of surgical wisdom to me.

"Williams, if there's something that can't be done, you get it done."

"Yes, sir."

"If there's something we can't get, you find a way to get it."

"Yes, sir."

"You're always running, from the time you hit the door 'til the time you go home." He grinned again.

"Yes, sir."

"And when a patient tells you they feel like they're dying, believe them."

"Yes, sir."

"And dude. Stop calling me sir. This is surgery, not boot camp."

"Yes, s——. Got it."

Maybe it wasn't a return to basic training, but it was a Beast of another species, and the hierarchical nature of surgical residency fit me like dress blues. Many of the habits I internalized at the Air Force Academy never died: to place service above self. To provide solutions, not excuses. To respect the rank even when you don't respect the person.

And to never bother my commanders unless shit is flying (proverbially and, sometimes, in surgery, literally).

"Williams," Dr. Lee bellowed without breaking stride while we continued patient rounds, "Do you know the worst thing about being me?"

"No, I don't."

"It's that I can't operate with myself. You know, be my own assistant." His head snapped backward in a full-throated laugh at his own joke that filled the halls. I'd hear that same joke from him countless times until he graduated. His grin gleamed through morning rounds, a day of colorectal surgery, afternoon rounds, and I'm certain when he drove home that night.

Surgery interns often don't yet know what they don't know. This can be a problem because something they diagnose as a minor condition could actually be life-threatening. In the summer of 2001, I began my journey as a surgeon. I learned a lot during medical school, but not enough. It's what surgery interns don't know that can make us highly educated lethal weapons to strangers entrusted to our care—or merely a nuisance who could give you quite a bruise, as I learned one night while doing evening rounds.

"Good evening, Mr. Linden," I said to the elderly man lying in bed. No response.

"Mr. Linden?" Still nothing.

"Mr. Linden!" My heart began to gallop, and my brain kicked into overdrive. I froze.

The nurse with me stopped pressing buttons on Mr. Linden's infusion pump and looked at me bug eyed. I already knew that most nurses know plenty more than any intern, and I respected their experience and knowledge. As an Air Force officer, I had learned to respect enlisted troops I outranked but who would sometimes save me from myself. The nurses who worked with medical students and interns had developed skillful methods to get us trainees to do what we didn't know we should do. Sometimes the nurses were subtle with us, other times more directive. The nurse's look of abject terror horrified me: an unresponsive patient plus a nurse who looked terrified equals disaster. I leapt into action.

"Call a code!"

As the words to activate the emergency code team rushed from my mouth with military authority, everything I learned to earn my certification as an advanced cardiac life support provider departed with them. I no longer had any idea how to run a code. And Mr. Linden might die because of it. The various cardiac rhythms, medications, and appropriate advanced cardiac life support algorithms had simply vaporized from my mind.

The nurse smacked the code blue button on the wall, activating a battalion of nurses, doctors, and technicians. But in the alternate universe born in the crisis moment of life and death, time became relative. The minutes it would take for the cavalry to arrive felt like hours. Even I, as an intern, knew nobody could survive more than a few minutes of cardiac arrest. I had to do something.

"Mr. Linden! Tell me your name, sir!" No response.

I pleaded for him to wake up before the nurses arrived because I'd have to run the code. The steps needed to save this man's life—even the presence of mind needed to retrieve the bright red life support algorithm cart nearby—were beyond my grasp during that millisecond. My only thought was Mr. Linden had to wake up before they connected the defibrillator, which would spit out a white strip of squiggly black lines another nurse would hand to me to interpret in front of everyone. And then I'd have to decide if his cardiac rhythm was this, that, or the other thing. And if he was coding, did I give him meds? Which one? Would I shock him? How much? I had to do it right or Mr. Linden would die.

The staff would roll in with the red crash cart with needles and medications, and I would have to decide which one to give.

Or Mr. Linden would die.

On the crash cart would be the defibrillator with sticky white pads they'd slap upon his chest, and I'd have to decide whether to defibrillate.

Or Mr. Linden would die.

And if I decided too slowly, or interpreted the rhythm incorrectly, or defibrillated when I should order medication, or ordered medication when I should defibrillate—then Mr. Linden would die. Right then, right there, Mr. Linden would die, and it would be my fault. And I would spend the rest of my shift completing death paperwork and dictating a death summary and asking the family to consent to a post-mortem to see what had killed Mr. Linden. I could see the medical examiner's writing on the death certificate now: "Cause of Death: Dr. Brian Williams."

As the code team stormed the room, rolling in battle equipment, I, a doctor only a few weeks out of medical school, assumed my position of authority, and did what I could do best.

I did it with vigor.

I did it with confidence.

I did it with military authority.

Channeling all my fear and desperation and angst into a tight fist, I ground two angry knuckles into his sternum as if drilling a hole to China. Inches from his face, I barked: "Mr. Linden, *wake . . . up!*"

"Ouch!" Mr. Linden yelped, backhanding my fist away and nearly dislocating my wrist. He blinked in the light, sleepily processing the army of doctors and nurses gathered for his rescue.

Stunned, I straightened up, my chest puffing outward. It worked! I saved his life!

But the seconds of self-adulation were few. Soon it became clear what happened. I had subjected Mr. Linden to one of the most uncomfortable maneuvers in medicine: the sternal rub. It's a maneuver so painful it will get a reaction from anyone not on the brink of death and is now discouraged by many practitioners. But, when done, the sternal rub is the third step in a sequence to evaluate an unresponsive patient. The first is verbal stimuli, which I did. The second step will sound familiar if you've ever watched a television medical drama: check for a pulse.

Before I so expertly revived Mr. Linden, I failed to place two fingers on the side of his neck to feel for a pulse. Nor had I taken time to observe his chest, which rose and fell rhythmically, indicating he was breathing on his own. Nor did I learn until later that the "experienced" nurse was merely weeks out of nursing school. A senior nurse assuredly would have saved me from myself. This new graduate would mature into a phenomenal nurse, and we would joke about that night for years.

Do not attempt to perform a life-saving procedure on a patient who does not need one: it's pretty basic. In medicine we joke that when arriving at a code, first check your own pulse. Second, check the pulse of the patient. By the time the operating rooms were humming in the morning, I was infamous. Top of the list for bonehead intern maneuvers. The green trainee who diagnosed a cardiac arrest in an elderly man, sleeping soundly.

I will say this for myself: times of medical crisis do require decisive action, expertise, and technical skill. An indecisive trauma surgeon can be as dangerous as an unskilled one. Mr. Linden received a bruised sternum, and I can tell you I've learned a lot between those early days and now. But as an intern, I still epitomized another Dr. Lee dictum: "frequently wrong, but never in doubt."

Weeks earlier, on July 4, 2001, shortly before the fireworks show started over the Boston Esplanade, Kathianne Sellers strutted past me at a restaurant bar. I'd later learn as a preteen, she stopped in Colorado Springs while on vacation with her parents and sister. On their way to tour several national parks, they paused to visit the United States Air Force Academy Cadet Chapel. Visitors can watch the Academy noon meal formation, when the entire cadet wing gathers ceremonially before marching to lunch. During one of those formations, my future wife might have seen her future husband marching in a sea of cadets.

Now, fourteen years after our serendipitous crossing at the Academy, it was she who marched past me exuding an aura that announced, "Step aside, I'm here." I almost jumped to attention and saluted.

Dressed in black cropped pants painted onto her toned physique, she wore her shoulder-length brunette hair pulled into a ponytail. Knowing we only miss 100 percent of the shots we don't take, I took mine and introduced myself.

"I'm Kathianne," she responded. "It's one word. And don't call me Kathy."

She set her boundaries from the start. Kathianne had actually been recruited by the Academy herself, but she chose to go to the University of Minnesota on a track scholarship. Once ranked third in the nation for high school high jump, she was also a Pennsylvania state champion and held a district high jump record that remained unbroken for thirty years. In college, she ran the anchor leg for the record-holding 4x100 relay. A registered dietitian, she loathed organic chemistry and was fascinated with psychology. Her direct-ness, confidence, and openness impressed me. My own list of accom-plishments, which most people found impressive, she found to be underwhelming.

That evening, in an endearing non sequitur, she said, "I can't marry a doctor. I'll never be your priority." Since we had met mere minutes earlier, marriage was the furthest thing from my mind. Six weeks after we met, she left Boston, moving back to her home state of Pennsylvania to earn her master's degree in health education. We maintained dwindling contact over the intervening weeks, as I worked hundred- or even hundred-twenty-hour weeks as a surgical intern.

Then came 9/11. I was at work in the early months of my surgery internship when Kathianne called to tell me a plane had crashed into one of the twin towers. Even as the second tower collapsed, the magnitude of the tragedy escaped me. I knew something historic was unfolding beyond the sterilized world in which I was immersed, but I could not stop my work to absorb the news. In an era of flip phones and mobile plans charging by the minute, television, not social media, was still king for breaking news.

While much of the world stopped, engrossed by the footage of the World Trade Center attack, interns and residents and doctors and nurses did the litany of medical chores required of us. I was in a dead sprint: examining patients, writing medication orders, checking lab results, and dictating discharge summaries. Entering patients' rooms that day, I'd catch snippets from the television: talking heads speaking of a nation at war. But it seemed to be happening a universe away. Right then I had to pre-op Mr. Jones, discharge Ms. Brown, and adjust Mr. Smith's pain medication. Interns occupied the lowest rung of the hierarchical surgical ladder. An intern does not question or think or complain. An intern gets it done—at least the good ones do. And I intended to be great.

As the day of 9/11 morphed into the era of post-9/11, the world around me changed significantly. But I changed little. Why should I? I could lie low for now, as many Americans focused their ire on people who appeared to have familial roots in the Middle East. Their skin was not as dark as mine, but most were still easy to identify. Instead of wearing baggy denim jeans, the men dressed in tunics. Instead of locs, the women wore hijabs. Nations at war are skillful at dehumanizing their perceived enemies. In World War II we had the *Japs* and *Krauts*. Vietnam gave us *gooks* and *dinks*. After 9/11 little time passed before the verbal attacks rained upon *ragheads* and *camel jockeys*. For the moment, Black people were no longer the most derided racial group in America.

The period was short-lived. In the early days following 9/11, I entered a clothing shop and somehow managed to walk headlong into the tirade of an apoplectic Sikh. His arms flailing as he spoke in a near falsetto. Within seconds, I understood he and a customer were in a heated disagreement that involved a racist epithet. Having been in the situation myself many times, I sympathized with the shop owner—until he suddenly spat his venom toward me.

Spotting me, the owner's eyes widened. He pointed and boomed, "I am no sand nigger! *He's* the goddamn nigger!"

I did an about-face and walked out. I knew what I wanted to say would get me nowhere, and what I wanted to do might get me arrested—or worse. Seeking acceptance from the handful of speechless white customers, the store owner had reestablished his place on the racial pecking order. He'd get none of my money, but I'm certain his business suffered little that day.

War-time racist epithets eventually fade from the American lexicon, but *nigger* is timeless. It is the "epithet that generates epithets," as Randall Kennedy writes—the root of the root. "That is why Arabs are called 'sand niggers,' Irish 'the niggers of Europe,' and Palestinians 'the niggers of the Middle East,' " writes Kennedy, explaining what I experienced. *Nigger* perpetuates the caste system by crushing the core of what makes us human. It dehumanizes.

"What white people have to do is try and find out in their own hearts why it was necessary to have a nigger in the first place," James Baldwin wrote, "because I'm not a nigger, I'm a man, but if you think I'm a nigger, it means you need it."

After grad school, Kathianne returned to Boston to be with me and, four years after we met, we were married. Our peripatetic life together began with our first move to Atlanta for my trauma fellowship. Through it all, as an absentee partner, I proved her right in her concern about marrying a doctor. On my way to becoming a double board-certified trauma surgeon, I dedicated barely enough energy to keep the marriage aloft.

Yet in the decades we've been together, from my internship in Boston to becoming an attending on Chicago's South Side, she has been a persistent and sometimes forceful presence. Even now, when I am hyperfocused on work, she grabs me by the scruff of the neck and forces me to stop and take notice of my surroundings. Better than anyone, she knows how skilled I am at remaining unaware of the obvious, how unconscious I can be of the reality unfolding around me.

6 | THE GRADYS

Grady Memorial Hospital in Atlanta, Georgia, first opened as a fourteen-bed public hospital in 1892, the same year the first immigrants passed through Ellis Island. Also, that year more than 160 Black Americans were lynched. The current incarnation of the hospital, like the three previous ones, was constructed as a segregated facility, and it remained so until 1965. The same year saw Malcolm X assassinated and civil rights protestors beaten, attacked by dogs, and firehosed by law enforcement as they crossed the Edmund Pettus Bridge on Bloody Sunday.

It's hard to imagine a clearer manifestation of the racialized US healthcare system than Grady Hospital. In fact, during the Jim Crow era, Atlantans referred to the hospital in the plural form—"The Gradys"—because it was essentially two different hospitals contained in a single building. During my fellowship training, many of the elders I cared for still referred to it as such. For many years, Grady had four wings: A and B wings for white patients, with enviable views of the city, and D and E wings on the opposite side for Black patients, with views of neighborhood blight. A long hallway connected the two segregated wards, and Black doctors were disallowed into the hospital to care for their own patients who had been admitted.

Grady Hospital is also where I trained to become a trauma surgeon and critical care specialist. A few weeks after I began my fellowship, the American Medical Association, recognizing the transgenerational damage of the Flexner Report it had commissioned a century earlier, formally apologized for its treatment of Black doctors and patients. I started my fellowship in 2008, the year we elected our first Black president, and finished in 2010, the year after President Barack Obama signed into law his signature legislative victory: the Patient Protection and Affordable Care Act. I paid little attention to this landmark legislation, focused as I was on the bullet-ridden bodies in front of me. And if you'd asked me about any connections between my work, the Affordable Care Act, and creating health equity, my answer would have been vague and uninformed.

What I *did* know were all the ways racism manifested in my day-to-day life.

A few years after Hurricane Katrina displaced thousands of residents from New Orleans, I sat amid a sea of white faces at a national conference of trauma surgeons. I spied a few Black faces peppering the auditorium, but not many. On stage were the self-professed deities of trauma surgery, the surgeons who, throughout all of my training, I was told to emulate. They'd earned their fame cutting on the bodies of bullet-riddled Black men. They were mostly men who had been awarded million-dollar grants, who had published their research papers, and who had cocktails and fancy dinners with others who had done the same.

A famous white surgeon commanded the dais, speaking about some topic I can't remember. The demographics of his city had changed with the influx of Black citizens, most of them displaced by Hurricane Katrina. "We have a lot of Katrina refugees," he said. "You know, the kind that get shot while walking Grandma to Bible study. I'm guessing most are the kind New Orleans does not want back."

Raucous laughter ensued, engulfing the auditorium. These were my mentors. My colleagues. My friends? I glanced at the faces of the few Black surgeons in the room. To be Black in medicine is to give the nod, remain silent, and pretend this kind of talk doesn't matter. We know pounding our fist on the table for justice means that another who looks like us may never be offered a seat.

As the years progressed, I took for granted how much care patients received without oversight by more senior doctors. Day-to-day decisions at Grady were relegated to fellows, residents, and interns. We can debate whether this was a superb learning environment for surgical trainees or medical exploitation. What is beyond debate is that when the same trainees cared for patients across town at the university hospital—which mostly served wealthy, white patients— they had more stringent oversight. Such was the case from day one of my medical training, and it would remain true in the years to follow.

We praise the "science" of medicine. Yes, becoming a doctor requires burying yourself in textbooks for thousands of hours, learning this science and that. We articulate a thesis, design an experiment, review the results, and come to a conclusion. We hope the conclusion supports our thesis. When it doesn't, scientists retest or change their view. The intransigent will beat the data into submission to get the desired answer.

We also praise the "art" of medicine: the intuitive side of the profession, a physician's educated opinion that a "clear" diagnosis might not be right. Some say what matters most to patients, in order of importance, are the three "A's" that define a good doctor: affability, availability, and ability. Sometimes, how we make our patients feel is as therapeutic as finding the cure.

Yet sometimes medicine is neither art nor science. It is exploitation. A roiling history of exploitation of, and experimentation on, Black people has fostered distrust of the medical establishment. A brief survey of history includes Dr. J. Marion Sims, past president of the AMA and often revered as the "father of modern gynecology," who performed barbaric vaginal operations on enslaved women. They were denied anesthesia, physically restrained, and repeatedly mutilated. A larger-than-life marble statue in his honor was finally removed from New York's Central Park in 2018. Involuntary hysterectomies—what Fannie Lou Hamer came to call the "Mississippi appendectomy"—were frequently performed on Black women, often by medical students in training. These are part of the legacy of "dehumanizing attempts to control Black women's reproductive lives," as Dorothy E. Roberts describes in *Killing the Black Body*.

You are likely aware of the Tuskegee Syphilis Study, but do you know its formal name? It is *The US Public Health Service Syphilis Study at Tuskegee*. Yes, in a multigenerational study run by the federal government, the US Public Health Service denied 600 Black men therapeutic penicillin from 1932 to 1972 to allow the study of the natural progression of latent syphilis. Their health was compromised, as was the health of their partners and children, who were predictably exposed to the disease.

You may not be aware that the Pentagon funded a study of non-therapeutic, whole-body irradiation from 1960 to 1971. All the subjects were poor, most were Black, and 25 percent of the subjects died within one month of exposure. The Radiological Society of North America awarded the lead researcher-physician its highest honor. They conducted this research through the 1960s, as the United States prepared to land men on the moon, and the study did not end until the year before my younger sister was born.

Harriet Washington documents these studies and more in *Medical Apartheid*, her book about the medical establishment's experimentation on Black people. And as Washington demonstrates in *Carte Blanche: The Erosion of Medical Consent*, academic medical centers, like the ones where I have spent my entire career, were placed geographically precisely to exploit this reality. But Washington says it best: "Many medical institutions are located in predominately African-American and poverty-stricken areas. . . . This is not accidental but by design. The proximity of Black bodies for display, teaching, practice, and training material was an economic boon for medical schools and a selling point in recruiting medical students." To be clear, academic medical institutions were collocated, by design, adjacent to racially segregated, poverty-stricken neighborhoods. What better way to recruit medical trainees than to boast of the amazing opportunities to hone their craft? Where better to literally "practice" medicine than in a community of de facto experimental subjects who have no other options for medical treatment?

One might think this is ancient history, but it is not. When I came of age in the 1980s, Black women, many of them in their teens like me, were still the prime target for controlled reproduction through forced sterilization. And in the 1990s, the Medical University of South Carolina enrolled pregnant Black women in drug addiction research without their knowledge. Take a critical look at your nearest academic medical center, and you are likely to find the exploitation still thriving.

Even today, Black Americans, identified with euphemisms like "urban poor" or "socioeconomically disadvantaged," still serve as a ready supply for medical research. The era of involuntary experimentation has evolved into a complex system of "waiver of consent," used as a procedural means to circumvent obtaining informed consent. Here's what I mean: From 1996 to 2017, 46,964 patients were enrolled in forty-one trials for modern therapeutic drugs and medical devices, in which the FDA granted an "exception from informed consent," or EFIC. In EFIC trials, which are designed for patients with life-threatening conditions, subjects are required to opt *out*, rather than opt *in*. That means that in certain situations, you can be enrolled in a study without your informed consent. Of the nearly forty-seven thousand patients enrolled in these studies, 96 percent were enrolled *without their consent*. Many interventions had adverse effects, including death. And nearly one-third of the research subjects were Black Americans.

You can make cogent arguments that this work is legal and necessary to advance medical science. But legal does not mean ethical. Ethics and equity demand a higher standard, and research requires relationships, not paternalism. It requires respect, not exploitation. Black people's legacy of distrust of the medical establishment, rooted in its history of experimentation and research without consent, will be hard to overcome.

I am the beneficiary of research built upon the horrors inflicted upon my ancestors. From the treatments I've received as a patient, to the operative techniques I use to save patients, to the redactive history of medical innovation I taught: I have benefited from and been blind to this history. When I started medical school, I wanted to save lives and rise to the top of my field. I had no idea my life as an academic surgeon would make me complicit in a system built on the invisible exploitation of the bodies of my people. There's no way around the truth: we who heal people also hurt them. We practice medicine on vulnerable Black people. We perfect our surgical techniques on broken Black bodies. In doing so, I have gained knowledge, prestige, and wealth.

Dying patients do poorly when their doctor arrives with a racing heart and a gaping mouth gasping for breath. Unlike Hollywood medical dramas might suggest, I do not sprint to the scene of an emergency. I walk with a purpose, but I never run.

So when I met the ambulance as it pulled into the emergency bay at Grady Hospital in downtown Atlanta, I was unhurried. The blaring stopped, and the driver reversed into the loading dock. As the medics unloaded the stretcher, one hitched a ride, straddling the limp body and continued chest compressions.

"What's the story?" I asked the medic.

"Gunshot wound to the chest. We lost his pulse just as we pulled in and started compressions." The ensemble rolled past the emergency department triage desk, with me guiding the foot into the trauma bay.

To learn not much time had elapsed was comforting. It meant we had a chance to save him. If too much time had passed, even if we revived him, he would likely have irreversible brain damage due to lack of oxygen, also called cerebral anoxia. His body would live, but whatever sort of person he was—serious or playful, extrovert or introvert—would die along with the brain cells starved of oxygen. Without a functioning brain, he would need high-level medical care for life.

As I neared the end of my fellowship in trauma surgery, reports of a victim with multiple gunshot wounds didn't necessarily worry me. I knew not all were in critical condition. Many could get their wounds cleaned, dressings applied, and be discharged home straight from the emergency department.

And seconds matter in trauma. Any delay could mean death.

The emergency medicine resident at the head of the bed did a sternal rub, grinding his knuckles into the patient's breastbone, like I had done on poor Mr. Linden during my residency. That painful maneuver usually wakes the most moribund patient. But our multiple-gunshot victim did not respond, and a gunshot wound to the chest in traumatic arrest meant only one life-saving option.

"Set up for a thoracotomy."

I had first heard those five words from the trauma fellow when I was a wide-eyed medical student ten years earlier. Now the trauma fellow saying those words was me.

The nurse arrived with the metal instrument container and dropped it with a metallic clang onto the workbench wheeled to our patient's left side. As she unlocked clasps, removed the cover, and began extracting instruments, I summoned the medical student who stood wide-eyed watching the action. "You. Come here."

I positioned the patient's limp arm above as if he were reaching for the sky, except he lay flat on his back, stretching to the wall behind him.

"Hold his arm like this," I said, looking directly into the student's eyes to ensure she understood the importance of her role. "And do not move. Got it?"

"Yes, sir."

The student did as told while bumping elbows with the emergency medicine resident and the respiratory tech as they intubated our patient. A junior surgical resident emptied the bottle of brown sterilizing liquid onto the patient's chest and stood ready with the Finochietto retractor, better known as the rib spreaders.

With the scalpel in my right hand, I said, "Everyone, hands out of the field." My left fingertips dug along his ribcage, searching for the fifth intercostal space: the valley of soft tissue between the fourth and fifth ribs. Grinding my fingers between his ribs, I confirmed the correct anatomical location with adequate force to cause enough pain to awaken the deepest sleeping patient.

Our patient didn't flinch.

Time slowed, and my training kicked in. I filtered out the chorus of alarms and monitors and voices and scurrying team members and became hyper-focused. Mentally several steps ahead of the scalpel in my hand, I had to anticipate the injuries I might find and ran through a checklist of what to do for each scenario. I made a foot-long incision and could feel the skin and muscle give way, but refused to surrender the contents within. On my second pass with the scalpel, the remaining tissue opened and blood cascaded from the chest cavity, soaking my legs and shoes and splattering the floor. It was like a shopkeeper had dumped a bucket of mop water on the sidewalk.

I placed the lips of the retractor between two ribs and ratcheted it open, to provide a view of the vital organs resting in a pool of blood and clots. He had a hole in his chest cavity somewhere hosing blood, and I had to find it. It could have been his aorta or his lung or his heart, and I had to stop it. I cupped my hand to scoop out handfuls of blood and clots, so I could get a better view. Elbows deep in his chest, I pawed a pool of crimson to the floor as my hands retraced a sequence of familiar steps I had learned through practice on bullet-riddled bodies, mostly those of young Black men and boys like him.

"Clamp."

The resident handed me the special metal cross-clamp to place around the aorta, the main blood vessel leading from the heart to the rest of the body. The average adult has five liters of blood, which is a little more than a gallon. When there is an injury to a major blood vessel, the entire blood volume can drain within minutes. Seconds matter in trauma, and transport time is so important because every minute spent traveling to a hospital for a patient bleeding out from a gunshot wound is more time to bleed and less time for me to stop it. Our patient was bleeding to death, and I had to get the clamp on quickly to compress the aorta, stop the massive bleeding, and redirect blood to his brain to prevent irreversible brain damage. His brain needed blood more than his legs did.

In that moment, our lives, mine and his—bound by race and separated by degrees—diverged. My life as a trauma surgeon began as his life slipped away.

"He's starting to brady," a nurse said. Bradycardia: his heart was slowing down. Unless I stopped the bleeding, it would slow, then stop. Flatline. He would die.

I continued to scoop blood onto the floor, trying to get a clear view of the injury. I opened the pericardium and held his heart in my hands. I moved the lung this way and that way, looking for an injury. Nothing. Whatever was hosing blood was beyond my reach, and I simply could not stop the blood pouring into his chest cavity and away from the vital organs.

After a few minutes of emergency surgery and several rounds of epinephrine, the monitor flatlined. The entire team worked feverishly to revive him, and I stayed focused on doing the same. Eventually my attending, peeking over my shoulder, said, "That's enough Brian. I'm calling it. Time of death: 2:15 a.m."

Today, I remember little about this young man who died on my watch. I don't remember the faces or names of his family members, who I informed of his death. But I do remember what I felt for him: nothing. Emptiness. To me, the cause of death was nothing more than a physiological riddle to solve. What was the bullet trajectory? What organs were injured? Did I miss something? What could I have done differently to save him?

My laser-focus was to become one of the top trauma surgeons on the planet. To do so, I remained detached and indifferent to his story, his neighborhood, and his exposure to violence. At the time, I did not believe I could do anything more than perfect my skills, save lives one at a time, and teach others what I knew. These were nothing more than bullet wounds to me; as a trauma surgeon, I could repair the wound. But to question what kept the bodies coming to my trauma bay in the first place? To repair the upstream societal ills that funneled the bodies toward the hospital? I didn't even think to ask. I kept my head down and scalpel ready for the next trauma.

Besides, I was having the time of my life.

"Come here and get a closer look," I said to the mute medical student.

On a summer night one decade earlier, a trauma fellow had explained anatomy to me on the body before us. Now it was my turn to pay it forward. There is a saying in medical training: see one, do one, teach one. When learning a complicated procedure, a trainee first watches someone more experienced do it before she is allowed to perform the procedure. Eventually, that trainee is unleashed to instruct other junior trainees.

That night in Atlanta, having lost the fight to save our patient's life, with the pride of a young trauma surgeon, I described to the medical student how we gained access to the chest cavity through the left fifth intercostal space. I explained why we always position the rib spreader with the ratchet toward the bed and showed her the anatomy of the non-beating heart. I pointed out where I had incised the pericardium anterior to the vagus nerve, and I explained how she should trace her hand along the posterior wall of the interior chest wall to find the aorta.

"And be careful," I warned, as I guided her hand along the path to the aorta. "Don't catch yourself on a rib. They're sharp—and you don't want to catch any diseases."

PART II

Code Yellow

The state calls its own violence law, but that of the individual, crime.
—Max Stirner

7 | "BALD, BLACK, AND SUSPICIOUS"

"Because I didn't want to get *shot!*" I looked at Kathianne incredulously, stating what I felt should be obvious. She tossed her head and rolled her eyes in disbelief.

"Oh, come on. Be real. You don't have to show them your ID. This is your house!"

"Apartment."

"You know what I mean," she fired back. "You *live* here!"

"Oh, please, Kats. That doesn't mean jack. Cops have killed Black folks for much less."

A few days earlier, I had been standing outside the door to our building, wearing designer denim jeans and an Air Force Academy athletic pullover. It was snowboarding season, and my gear lay on the concrete beside me while I waited for my ride to the airport. We had recently moved to Dallas, Texas, and I was eager to get to Colorado for a weekend on the slopes. Engrossed in the ski and snow report on my cell phone, I did not notice the Dallas police cruiser roll to a stop and two uniformed officers step out.

At first, I paid no attention to the man and woman in blue uniforms with shiny badges and lethal weapons as they approached. I had done nothing wrong, and I lived right there. Once I realized what was happening, my throat tightened and my heart pounded and I stood frozen and straight. I knew the encounter could turn deadly even if I did everything right. One officer flanked me, blocking any escape route—not that I intended to run. I knew better. The other officer came from the front and asked to "see some identification." I didn't even think twice before slowly reaching into my back pocket, pulling out my wallet, and handing over my driver's license.

After a few tense minutes, the officer returned my license and said, "Thank you. We were just responding to a call. You're free to go." Finally, I could breathe; but my peace of mind was fleeting.

During the ride to Dallas-Fort Worth airport, I silently fumed. By that point in my life, I had done everything America asked me to do: I had graduated from a prestigious university, served my country, and become a doctor. And this was my thanks: cops rolling up on me for Standing While Black?

Days later, I learned more about the incident from an acquaintance who had access to the police report. He explained to me that someone had called 911 to report a "bald, Black man acting suspiciously."

My temperature rose as I recounted the incident to Kathianne and as she tried to comprehend the story. At the time, we had been together eleven years, married for seven, and I had never before initiated a deep discussion about my fear of police. "I am your wife," she now said. "How could I not know you felt this way?" It was true: I had never told her about being spread-eagle as an Air Force officer, or stopped late at night in Alabama when driving to visit my sister, or stopped during the day in Virginia while visiting my parents. Day or night, east coast or west coast, north or south, my distrust of police knew no boundaries. I feared cops more than I feared random acts of violence.

So I took precautions. My car displayed a United States Air Force Academy alumni license plate, my driver's license was stamped with "Veteran" (and organ donor), and I usually had my hospital badge draped around my neck while driving. Visible items to broadcast, "No need to fear me, Officer." So when the police officer asked to see my

ID, I did not ask why. Nor did I assert my right to refuse, as my wife suggested I should have done.

Sometimes your survival instinct compels you to simply comply.

Just over a year prior, we had shoehorned our life into the back of a royal blue Mini Cooper and made the cross-country drive from Atlanta to begin the next phase of our life in Dallas. I was to begin my dream job as an assistant professor of trauma and acute care surgery at the University of Texas Southwestern Medical School and as an attending trauma surgeon at Parkland Memorial Hospital. As a graduation gift to myself to celebrate thirteen years of medical training, I bought myself a Rolex. I had always wanted a nice watch, and after years of buying throwaway timepieces, I now owned a timeless classic I could pass along as an heirloom. And to extend the celebration a bit, we took several days to drive leisurely from Georgia to Texas, connecting the interstate dots through Alabama, Mississippi, and Louisiana.

We were aware that an interracial couple like us, doing such a trek a few decades prior, would have been tempting deadly fate. In the arc of American history, we lived only a blip away from the Jim Crow era, when Black Americans used the *Green Book*, first published in 1936, to navigate safe places to eat and sleep when traveling. And, of course, our marriage would have been illegal in the many states with anti-miscegenation laws until 1967, when the Supreme Court ruled them unconstitutional in Loving v. Virginia. That was just two years before my birth.

We arrived in Dallas safely, settled in, and were soon enjoying high-rise living with concierge service in an upscale section of the city. Our neighborhood had once been a thriving Black community known as Freedman's Town. Founded by formerly enslaved Black Texans, the town was leveled to make way for two major highways linking downtown to the rest of Dallas. The displacement of Black Americans was a pattern replicated across the nation, as part of President Eisenhower's effort to create an interstate highway system.

Planners routed some highways through Black and brown communities to further a segregationist agenda. Deborah N. Archer explains in her article "White Men's Roads through Black Men's Homes" in the *Vanderbilt Law Review*, "In states around the country, highway construction displaced Black households and cut the heart and soul out of thriving Black communities as homes, churches, schools, and businesses were destroyed. In other communities, the highway system was a tool of a segregationist agenda, erecting a wall that separated White and Black communities and protected White people from Black migration. In these ways, construction of the interstate highway system contributed to the residential concentration of race and poverty, and created physical, economic, and psychological barriers that persist."

In Dallas, gentrification followed the highway, land value rising in tandem with real estate prices. All that remains of Freedman's Town today are unmarked gravestones and a memorial recognizing formerly enslaved people. The memorial was a ten-minute walk from my front door.

Three years later, we moved into a four-bedroom, five-bathroom, three-thousand-square-foot house. Although we became close to our neighbors, I was cognizant of being the only Black person in the neighborhood. When we lived uptown, I'd be up before dawn for an early morning run or would take an evening stroll by the park after work. I stopped both routines after we moved. In fact, the idea of taking a dawn run or evening walk in the neighborhood where I owned a home never crossed my mind. I knew I had to be careful lest I be found guilty of being Black in a white neighborhood.

The year 2012, when police questioned me for standing outside my apartment building, was a notable year for gun violence. In February, George Zimmerman, a wannabe cop, shot and killed

Trayvon Martin, an unarmed seventeen-year-old walking home one evening to his father's house. In April, a gunman killed seven at Oikos University in Oakland, California; in July, a gunman killed twelve and injured fifty-eight more at an Aurora, Colorado, movie theater. One month later came another mass shooting of six worshipers at a Sikh Temple in Oak Creek, Wisconsin. And that's not an exhaustive list.

Then came December 14, 2012. Adam Lanza shot and killed his mother before fatally shooting twenty children, most of whom were six and seven years old, and six adults at Sandy Hook Elementary School in Newtown, Connecticut. Shock, grief, and a call to action followed. It was a moment when our nation could address the epidemic of gun violence, and we failed. An attempt to pass meaningful federal gun safety legislation withered on the vine, kneecapped by lobbying from the National Rifle Association.

Throughout those years I felt horrified at the scope of mass school shootings, which were often perpetrated by white shooters in suburban and mostly white school districts. I was also dismayed that the lives and deaths of my Black and brown patients, victims of gun violence, never received the same level of collective national attention. If we showed such little regard for the health and safety of white suburban children, I knew there was no chance for my patients, who were mostly urban Black boys and girls. And if we don't care about kids, white or Black, what chance do any of us have?

"Get your white coats," I commanded. Like Cadet Jackson, I eyed the group before we began morning rounds. If I could make them do push-ups, I would.

"Three buttons. Not two," I said, pointing to the junior resident who bowed sheepishly. "Not zero," I said to the senior resident. "You would be fine," I said, nodding toward the chief resident, "except for the coffee stains and a coat that is more gray than white." I made a mental note to pull him aside later and explain how, as a leader, he must set the standard for the junior residents to follow.

Medical degrees and fancy titles do not excuse sloppy appearance. I wanted the residents to know that patients, families, and staff make judgments about you within seconds of seeing you. I also needed them to know this: our patients at the county hospital deserved the same respect given to the wealthy patients at the university hospital across the street.

Dallas is the ninth most populated city in the United States, and Parkland Hospital is a major public hospital serving an impoverished population. As a safety-net hospital, Parkland cared for poor people, most of whom were Black or Hispanic. Nearly 100 percent of our patients were uninsured or underinsured. Still, we cared for everyone, regardless of their ability to pay, and Parkland was usually their only option for healthcare. I adhered to the ethos that they deserved world-class medical treatment and that they deserved the highest respect. Pride, uniform, first impressions.

Walking with purpose, I led the gaggle of white coats on morning rounds en route to the Surgical Intensive Care Unit (SICU). I was now a trauma attending, the surgeon atop the training hierarchy. I was also the only Black person on rounds and the only Black trauma surgeon of thirteen in the department.

Leaving the OR suite after examining a preoperative patient, we walked past a wall of photos dedicated to the "Giants of Surgery" who had worked at Parkland. The memorial was greeted with great fanfare when it was unveiled. To me, it was another commemoration of white men, in one of the most highly trafficked areas of the hospital. I had nothing against the men in the pictures; two of them were my partners, and others had made contributions to surgery that I now incorporated into my practice. But the exhibit excluded the medical students, trainees, hospital staff, and patients who did not resemble that lionized ideal. Every time I passed, I could feel their maleness, their oldness, and their whiteness. In some ways, their presence motivated me. I intended that someday my photo would adorn the wall so staff, students, and trainees could see how we, Black people, had progressed—and how far we still had to go.

Swiping my badge to enter the secure unit, the doors opened to the chimes and beeps of alarms as nurses, therapists, and aides in the SICU transported patients, gave medications, and typed at computer workstations. It was a beehive of activity, although with much less intensity than a trauma activation. If the emergency department was my primary residence, the SICU was my vacation home. Outside the room of our first patient, the junior resident began his presentation as the senior ICU resident, Dr. Luka Cyrus, joined our group to listen.

"This is a 57-year-old woman injured in a high-speed MVC [motor vehicle collision] two days ago, restrained front-seat passenger T-boned on the passenger side, two days status post-exploratory laparotomy where she underwent a splenectomy. Her injuries include a subarachnoid hemorrhage, C5 transverse process fracture, left T9 through T12 non-displaced rib fractures, and a left humerus fracture. She was extubated first thing this morning."

That meant the patient had been sedated since her operation two days prior. She likely could not recall the intervening forty-eight hours—or that I had saved her life.

I entered her room first, as the team trailed behind me. The patient, who was white, lay upright in the bed. The monitor hung from an adjustable arm over the right side of the headboard, displaying heart rate, oxygenation, and respiratory rate with squiggly lines of various colors. Her disconnected ventilator, the size of an office mini-fridge, was still by her bed. Another woman, who appeared to be in her late twenties, sat beside the patient, texting on her phone until we came in. Our patient had a remote in one hand, channel surfing. As I approached her bedside to introduce myself and examine her.

"Don't touch me," she ordered. "I'll wait for my real doctor."

"Mom, this is your doctor," the woman beside her said. "He saved your life!"

"I don't care. He's not touching me."

I stood a few feet away. She spoke as if I were standing in the next county. I don't know what thoughts circulated in the heads of the trainees—my trainees.

"Ma'am, it's okay," I calmly replied. Suppressing my indignation was, by that time, a well-honed skill. "Just letting you know we're transferring you to the floor today. That means you're one step closer to going home."

"Thank you, Doctor," her daughter said. She pleaded with her eyes, hoping I'd accept her silent apology on behalf of her mother.

Leading the team out of the room, I slammed the lid on my bubbling rage. I was not surprised. It happened in medical school, residency, and fellowship; why would the treatment suddenly change now? Because I was an attending? Even with two certifications from the American Board of Surgery and a faculty appointment to one of the biggest medical schools in the country, I couldn't escape. As the most senior doctor in the room, I was ostensibly the most powerful. Racist encounters like this take a toll, and we exit each one changed in some small way. By saying nothing to this patient, who might be dead were it not for me, did I relinquish my power or strengthen it?

Later that afternoon, Kathianne hovered as I scoured the refrigerator and cupboards for food. Finding nothing appealing, I grabbed a few snacks, shoveled them into my bag, and made a mental note to stop at the fresh market for a pre-made meal on my way back to the hospital.

"You're working again? Tonight?"

"I know," I mumbled. It was July 7, 2016, and I agreed to cover the shift of one of my partners who was away on vacation. "I switched with Hardison and forgot to update the calendar." Earlier, when I realized my oversight, I raced home during a lull at the hospital to stock up for the night shift.

"When someone needs time off, why is it always you?"

"Gimme a break, Kats. It's not always me, and I'm sure he'd do the same for me."

What I didn't say was, even if he wouldn't, I'd still say yes. It was my sixth year as a trauma surgeon and critical care specialist. During those years in Dallas, I had excelled at my job, sharpened my skills, and taught hundreds of students, residents, and fellows. I served in leadership positions in local, regional, and national medical societies. I received accolades and awards, promotions and pay raises, and validation from patients, colleagues, friends, and family. I earned a faculty promotion to associate professor and was appointed as the program director of the surgery residency, the first Black surgeon in the history of UT Southwestern to hold the position. It was the largest surgical residency program in the country, and I took the reins when not a single resident was Black.

Still, I felt obliged to sprint when those around me walked. The rules for career progression that applied to my white colleagues did not apply to me. I rarely said no and even more rarely asked for help. I knew my white colleagues' perception of my commitment mattered more than the truth did. As long as I smiled and danced and didn't complain, relationships were fine. But to slip, even once, was never an option.

"Kats, that's just the way it is," I told her. "Work twice as hard for half as much. That's how it's always been, and that's how it will always be."

Married to a Black man for eleven years and she still didn't get it, I thought harshly. Then again, maybe she did. It wasn't as if I ever explained my experiences to her or let her into my head and heart, which she often asked me to do. So how would she know?

"How is it you have plenty of time for work, but none for your family?" Kathianne asked. Her voice slipped in around the edges of my own thoughts, barely gaining a space in my brain. She was as exhausted as me but for different reasons. My exhaustion stemmed from the perpetual mental gymnastics needed to subdue my internalized anger. Hers was from being a de facto single mother raising a hyperkinetic five-year-old daughter. We were at a fragile point in our marriage, and for months I had promised to make her a priority. Instead, once again, I shoved her to the back of the line so I could work. When duty called, my family, once again, heard a busy signal.

"Kats, I do not need this right now. This is the job. It's always been the job. You know this."

Arms crossed, she pursed her lips and narrowed her eyelids, her ire searing. I broke the standoff.

"Where's Abeni?"

"She's at gymnastics practice."

I understood what she left unsaid: *If you were around more, you'd know that.*

"Kats, I gotta go." I kissed her on the cheek. "Tell Abeni we'll video before bed. I love you."

"I love you too." But the way her words dripped like molasses, I wasn't so sure.

Still, we were living the American dream. We had started a family, bought a house, and even added a dog (and later a second) to the mix. During that time, I gave all I had to the hospital. I loved my work, so it was easy. The day after our daughter was born, I hopped on a plane to get back to work, leaving Kathianne alone for over a week in a hotel with my mother, until she could legally bring our adopted newborn across state lines to her future home in Dallas. My patients needed me. My colleagues needed me. Parkland needed me. I ignored what the people closest to me needed. That included myself.

I thought of myself as an accomplished Black man living in a majority-white world, masterful at navigating the daily challenges of being too Black for some people but not Black enough for others. My white coat inspired respect in some people and my Black skin engendered disdain in others. It was sometimes confusing, often infuriating, and always exhausting. But still I assimilated, achieved, and ascended. I enjoyed the validation from the accolades, awards, and a six-figure salary, content to ride the bullet train of success.

Occasionally, however, I paused to look out the window and contemplate the landscape whipping past. Surveying my surroundings left me dismayed. Black and brown people were poor and sick and dying all around me. After three decades of chasing whatever I was chasing and nearly two decades in medicine, I sometimes worried that not much separated me from my patients who were dying. The deaths of countless Black men and women—from police violence, from gun violence, and from structural violence—frustrated me. But as an urban trauma surgeon, I felt my place was at the hospital caring for patients, not joining protesters in the street.

And sometimes I could not tell if the healthcare system eliminated health inequities or perpetuated them. Safety-net hospitals where I chose to work, like Parkland in Dallas and Grady in Atlanta, were valorized for catching people who would otherwise fall through the cracks. But I began to wonder if such hospitals exist only because we as a nation have abandoned millions of people to fend for themselves in the first place. During those moments of reflection, I saw a landscape riddled with injustice and inequality—and now, quite possibly, the wreckage of my own marriage.

But neither Kathianne nor I could anticipate what would come later that summer night, when a sniper unloaded his AK-74 on fourteen Dallas police officers.

That was the night everything changed.

8 | TRAUMATIC ARREST

Everything happened all at once, and much of it was a blur. But I remember the blood. Lots of blood. The first police officer arrived at 8:45 p.m. The trauma nurses had placed him on the stretcher like a sack of potatoes and sped around the corner from the ambulance bay while one gave him chest compressions. A gaggle of cops with assault weapons slung over their shoulders trailed after the stretcher.

"Gunshot wound to the chest," one said, as I kept pace alongside the speeding gurney. Despite the man's midnight blue uniform, it took a moment for me to realize he was a cop. I didn't have a frame of reference for what was unfolding before me. Gunshot victims were routine in my world. But a bullet-riddled cop shadowed by an armed posse? I'd been through a lot of wild trauma activations, but I had never seen that before. It didn't make sense.

I removed my white coat, draped it over a chair as I entered the resuscitation bay, and snatched a pair of purple nitrile gloves from the red crash cart. Vanessa, the head trauma nurse, redirected the ensemble headfirst through the sliding glass doors into Trauma Bay 1 where a dozen nurses, doctors, and trainees took center stage. Surveying the scene, I processed the flood of information while a quartet of gloved hands grasped the edges of the sheet beneath the officer.

"Ready. Three. Two. One. Lift."

Pulling it taut like a parachute, they lifted him onto the stretcher in the center of the room and I pushed the bloodied gurney into the hallway. Two nurses untangled the laces of his boots, which fell with a dull thud on the concrete floor. Another nurse with heavy-duty trauma shears fileted open his uniform, the fabric melting away as she cut a path from ankle to thigh through his waistband, repeated the path on his other leg, then completed the mutilation of his uniform top. The discarded clothing joined his boots on the floor in a heap. Completely exposed, he looked like a newborn baby, naked and dependent upon us for survival.

"Continue chest compressions," I said, becoming aware of more activity on the other side of the trauma hall.

Eight trauma bays were arranged in a horseshoe around a central-ized common area of computer workstations. Across this common area, another team of nurses was wheeling a second police officer into Trauma Bay 8. He lay perpendicular on the stretcher, his torso and legs dangling from the sides. That too, was abnormal, and like the first officer, he was getting chest compressions. I later learned his partners had rescued him from the scene of the shooting, tossed him into the back of a squad car, and raced to the hospital. "Who in the hell is shooting cops?" I thought to myself, although I had no time to dwell on it. The pager on my hip demanded my attention, alerting me that more gunshot victims were on their way. Several time-sensitive tasks had to happen at once. By now Dr. Jon Ashton, the trauma fellow, had joined me in Trauma Bay 1.

"Ashton, I've got this," I said and pointed across the hall. "You take the team and go see what that's about."

Ashton was one of the top residents I'd worked with—ever—but at the time, it was the first week of his trauma fellowship, and a multiple-casualty event might exceed his skills. At the moment, he was all I had, and with an unknown number of gunshot victims soon to arrive, I needed another qualified trauma surgeon ASAP.

"Vanessa, page my backup."

Now I was with the team in Trauma 1, and Ashton had another team in Trauma 8. That all took about ten seconds, which meant I could focus on the body in front of me.

We began with the primary survey: the life-saving algorithm I learned as a resident, mastered as a fellow, and now taught as an attending in a course called Advanced Trauma Life Support. The step-by-step algorithm helps us assess life-threatening injuries needing immediate intervention. It is sometimes known as the "ABCs of Trauma": A—Airway, B—Breathing, C—Circulation, D—Disability, E—Exposure. The primary survey is a standard sequence for those initial moments of a trauma when we have minimal information and have to make life-saving decisions within seconds.

After the primary survey, we do the secondary survey to look for additional non-lethal injuries, such as skin lacerations or broken bones. Painful? Yes. Life-threatening? No. Eventually, usually within twenty-four hours of admission to the hospital, we do a tertiary survey, to ensure we missed nothing in the secondary survey.

But tonight, we would not make it past the primary survey.

"Continue chest compressions," I said. "And activate MTP."

In an extreme emergency, when a dying patient needs large amounts of blood, the blood bank will keep sending coolers of blood products—packets of red blood cells, fresh frozen plasma, platelets, and cryoprecipitate—until we say stop. We need the proper combination of all these blood products to prevent someone from bleeding to death. This is the Massive Transfusion Protocol, or MTP.

The trauma team was in full throttle. At the head of the stretcher Dr. Alice Waterson, the emergency medicine attending, set up equipment, tubes, and medications for intubating any patient unable to breath on their own. This involves sliding a plastic tube into the patient's throat, a tube connected to flexible tubing snaking to the ventilator. The brain cannot live without oxygen for more than a few minutes, which is why CPR is critical in order to keep blood flowing. Our patient did not breathe on his own, so the ventilator would deliver oxygen-rich air to his lungs, where it would diffuse into his blood and keep his brain alive.

On his left and right, nurses poked his limp extremities with intravenous lines, hung bags of blood products, and slapped EKG leads to his chest. Equipment drawers slid open and slammed shut amid a choir of voices. There's a rhythm and grace to a team working together during a trauma activation, one indecipherable to me nearly twenty years ago, as a medical student. It's like a call and response, in which everyone knows their part. Now I'm fluent.

And an interesting paradox occurs during a medical crisis, particularly at a training institution: the more senior the team member, the less they speak. As the one in charge, I had still only spoken twice. I was thinking three to four moves ahead as I monitored the team at work, continually assessing the monitors and listening to the flood of verbal information.

"14-gauge in the right AC," said a nurse.

"First unit of blood is hanging," said another.

"We're ready to tube him," said the resident.

Less than five minutes after his arrival, our motionless, pulseless patient had a stranger's blood flowing into his veins and lay ready for intubation. While the rest of the team worked on every part of his body, Dr. Waterson readied a lighted, curved retractor to compress the tongue and provide a clear view of the back of the throat; the endotracheal tube to insert into the windpipe; and a supply of sedative and paralytic medications.

On the monitor I watched as a disorganized heart rhythm, incompatible with life, began snaking across the monitor.

"Check for a pulse," I said.

"No carotid," said Dr. Waterson, placing two fingers on the side of our patient's neck as she prepared to intubate.

"No femoral," said Nurse Vanessa, pressing on his groin.

I was watching the last gasps of a dying heart, and a patient in traumatic arrest, with a gunshot wound to the chest, has only one life-saving option. Only one procedure would give this police officer the chance to live. And only one person in the room was qualified to do it. Me.

The experienced members of the team knew what was coming. We had done it many times before, and not once did the patient survive. Vanessa, with her many years of experience, most definitely knew. She had already reached for the tray of supplies.

"Listen up, everyone," I said. "Set up for a thoracotomy."

With that directive, the team blasted from full throttle to rocket launch.

The most important machine powering the body resides in the chest. The heart. In a brain-dead person, the heart can survive and keep beating. This is why victims with gunshot wounds to the head are coveted organ donors: they are usually young and have healthy organs. But stop the heart and within six minutes, brain death follows. To survive, that patient needs an emergency thoracotomy.

Tens of thousands of activations and hundreds of thousands of hours of training had prepared me for this, my singular job: save the patient.

Time was my enemy, so I broke from routine and did something I have admonished countless trainees for doing: ignored my head-to-toe personal protective equipment, also known as PPE. In the critical rush to get started, I disregarded the gear used to protect me (and also my wife) from blood-borne diseases such as HIV and hepatitis. I did this not because he was a cop but because we had a worsening multiple casualty event and seconds mattered. Any delay could be the difference between life and death. I already had my gloves, I put on a face mask and eye shield, and ignored the rest. Deviating from the mandated routine was usually unthinkable for me, but my pager was screaming that more injured police officers were coming our way.

Since that summer night as a wide-eyed student watching my first ED thoracotomy, I had done the procedure more times than I could count. At each phase of my career, as I watched or assisted or performed thoracotomies, there was one constant: the Black body on the stretcher in front of me. Almost all the patients were young Black men and women in traumatic arrest from a gunshot wound. Most died in the emergency department; some survived long enough to make it to surgery, where they died on the operating room table; the remaining survived surgery only to die in the intensive care unit.

I rarely perform ED thoracotomies because of these abysmal outcomes, and I sometimes critique my contemporaries for their eagerness to do them. Sometimes physicians operate out of the "maximum resident benefit" mindset, as I also learned as a medical student, encouraging trainees to practice the procedure on people unable to refuse. In the throes of a futile emergency, I would not want a thoracotomy done to me or a member of my family for MRB. To this day, it is a dichotomy I have not reconciled.

But on that night, at that moment, in that room, the only chance for that cop to live was an ED thoracotomy. With a melodic clang, Vanessa dropped the thoracotomy tray on the bedside workbench as I positioned his left arm above his head, reaching past Dr. Waterson's hip for the back wall. With my right hand I grasped the scalpel, and with my left I felt for the valley of soft tissue in the fifth intercostal space.

"Everyone, hands out of the field!" I ordered.

I can recite the steps of an ED thoracotomy like I can recite the alphabet, minus the memorable melody. I studied voraciously, internalized the teachings of my mentors, and watched intently whenever they did the procedure. I can perform the procedure only because I've had a lot of practice. My focus is always on the body before me. Not the bodies I have already treated and discharged, nor the ones likely coming later in the night. It is the body on the gurney in front of me that matters. And for years I had been perfecting this disfiguring skill on the bullet-riddled bodies of scores of dying Black men and women lying before me. None of them had left the hospital alive. That reality changes a person.

In trauma surgery, heroism and futility often walk hand in hand, and sometimes it's hard to know the difference. But my duty is to always be a voice for humanity. Soaked in his blood, I cradled the police officer's heart in my hands, trying to pump it back to life. It would not beat. I checked his carotid and his femoral pulses. He had none. Were it not for the ventilator, he would not breathe. The decision to end life-sustaining treatment—or death-prolonging treatment, depending on your point of view—falls to me.

"Before I call it, anything else we can do?" I asked Dr. Waterson.

"I agree. We've done everything," she said.

"Does anybody think we missed anything?" I scanned the room, looking everyone in the eyes, so they knew I sincerely wanted their input. Before I call a death, any death, I give everyone a chance to speak. If you are in the room, I do not care if you are a medical student or an experienced attending physician. If there is anything we can do—any sign we've missed, any possibility left—I want to hear it.

I stopped pumping. I glanced at the digital clock on the wall and called the time of death, which Nurse Vanessa logged in the medical record. Other nurses turned off the monitors, stopped transfusing blood, and removed the crash cart equipment. Nobody said a word while the frenetic pace slowed to routine post-mortem care. Only the high-pitched monotone on the cardiac monitor remained, along with the clicking from the mechanical breaths of the ventilator as the trauma team regrouped for the next patient.

For the moment, this death was barely a blip on my emotional radar. I had been here countless times before. Besides, another patient in Bay 8 needed my help, and more were arriving in ambulances, their lights and sirens screaming. I filed away this death, thanked the team, and peeled off my gloves to find blood coated my forearms, Rolex, and hands. There was so much blood that it slipped over the lip of the gloves at my wrist to coat my hands. After a quick wash in the sink, I fisted my white coat from the workstation chair where it rested and was on the move.

But two surgery residents cut me off before I had both feet out of the door.

9 | HAIL MARY

"Dr. Williams, I've called all the residents in house to come help. What can I do, sir?"

It was Dr. Cole Jacobsen, a third-year surgery resident and not scheduled for trauma call that evening. He was sharp and would mature into a great surgeon. At the moment, he took the initiative to mobilize all the surgical residents in the hospital. Beside him stood Dr. Luka Cyrus, the resident from SICU rounds earlier that day.

"Dr. Williams, how can I help?"

He should have been covering the Surgical Intensive Care Unit. Those patients were sick, needed constant monitoring, and were also my responsibility during my night shift. But I did not question why he left his post because we needed all hands on deck. In my peripheral vision, I saw two more officers arriving, one on a stretcher and one on foot. The man, lying upright on a stretcher, appeared alert and stable. A woman in uniform followed the gaggle surrounding him.

Pointing to the cop on the stretcher, I said, "Cyrus, that one's yours." Dr. Cyrus was a fourth-year resident and had plenty of experience running traumas. Less experience than Dr. Ashton, the trauma fellow in Trauma Bay 8, but more than Dr. Jacobsen the third-year resident who had herded all the available residents.

Within minutes we had received three gunshot victims, all of them cops. One I had already pronounced dead, one was across the hall in Trauma Bay 8, another had just rolled in, and several more were expected to arrive. How many more, we didn't know. But having trained for multiple casualty disasters, I put several tasks in motion at once.

I had a mid-level resident, Dr. Jacobsen, calling for the backup trauma surgeon. I had a senior resident, Dr. Cyrus, assessing the third officer who arrived. In Trauma Bay 8 I had the trauma fellow, Dr. Ashton, treating the second officer who was obviously in critical condition when he arrived, hanging off the stretcher and getting chest compressions.

That is where I needed to be.

"Ashton, what have you got?"

"Gunshot to the chest."

Ashton gave me a report on the critically injured police officer before us in Trauma Bay 8. He was in training to lead a crisis like this without any supervision, learning to make the time-critical, life or death decisions. As an attending, I tried to allow trainees autonomy to make medical decisions without jeopardizing patient safety. It was a delicate balance. Intervening too soon impairs training, and waiting too long can lead to patient death. Any indecision or misstep and I would quickly take over. I waited a breath for him to verbalize his decision.

Long enough.

"Ashton, he needs a thoracotomy."

As the team launched into preparations for another ED thoracotomy, Dr. Cyrus, who should have been with the stable officer in another room, came into Trauma Bay 8.

"Dr. Williams, I think my patient needs a chest tube."

"Is he crashing?"

"No, sir. He's stable."

Standing over Ashton's shoulder, I focused on his every move. He positioned the left arm, poured brown sterilizing fluid on the left chest, and reached for the scalpel. I stood beside him with the rib spreaders ready.

Surgery residents learn the technique of placing a chest tube within weeks of starting their first year of training, so I had no doubt Dr. Cyrus could do it unsupervised. Knowing when to do a procedure—and when *not* to—is the judgment residents gain from experience. We don't do invasive procedures on patients who do not need them. (An ED thoracotomy is a maximally invasive procedure compared to a chest tube, which only requires an incision a few inches long.) My experience with Dr. Cyrus was that he was a dedicated resident who made excellent clinical decisions. For a chest tube, I trusted him.

"Okay, Cyrus. Go ahead and do it. Don't wait for me."

"Yes, sir."

"And if his status changes, send someone to get me ASAP."

Dr. Ashton's first pass with the scalpel barely sliced through the skin and superficial layers of the fifth intercostal space. The second pass cut deeper, but still no entry into the thoracic cavity. I never enjoyed depriving a trainee of a procedure, but seconds matter.

"Ashton, give me the knife." In one stroke, a crimson tide cascaded to the floor as I handed the scalpel back to him. "Now curve the incision down to the bed—and don't lacerate the lung."

He did as he was told. I two-fisted the rib spreaders, slipped the edges into the incision, and ratcheted it open.

"If they arrive alive, they should leave alive," is a maxim of trauma surgery. It is our goal and failure is not an option. But the inverse is also true: a trauma patient who arrives dead stays dead, with or without an ED thoracotomy. That means a thoracotomy is a clinical Catch-22.

As I've said, the chance of saving a patient with an ED thoracotomy is almost zero. It is also invasive and disfiguring. The trauma surgeon who chooses not to do an ED thoracotomy will endure reproach from the zealots who ask, "Why didn't you do a thoracotomy?" Then again, if you do a thoracotomy, you'll suffer indignation from the restrained—I'm usually among them—who ask, "Why did you do a thoracotomy?"

At this stage of my career, I can "crack a chest" and cross-clamp the aorta in less than a minute. A few seconds later, I will have split open the pericardium, the leather-like covering encasing the heart, and hold that heart—their life—in my hands. If it is not beating, I can sometimes bring it back to life with bimanual massage, plug a hole spouting blood with my finger until I repair it, inject epinephrine into the muscle of the left ventricle, or use internal defibrillators to deliver electricity and shock it back to life.

But now, for the second time within minutes, I was pronouncing another Dallas police officer dead. I still wasn't fully processing the facts: that we'd lost two police officers. I was thinking a few steps ahead to manage a worsening tragedy I knew little about, other than somewhere in Dallas, cops were being shot. Were they still getting shot? How many would we receive? Was my backup on the way yet? More patients were coming, and the team had to move on. As I left Trauma Bay 8 to join Dr. Cyrus placing a chest tube on the stable officer, Jacobsen stopped me to say the backup trauma surgeon could not be found.

The trauma team ran smoothly despite the austere conditions. It was still early in the crisis; the team had drilled for this type of disaster. Nurse Vanessa, a product of those extensive drills and preparation, wedged herself between Jacobsen and me.

"Dr. Williams, they say there may be bombs around the city."

"Bombs?" I echoed, trying to wrap my head around the idea of potential explosions in downtown Dallas.

"They're not sure, but they're concerned. Should we activate the Code Yellow?"

A Code Yellow sends a group page notification to all critical hospital personnel to come to the hospital without delay. In my six years at Parkland before the shooting, I could count on one hand the number of times I called for backup. But a Code Yellow? Never. Vanessa always functioned by the book, and she was not given to hyperbole. If there were truly bombs scattered throughout Dallas—well, you don't need to be a trauma surgeon to know that would worsen the crisis. I needed more trauma surgeons—as many as we could mobilize—and I needed them as soon as possible.

"Call the boss and tell him we have a multiple casualty event with an unknown number of GSWs en route," I told Dr. Jacobsen. "Let him know there is a report of possible bombs in the city and that we need all hands on deck." With no response from my backup, more injured cops en route, and reports of bombs, I wanted him to know we were in the midst of an evolving disaster.

And in response to Nurse Vanessa's question about whether to activate a Code Yellow, I said one word: yes.

Activating the Code Yellow resulted in a scene I could have never envisioned. We set up an incident command center run by a mix of clinicians and administrators, and we began transitioning the hospital to disaster operations. Officers from the Dallas Hospital District Police Department donned body armor, grabbed AR-15s, and began patrolling the hospital. They stopped visitors from roaming the halls, controlled access to the emergency department, and secured all points of entry to the hospital.

By activating the Code Yellow, Parkland not only responded to a multiple casualty event; it prepared to defend itself from attack.

10 | SECONDS MATTER

Two cops were dead. A third had a gunshot wound to the chest but did not appear critical. We were expecting more to arrive, but for the moment, the third officer became my priority. He was sitting upright on the stretcher in his blue uniform, conversing with the team who were sticking needles in his arm veins, positioning him for x-rays, and asking about his medical history. He appeared stable as he talked with the nurses and techs. His partner, also in uniform, stood beside him at the head of the bed.

Dr. Veronica Morris, an anesthesiologist, gathered equipment and medications for possible intubation if necessary. She, like dozens of other doctors in the hospital, had left her normal post to come help. There were so few Black doctors at Parkland that whenever I saw one, even during times of crisis, it left an impression. Dr. Morris and I exchanged a knowing glance, one communicating a lifetime of shared experiences. It's like a mental handshake saying, "*I got you.*"

"Good evening, Officer. "I'm Dr. Williams. I'm the trauma surgeon on call tonight." Turning to the resident, I asked, "What's the story, Cyrus?"

"Dr. Williams, Officer Smith has a gunshot wound to the chest. I put in a left chest tube, which has put out over a liter of blood, and his pericardial FAST was equivocal."

FAST is an acronym for Focused Assessment for Sonography in Trauma. It's like doing an ultrasound on a pregnant woman, except in trauma we use it to look for life-threatening, internal bleeding. By saying *equivocal*, Dr. Cyrus meant he could not tell if an internal injury existed or not. And whenever I hear *equivocal* from a trainee, I default to the worst-case scenario—that there is a life-threatening injury. I have performed thousands of FAST exams, and I have taught the FAST exam to hundreds, maybe thousands, of trainees. Sometimes subtle signs are recognizable only after years of experience. And truncal gunshot wounds, like the one to Officer Smith, kept me hypervigilant. I processed what I knew: gunshot wound to the chest; patient alert, interactive, and appeared stable; *equivocal* pericardial FAST.

My internal alarms began to hum. "Let's repeat the FAST."

I scanned him and the monitors above his head and maintained an impassive facade, revealing nothing of my concern until I was certain. "I'm going to flatten the bed and have you lie down for a moment."

As I engaged the lock to lower the back of the bed, I kept my eyes on him, watching for any change in his demeanor. Did he grimace? Have trouble breathing? Resist lying down? I also took a mental snapshot of his vital signs on the monitors while he sat upright, and watched for any change when he laid down. Subtle changes in heart rate and blood pressure during this simple maneuver—transitioning a patient from sitting upright to lying flat—can speak volumes about what is happening inside a patient's body.

Dr. Cyrus rolled the ultrasound to the bedside, powered it on, and applied clear gel to the notch below Officer Smith's sternum. We all stared at the fuzzy images flickering on the screen. Dr. Cyrus slid the handheld probe across his chest as the four chambers of the heart came into view, then out, then back in again.

"See. Right there, Dr. Williams." He pointed at blurred portion of the image. "I wasn't sure about that."

I took the probe from Dr. Cyrus and maneuvered it to get a clearer image. I scanned the tubing from his chest draining into the pleuravac cannister on the floor, now filled with blood. Too much blood.

My internal alarms began to wail.

Officer Smith looked okay, but something was not right. The gunshot wound to the chest. The volume of blood in the canister. The abnormal ultrasound. We needed to move. And we needed to do it quickly.

More than a dozen extra surgeons were now in the emergency department. All were still in training except one: Dr. Gina Wallace, a plastic surgeon and classmate of mine from medical school. Gina was fully trained, board-certified, and capable of operating independently. There was one problem.

"Willie, I haven't done trauma in a while, but I'm here if you need help." Gina addressed me by a nickname only my closest friends used. She was skilled at performing reconstructive surgery, not dealing with gunshot wounds to the chest and abdomen. I needed another qualified trauma surgeon as soon as possible and did not want to draft her into something she might be unqualified to do. Still, all surgeons do some training in trauma during residency. Officer Smith could not wait, and I was the only trauma attending in the emergency department and unable to leave during a worsening multiple casualty disaster when more injured police officers were en route. I had no choice but to draft Gina as well as give the trauma fellow a battlefield promotion.

"Ashton, come here. Gina, I need you to take this patient to the OR with Ashton. He'll help you get positioned for a left thoracotomy. Just get him on the table. I'll be there in a few minutes."

At that moment, a nurse checking her phone for breaking news, announced to the team, "CNN says there's a shooting at a Black Lives Matter rally downtown."

Her pronouncement was matter-of-fact. It was the moment I learned details about the Dallas cops getting shot. Later I probably would have forgotten when, exactly, we learned what had happened— except for what came next.

"I hate Black Lives Matter," a second nurse said.

The first nurse took the baton, glaring toward Dr. Morris, the Black anesthesiologist preparing to take Officer Smith to the OR.

"Yeah. *This* is what happens when Black Lives Matter."

Armed hospital police were patrolling the trauma center. More Dallas police officers, on and off duty, were arriving to support their injured colleagues. And more doctors and nurses, not directly involved with the trauma, watched from the sidelines, ready to help as needed. As I ping ponged from exam room to exam room, I walked by those extra medical personnel and officers so many times they became part of the background scenery. Hyperfocused on the bodies before me, I didn't notice my shadow: a silent man in faded blue jeans and a button-down shirt.

"Blake?" I stopped and furrowed my brow. There he stood: another qualified trauma surgeon, but not the one I expected.

"I'm here, man. Whaddya need?"

Dr. Blake Michaels was one of my senior partners. I assumed he responded to the Code Yellow, but I didn't ask. I was just so relieved to have another trauma surgeon on hand.

"Blake, this is Officer Smith. He needs a left thoracotomy. Gunshot wound to the chest. Stable but pressure dropping and a lot of blood from his chest tube."

Like an aim, fire, and release air-to-air missile, Dr. Michaels took command, gave orders to the team, and within seconds they were rolling to the OR. The plastic surgeon and trauma fellow wouldn't need to do the procedure after all. The anesthesiologist, Dr. Morris, still reeling from the racist remark by a nurse standing over a conscious police officer, joined the team, racing to the OR for emergency surgery.

Again, I paused to regain situational awareness. Three gunshot wounds so far. Two deceased. One going to the OR with Dr. Michaels. Code Yellow activated. As I walked the line of exam rooms, checking on the teams preparing for more patients, Monica, the director of operations for the emergency department, approached.

"Dr. Williams, do you want to go on divert?" Going on divert would mean shutting down the emergency department. In the midst of a Code Yellow disaster, with potentially more gunshot (and maybe bomb) victims coming in, the number of patients might exceed Parkland's logistical ability to respond. Going on divert meant refusing to accept additional sick or injured patients from anywhere. Diversion would preserve our resources and personnel, but it meant turning away strokes, heart attacks, motor vehicle collisions, falls, gunshot victims, and more. We would also refuse transfer of patients from lower-level trauma centers in the area, patients who needed the resources and expertise only we could provide. In short, we would redirect any calls from EMS and divert the ambulances to our sister hospitals in the area. Essentially, we'd temporarily close down. And for the premier Level 1 trauma center in north Texas to do that would be a big deal.

Considering the circumstances, it was not an unreasonable question, but I was never in doubt about my answer.

"Monica, absolutely not. This is Parkland. We never shut down."

How much time had passed since the disaster began? An hour? More? Moving from examining a patient to speaking with a nurse to checking information on the computer, I had no idea. Time didn't matter. What mattered were the bodies of two deceased cops the nurses were preparing for family viewing. What mattered was Officer Smith in the operating room, hemorrhaging on the table. What mattered was a fourth officer who had also arrived, who appeared stable and was on his way to get a CT scan of his chest.

I took the stairs to the third-floor OR suite and changed into a clean set of scrubs. How long I had been in those bloody scrubs, I didn't know. Entering the OR, I saw my two senior partners, Dr. Michaels, who magically appeared in the trauma hall, and the boss, who also came to help, bent over the patient. Dr. Ashton, the trauma fellow, also assisted in the operation. Monitors beeped, anesthesiologists hung bags of blood, and a nurse brought in another cooler of blood products. Clearly, the massive transfusion protocol was still ongoing.

Watching the action, I felt a mix of guilt and relief. I was relieved to see two experienced trauma surgeons working to save Officer Smith. The patient was in expert hands, yet I could not shake the feeling that I should have been doing the case—that I had somehow ignored my duty to treat this cop. He came in on my watch. He was my responsibility. But I couldn't; there were simply too many critical tasks downstairs to manage. So I left to get back to it.

Nurse Vanessa stopped me when I returned to the emergency department from the OR.

"Dr. Williams, the family of Officer Zamarripa is here."

"What's his first name?"

"Patrick."

Patrick Zamarripa was the first wounded officer to arrive. I usually didn't know the names of my gunshot victims until I notified the next of kin. Until that moment, I had known Officer Patrick Zamarripa only as "the officer in Bay 1." Now, as I had done for countless gunshot victims, I had to deliver the news of his death to his family.

11 | END OF WATCH

The family room at Parkland Hospital is a windowless room with white walls tucked away in a back hallway near the trauma center. Straightening my white coat over a set of clean blue scrubs, I slid into a chair across from a woman with wavy Black hair gripping the hand of a man in a US Army Veteran baseball cap. They were Officer Zamarripa's father and stepmother, Rick and Maria, and their eyes locked on me as I extended my hand.

"I'm Dr. Williams. I'm the trauma surgeon on call tonight. I'll walk you through what happened with Patrick after he arrived at the hospital. You can stop me at any time if you have any questions."

Rick nodded. Maria stared, gripping her husband's hand more tightly.

No matter how many times I do this, I always want to do my best with this conversation. It is humbling to guide strangers to a dark place they do not want to go, especially when they already have some idea of the horror awaiting them. This may be one of the worst days of someone's life, and they deserve a doctor who delivers the news with sensitivity, compassion, and respect.

"There was a shooting downtown," I said, speaking in a measured monotone. "I do not know much about that, so I can't tell you what happened. But when Patrick arrived here, he was in critical condition."

I never assume people know what medical terms, even the more common ones, mean. Even if they do, during crisis moments, the mind works in mysterious ways and ignores words or misinterprets them. I often repeat myself, but in different ways, so it sinks in.

"By critical, I mean Patrick's injuries were life-threatening. He had a serious gunshot wound, and when he arrived here at the hospital, his heart had stopped. They were already doing CPR to restart his heart."

Having prepared them the best I can, I began to say the words no parent should ever have to hear. But Officer Zamarripa's father stopped me.

"It's okay, Doctor," Rick said somberly. He looked me in the eye with a dignity I have not yet, all these years later, been able to find words for. "I know Patrick is dead. And I thank you. I thank everybody. I know you did everything you could."

I sat in stunned silence. Many families had thanked me in moments like this, but 7/7 was a different tragedy in so many ways. I had been unable to save this man's son, a Dallas cop killed in the line of duty. Yet, when he heard the news, he had found the composure and the kindness to thank me. I offered to answer any questions later if needed, stood, straightened my white coat, and excused myself from the room. Years later, Rick's words, and belief in me, remain an immense gift.

Outside it was past midnight, but well before dawn. Through a set of double doors to my right, the work of the hospital continued. Cleaning staff prepared the trauma bays for more potential patients from motor vehicle collisions, falls, and gun violence. Doctors and nurses tapped computer keyboards, pushed patients on stretchers, and prepared the bodies of the deceased for family viewing. We were past the initial critical phase of the disaster. During this lull, in which routine post-injury care occurred, the team did not need me in the trauma center.

I looked at the police officer on post outside the family room I had just exited. We locked eyes for a whisper of a second. He stood silently. Stoic. Statuesque. Police officers were posted outside the trauma bays where the deceased officers lay, and outside the private rooms where their families waited. Through the night, my interactions with the officers remained cordial. Business-like. The officer posted with Officer Zamarripa shared intermittent updates on the progress downtown, which is how I learned about the manhunt for a Black shooter.

That night it was hard to imagine what was happening beyond the walls of the hospital, to fathom anything beyond saving the lives of the gunshot victims right before us. I looked to the doors on my right and instead turned left, walking through a set of restricted-entry double doors. Those doors led to a back hallway I'd never before seen.

The doors exhaled shut behind me, enveloping me in silence.

Two nights earlier, while I slept beside my wife, Alton Sterling lay dead on the ground in Baton Rouge, Louisiana. The police responded to a prank call about a man threatening customers. Sterling was no threat. He was simply the wrong color in the wrong place at the wrong time. Restrained by two police officers outside a convenience store, where he had been selling compact discs, Alton heard the last words of his life—"I'll kill you, bitch"—from an officer before suffering multiple gunshot wounds, at point-blank range. He was thirty-two years old.

The next day in Falcon Heights, Minnesota, two police officers pulled over thirty-two-year-old Philando Castile. From a distance and in a moving vehicle, they said, he "fit the description" of a robbery suspect. Within forty seconds of initiating contact, one officer had fired seven shots, striking Castile five times. Two bullets pierced his heart.

The National Rifle Association had been tepid in its defense of Castile, a licensed owner who did everything right: inform the officer that he was licensed to carry a concealed firearm located in his glove box. The ultimate good guy with a gun, Castile followed proper procedure by disclosing his concealed carry status. That admission likely sealed his death. As Castile slumped over in the driver's seat and bled from multiple wounds, his distraught girlfriend live-streamed his death to a worldwide audience. Her four-year-old daughter witnessed the shooting from the backseat.

Sterling and Castile were the latest victims in a seeming epidemic of law enforcement officers killing unarmed Black men. Two of those killings were now recorded and broadcast for the world. As we kept hearing more news, Philando Castile's death particularly disturbed me. Police officers had stopped Philando Castile forty-six times during his short life. On the forty-seventh stop, he was shot and killed: a law-abiding citizen pulled over for a routine traffic stop, gunned down for reaching for his ID while Black. The government, according to academic and activist Marc Lamont Hill, should "offer forms of protection that enhance our lives and shield our bodies from foreseeable and preventable dangers. Unfortunately, for many citizens—particularly those marked as poor, Black, Brown, immigrant, queer, or trans—State power has only increased their vulnerability, making their lives more rather than less unsafe."

I had long maintained an impenetrable barrier between my personal identity as a Black man and professional identity as a Black doctor. Segregating those identities was self-destructive and, in many ways, self-serving. I was a veteran, surgeon, and scholar struggling with what it meant to be Black and routinely dealing with the worst kinds of violence perpetrated against my people. By now I knew enough about the history of policing to know that police departments, in their earliest colonial incarnations, served to maintain the racial caste system. That system had begun during the period of chattel slavery and continued during Reconstruction, through Jim Crow, to the present.

Contemporary policing traces its history to the eighteenth-century slave patrols hunting escaped enslaved people, which evolved into the militarized police departments of the present day. Radley Balko, author of *Rise of the Warrior Cop*, writes that police officers often "see streets and neighborhoods as battlefields and the citizens they serve as the enemy."

Still, as a Black man who had cleared every hurdle to prove my worthiness, I found America still could move the bar of conditional acceptance out of reach. Like America had done to Alton Sterling on July 5, 2016, and Philando Castile on July 6, and so many more Black people throughout history, America could also snatch my life from me with impunity.

Years earlier, when I explained to Kathianne the full extent of my fear when I was questioned by the police outside of our high-rise apartment, she thought I was overreacting. But on July 7—two days after the death of Alton Sterling and one day after the death of Philando Castile—and right before the tragedy unfolded in Dallas, she said, "Oh my God, Brian. You were right."

There in the early morning hours of Friday, July 8, hiding in the secluded hallway, I leaned against the wall. The silence surrounding me was so strange, so rare, it almost seemed like noise. Staring at the floor, I raised my head in a deliberate arc, from floor, to floorboard, to wall, to ceiling. I inhaled deeply while staring upward. Exhaling as the ceiling slowly drifted up, up, and away. Images from the night flashed through my memory: the limp bodies, the chest compressions, the bullet wounds, and the blood. So much blood.

I slid to the floor and buried my face in my hands. Without warning, I began crying softly. Soon my sobs erupted into body-shaking convulsions.

What was this feeling? Where had these tears come from? I didn't cry. Ever. I didn't cry at my wedding. I didn't cry at the birth of my daughter. Kathianne, a fan of true crime TV shows, sometimes joked that if she died under suspicious circumstances, everyone would think I was guilty because I never showed emotion.

But now two police officers were dead, their vital organs having been no match for the scorching missiles that pierced through them. Nurses were preparing the bodies for family viewing, bodies that were now crime scenes. A third was hemorrhaging in the operating room.

Had I missed something? Could I have done anything differently to save them?

I had already told one set of parents their police officer son was dead, and I wondered how many more such conversations remained before the crisis ended. I had become the dead pronouncing the dead.

My pager broke the silence. Three more officers had arrived, bringing our total to seven. I had no more time for reflection. I peeled myself from the floor, dried my eyes, and straightened my coat. I took a deep breath, swiped the badge, and re-entered the emergency department.

Rounding the corner to the trauma bay, Nurse Vanessa stopped me.

"Are you okay, Dr. Williams?" I looked past her.

"Brian, are you okay?" she said again. Breaking our unspoken protocol, she called me by my first name.

"I'm fine." I said. I always said I was fine, even when I wasn't.

"Are you sure?" she said, narrowing her eyes.

"I'm fine, Vanessa," I said in a tone to end further inquiry. Like we must do on any trauma shift on any night, we had to move on. "Let's get back to work."

In the predawn darkness, I follow a group of Dallas police officers through the metal detectors and sliding glass door outside to the ambulance bay. Only a few hours have passed since the first officer arrived at the hospital, but it seems like a lifetime.

The police officers cover down into two lines, making a lane from the emergency department entrance to the back of the vans. There they stand in formation, erect and sober. We stand silently on the asphalt, where white lines demarcate individual parking spots. Three of the spaces are occupied—not by ambulances, but by vans from the medical examiner's office. These vans will transport the bodies of the three deceased officers to the morgue. Ultimately five officers will die from the shooting. Nine additional officers and two civilians will suffer non-lethal gunshot wounds.

Standing in formation is not foreign to me. At the Academy, I stood at attention thousands of times. And I have stood ramrod straight and saluted, while taps played to honor a fallen soldier. I know what those police officers are about to do. I know I could join them. Except now I'm a civilian, and they are cops. I'm in scrubs, and most of them are in uniform. I am Black, and most of them are white. I hesitate, wondering whether they'll take offense or welcome me. But I have to do this. I've dropped into this moment and cannot walk away. I step forward and wedge myself into their formation.

"Uh-tench-hut!" one of the officers shouts, his voice shredding the silence. I snap my feet together, arms pinned to my sides, shoulders back and down.

"Present arms!" he barks, and I snap a salute. Family members of the fallen officers, assisted by Vanessa and her team, escort three gurneys rolling down the ramp to the vans. The sobs and the tears and the grief are palpable as the van doors close: three dull thuds in succession. In short order, the officers, doctors, and nurses disband and return to their duties. The hospital moves on. The officers move on. The team moves on.

Alone, I walk in the opposite direction to a corner of the ambulance bay. Watching as the vans rumble away, I wipe away another set of tears. The dawn sky above is becoming rimmed with light as the city awakens. Doing an about face, I walk with a purpose back into Parkland.

PART III

Shock

Any life, no matter how long or complex it may be, is made up essentially of a single moment—the moment in which a man finds out, once and for all, who he is.

—Jorge Luis Borges

12 | A FOOL FOR A PATIENT

I am sitting in an office, engulfed by a cannibalistic couch. Its massive cushions devoured me as soon as I sat down, and my back contorts into angles that would shame an Olympic gymnast. Pulling my phone from my back pocket, I press the power button until the screen goes black. I double check to ensure it's off, paranoid it might broadcast my secrets to some random person in my contact list. For a moment, the silence rests heavy upon me, pressing me further into this insatiable piece of furniture.

As the first anniversary of the shooting approaches, television, newspaper, magazine, and radio reporters all want to know, "How are you doing, Dr. Williams? How do you feel a year after 7/7?" Trying to strike the right tone, one respectful of the living and the dead, I usually say something like, "This was a terrible tragedy for our city. Like the rest of Dallas, I am working to heal." But if they want the truth—the one not tainted by my deft obfuscation—they would have to talk to the two women who could best answer. One is Kathianne, who has told me "You need to deal with your shit" more times than I can recount.

The second woman sits across from me now. Unlike me, she seems quite comfortable, sitting on a padded chair with her legs folded beneath a blanket. She cradles a teacup, never releasing me from her gaze. Holding the string of her tea bag delicately, she dips it in and out of the scalding water before allowing its remaining life to steep as it sinks to the bottom. I sit in silence waiting for her to begin the session.

My therapist knows the story of what had happened the night of July 7, 2016: 7/7, as it has become known in Dallas, is the largest loss of life for US law enforcement since 9/11. She knows the victims were cops, and the sniper, like me, was Black. She has seen the footage, and in earlier sessions I have narrated the story to her in dispassionate and even tones. By now, I am skillful at recounting the events of that night. I should not have even been working, it was supposed to be my night off. As the leader of the trauma team, I tell people, I treated seven officers from the scene, and the remaining officers were taken to a crosstown trauma center. And yes, I became the only surgeon in history to operate on multiple police officers victimized in a mass shooting.

I can narrate the wider story as well, to friends and colleagues outside of Dallas who call, text, and email to find out what happened and how I'm doing. I describe to people the peaceful protest in downtown Dallas, which had drawn eight hundred attendees and one hundred police officers who were providing security. Organized in response to the police killings of Alton Sterling on July 5 and Philando Castile on July 6, Black Lives Matter protests erupted nationwide on July 7. The wave of protests would serve as a prelude to the mass uprisings four years later after the choking death of George Floyd by a police officer less than five miles from where Philando Castile was killed. To this day, many still refer to the Dallas shooting as a "Black Lives Matter" rally. In fact, a local social justice organization had organized the protest. I'm not sure if Black Lives Matter receiving the credit, or the blame, for the rally is a testament to the penetration of its brand into the national consciousness or the perennial need for detractors to rewrite history to advance a comfortable narrative.

I tell people that while I worked elbows-deep in a chest cavity full of blood, Dallas police officers were cornering their suspect: Micah

Xavier Johnson, an African American US Army combat veteran. Johnson, armed with several weapons, had opened fire, targeting white police officers as cameras and phones streamed the event near Dealey Plaza, the site of JFK's assassination. It would take four and a half hours for a Dallas SWAT team to corner Johnson and kill him with a robot-delivered bomb, detonated by remote control. No police department in history had ever used a robot to kill a suspect. Johnson would kill four police officers before being killed. A fifth officer would die from his wounds the next day.

A protest for racial justice. Dallas, Texas. A Black shooter. Dead white cops.

I mean, what else do people need to know?

I wait for my therapist to say something. It's my second session (or is it my third?), and I'm getting used to these silences. She cradles the teacup and sips from it as a cloud of steam rises. Her hand movements are deliberate, her facial expressions comforting. Then she draws first blood.

"Have you written letters to the families?" she asks.

"To the families?" I'm suspicious and shift deeper into the maw of the couch.

"Well, you said you never reached out to them. So what's stopping you from writing to them now?"

Let me count the ways, I think: It's been a year. I'm getting hateful mail. There was a death threat. I feel responsible for their deaths. What would I say to them?

Shaking my head in a languid arc, I answer, "No. That would be intrusive."

"Why do you feel that way? What's different about these deaths that bother you compared to others you've had?"

I mentally roll my eyes, wanting to extricate myself from this damn couch and leave. But I suppress the urge. I know her therapeutic curiosity is genuine, but it still feels like an interrogation. I don't allow strangers to tug on my psychological weeds.

"It's just different," I say. "And I don't think sending letters is appropriate."

I have convinced myself that too long a period had passed. That to reach out now would seem disingenuous or traumatizing. That my silence is about respecting their privacy, when I know it is actually a desire to regain my own. By not sending letters, I can shield myself from more attention and avoid getting closer to anybody than absolutely necessary.

"You don't have to send them," she says. "Just write what you'd like to say."

We sit in silence while I process this madness. Write letters to the families of the dead police officers. My dead patients. But don't send them? What's the point of doing that?

Cradle.

Sip.

Silence.

A coffee table sits between us, a physical barrier reminding me this is indeed a reversal of my usual life. Now *I'm* the patient, and to heal, I have to place my trust in someone else. And my trust account is pretty close to bankrupt. I stall by grabbing a chocolate from the coffee table and rolling the candy from cheek to tongue and back to cheek. I scan the room—table, floor, wall, clock—looking everywhere but at my therapist. Might I be saved by the end of my billable hour? Seconds feel like minutes. Minutes feel like hours.

Finally breaking the silence, she spares me. "Just think about it," she says, with a barely perceptible nod. "You don't have to if you don't want to. But I think it might be helpful."

"I'll think about it." A committed noncommittal. That I can do. And I can do it very well.

Sip.

Cradle.

Silence.

Ordinarily, I would mentally trash her suggestion and move on. But she has proven surprisingly adept at her job. She works on me like I work on my trauma patients. Even when I cannot see the internal damage, my job as a surgeon is to decipher external clues—physical exam, heart rate, blood pressure, oxygenation, respiratory rate—and rapidly treat the destructive forces beneath the surface. Each clue by itself could mean nothing. Interpreted together, they often reveal enough to discern the difference between life and death. With experience, I have learned what to look for and what questions to ask. When a critical patient is unresponsive, I must intervene without their input. And then there are those challenging patients who *can* speak but refuse. Like I'm doing now.

This is not my first trip to her couch, although several times I've wondered whether it might be my last. Therapy is not my thing. But as Sir William Osler, the late nineteenth-century physician lauded as the father of modern medicine, said, "A physician who treats himself has a fool for a patient." So here I am.

I began our sessions intending to talk about the shooting, nothing else. But now my therapist casually strolls around in my psyche, shining a light into its dark recesses and pointing out unrelated secrets hiding in plain sight. At first, I wasn't concerned about what she would find. After all, I'm the one who hid everything there. But clearly, I have done a poor job covering my tracks. I wonder if she had me figured out the moment I offered myself to her carnivorous couch.

"For our next session, I have some homework for you," she tells me.

Like a hyper-focused college student wanting to ace the exam, I prepare to take notes. I grab a pen, paper, and liberate another chocolate from its foil.

With equal parts compassion and challenge, she says, "I want you to write a trauma narrative."

"A what?" I feel like I'm trying to comprehend a foreign language in real time.

"A trauma narrative. Try to describe the night of the shooting using your five senses. What you saw. What you heard. Any smells. How things felt."

She rubs a thumb and two fingers together. I'm certain she meant what I actually felt through my gloved hands that evening, but I felt as if she were a mafioso signaling the payment in kind for some unwelcome deed. The remembering would exact a psychological cost.

Absentmindedly, I rub my hands together and look at the floor. I think about that night every single day, and I have done so for an entire year. I am always watching a movie on an endless loop in my mind. I want to ask her why I need to write it down when I am always reliving 7/7.

The weight of bloodied scrubs against my legs. The alarms. The snapping ribs. The flaccid heart in my hands. The call and response of the trauma team. One officer crashing so fast I perform a thoracotomy. Another last-ditch emergency department thoracotomy failing to save the second officer. The third officer appearing stable at first, sitting upright on the gurney, only to make it to the operating room, then bleeding to death on the table. Three men whose lives I failed to save: Officers Patrick Zamarripa, Michael Krol, and Michael Smith.

Sitting in my therapist's office, I suddenly feel lonely. I have no words to describe my sense of emptiness and lethargy and guilt. Of wanting to crawl into a darkened closet and hide. I can hardly remember the days when I delighted in going to work because now I dread it.

As my hour expires, I thank her and leave, restarting my phone before her office door closes behind me. And, like some of my patients do to me, I promptly dismiss everything she has asked me to do.

Another year will pass before I take her advice.

Climbing into my car and pulling onto the highway, I feel a familiar mixture of failure and disgust. Failure because three cops died on my watch. Disgust because it never had to happen. I think of Shetamia Taylor, the mother who attended the protest with her four teenage sons, who frantically shielded her kids and was injured by shrapnel. I think of Larry Gordon, the SWAT negotiator who spent hours talking with Micah Johnson, bonding with him and trying to coax him into a peaceful surrender. I think of Mark Hughes, the Black man at the protest exercising his legal right to open-carry and helping protesters evacuate safely—the Black man who police misidentified as a suspect and who then received death threats.

And I think of the Black veteran who, like me, was enraged by the epidemic of police killings of Black men, enraged at the racial injustice written into seemingly every system of our national life. I think of the one who chose violence the night of 7/7: Micah Johnson, who told the negotiator, "I want to kill white cops. I want them to pay in blood." Having committed my life to service and to a profession of healing, I deplore the lethal actions Micah took to express his grievance. Whenever I think of him, anger and grief rise in my chest: fury, not at him, but for the actions he took to shoot the cops whose lives I tried to save, whose deaths still haunt me. And a silent admission that, on some level, I understand why he did it.

But unlike me, he is no longer alive to tell his story. He cannot counter the narrative now defining him: the angry, unhinged Black man who deserved to die. The sniper who asked to be wiped from the face of the earth by a bomb delivered by a robot.

Pulling into my driveway, I feel the familiar thrum of anger in my chest. It is my comfort and my pain. I know how internalized fury at persistent injustice can grow over a lifetime. So if all that is true about Micah Xavier Johnson, what does that say about me?

13 | GOD'S TOKEN

Four days after the shooting I stood in a secluded corner of the hospital, my forehead buried in one hand and my cellphone cradled in the other. "Brian, you have to go," Kathianne pleaded. "This country is tearing itself apart."

Parkland had scheduled an afternoon press conference, a chance to describe the hospital's response to the mass shooting. Since I was the trauma surgeon on call that night, leadership expected me to attend. Kathianne was trying to convince me to do what I never wanted to do: talk to the media. I had mastered avoiding the media, declining nearly every request over the years. I didn't have an active social media presence, and interviews were never my thing. This particular press conference meant recounting the most traumatic night of my career; live, in front of microphones, cameras, and strangers.

I had worked hospital shifts every day since the shooting. Each day I donned a clean white coat and spent another day at Parkland Hospital rounding on patients, teaching students and residents, and fixing people in the operating room. The day after the shooting, I even attended a disco dance party for my daughter's preschool friends and their parents. I was doing what I did best: compartmentalize, work, and soldier on.

I was also on a self-imposed media blackout: no television, radio, newspapers, or social media. The dominant news story was 7/7, and I wanted none of it.

"Just go so people can at least *see* you," Kathianne said. "The world needs to know that it wasn't just a Black man who shot those cops but that a Black man also tried to save them."

She paused to let it sink in.

"You don't even have to say anything. Just show up. Being there will make a difference."

She had a point. A divided nation reeling from another mass shooting needed to see that a Black doctor had been in charge, trying to do the right thing. In this story, not only the villain but some of the heroes were Black. Maybe just showing up would speak volumes without me opening my mouth. Besides, Kathianne was insistent.

"The country needs to see you. You're the only person in the world with this experience: a Black trauma surgeon who tried to save the white police officers shot by a Black man because of racist policing. I mean, come on."

She was relentless. Still, I felt reduced to something I had worked my entire life to avoid: being the token. A Black face present for the optics. I stared at the floor, computing the risk-benefit ratio. I'd be crazy to go, I thought; the risks far outweighed the benefits.

"Kats, I have to get back to work," I tried to sound nonchalant as nurses, doctors, and visitors passed within earshot. "I'll talk to you later."

Being married to someone who does not give up can be a blessing and a curse. Kathianne's tone shifted, assuming an urgency I rarely heard from her.

"If not you, Brian, then who?" she demanded.

(Anybody but me, I thought.)

"And, if not now, then when?"

(Never, and I was fine with that.)

The forcefulness of her speech gathered momentum. "This is bigger than you. You *have* to be there. *You* have to show up, Brian. Step into the arena!"

Per her insistence, we were both reading Brené Brown's *Daring Greatly* at the time, and the phrase "step into the arena" had become her mantra. Then Kathianne brought the spiritual heat: "That night, you were exactly where you were supposed to be. God put you there for a reason."

She should have stopped before invoking God, which is not a great strategy for convincing a faith-avoidant person like me to do anything. I had long grown weary of the stories told by white men about a white God and the celestial exploits of white people. I saw no place for a Black man like me in those timeless fables of redemption and salvation. God bless America? When neither God nor America seemed to value Black people? Please. When Kathianne said God put me there for a reason, my eyes rolled so far in the back of my head I nearly broke an ocular muscle.

Still, she was right: I should go. I didn't fully accept her logic, but I surrendered—not to any faith, but to my duty. This was about Black representation. I'd say nothing, just be present. I'd sit before the cameras, keep my mouth shut, look professional, and satisfy everyone. It was an act I had mastered over the course of my entire medical career. No confrontations. No controversy. No fuss. Get along to move along. And after the press conference I could shrink back to my life of comfortable anonymity.

"Okay. I'll go," I relented. "But if I speak, I'll lose it."

"Even if you do lose it and the world comes crumbling down, I will stand by you."

Given the preceding years of our withering marriage, that was a truly incredible thing for her to say. Although I trusted her and had told her more than anyone else in my life, I still kept her in the dark about my deepest thoughts.

"Let me know how it goes. Remember, God put you there for a reason. I love you."

"I love you, too."

Minutes later, when I joined my colleagues gathering in the hallway outside of the conference room, a man walked past holding a television camera emblazoned with the CNN logo. The minimal enthusiasm I had for the press conference evaporated, and I sent a final, desperate text to Kathianne.

No response. Having invoked God one last time, she went to the gym for a workout. After her incessant prodding and proselytizing, she had no plans to watch. In fact, we both assumed it was nothing more than a small, local press conference.

How wrong we both were.

Marching in a single file, six of my colleagues and I faced a phalanx of lights, cameras, and reporters. I ignored the murmuring amid the clicks and flashes and shuffling notepads. Like marching in forma- tion at the Academy, I caged my eyes on the back of my partner, Dr. Eastman, leading a few feet in front of me. Five more senior hospital leaders were in line with us.

The seven of us were chosen to represent Parkland and describe the hospital's response to one of the defining mass shootings in US history. As we filed into the conference room and took our seats at a rectangular table lined with microphones, I tried to ignore the standing-room-only gallery of attendees. So many people filled the room that some sat cross-legged on the floor mere feet in front of us.

Some of my colleagues wore black athletic jackets with the Parkland logo. I wore the white coat issued to every doctor on faculty at the medical school across the street. On the left breast of mine were two lines embroidered in blue—Brian H. Williams, MD, Trauma/ Critical Care—and on the right was the logo of the university and our employer, UT Southwestern. The white coat was my armor and resume, gleaming white and razor sharp for the world to see. Unlike me, my partners likely never had a patient ask them to take out the trash, or clear their meal tray, or call for their "real" doctor. If my role in this press conference was to be seen by white America, then I would leave no doubt that I was anything but a respected surgeon. Especially since I was the only Black person at the table.

I struggled to remain mentally present. I half-listened to the designated spokesperson, while the rest of us could choose to speak or remain silent. He began reading from a prepared statement summarizing the incident with sterile phrases: multiple shooting victims, critically injured, disaster response. The words sounded cut and pasted from the reports of other recent mass shootings.

At first, I barely paid attention, my mind replaying the bloody loop of the tragedy four nights prior. But occasionally the language of the official statement pierced my attention. As I began to listen in, what was *unsaid* was impossible to ignore. In the official statement, race was never mentioned. It was as if the shooting had happened in a vacuum-packed, sealed-off place with no history. No context.

Unbelievable, I thought. That's all he has to say? What about Alton Sterling and Philando Castile, Black men killed by police less than a week earlier? What about the larger context into which this tragedy had landed: the shooting at a gay nightclub in Orlando less than a month earlier? The presidential election with bigotry, intolerance, and violence on proud display? It was clear to me 7/7 was not an anomaly; it was the predictable result of America's refusal to reckon with her legacy of racism. A Black sniper had shot white cops at a protest for racial justice, and not a single person named the trumpeting elephant in the room. No one at this press conference—not my colleagues beside me nor the reporters asking the questions—was making any connections.

So there I sat, stone-faced, like a child forced to sit through church. Mentally adrift, I tried to hide in plain sight, eyes caged on the table. I ignored the cameras lining the back wall and the reporters sitting cross-legged on the floor, so close I felt I could have nudged them with my foot. I ignored my colleagues at the table, those who often professed they "didn't see color"—and who therefore didn't see what 7/7 meant to me. As I slumped and pouted and stared, the white-washed description of the shooting continued.

I was the mute trinket in a clean white coat playing my part: to be seen, not heard. To maintain everything I had achieved and to continue rising, on a semi-conscious level, I knew I had better stay in my lane. It was a reality I'm certain that my colleagues, pontificating in turn at the microphone, could not comprehend. I began to shift in my seat. I had spent a lifetime hiding my opinions and keeping my head down. But by remaining silent, I'd be giving tacit approval to a disingenuous narrative: one that deified the cops, vilified the killer, and nullified America's history of terrorizing Black people. But if I said what I felt—what I truly felt—I would most likely be fired.

As the microphone slid to me, I reached for it as if it were a cobra about to attack. I audibly exhaled, considering one last time if I truly wanted to do this.

"I want to state first and foremost, I stand with the Dallas Police Department," I began. A scratchy lump in my throat halted my words. "I stand with law enforcement all over this country. This experience has been very personal for me and a turning point in my life. There was the added dynamic of officers being shot."

The words flowed freely. The persona I had molded and polished for public consumption was displaced by this rogue entity who now commanded my actions.

"We routinely care for multiple gunshot victims," I said. "But the preceding days of more Black men dying at the hands of police officers affected me. I think the reasons are obvious. I fit that demographic of individuals."

My lips quivered and my voice thickened. Yet I could not turn off the spigot of words that continued to flow without end. In that moment, there were no cameras, lights, or people. No table, chairs, or walls. Nothing. Just me and the mic.

"But I abhor what was done to these officers, and I grieve with their families. I understand the anger and the frustration and distrust of law enforcement. But they are not the problem. The problem is the lack of open discussions about the impact of race relations in this country. And I think about it every day: that I was unable to save those cops when they came here that night. It weighs on my mind constantly."

By this time, I was choking back tears and barely able to talk. "This killing, it has to stop: Black men dying and being forgotten, people retaliating against the people who are sworn to defend us. We have to come together and end all this."

I didn't know what I was going to say until I said it. But suddenly it seemed like my whole career as a Black trauma surgeon—operating on patients, some who revered me and some who reviled me—had slid toward a pointed, jagged edge. In a room packed with people, likely watching me set fire to my career, I felt completely alone. And yet, for the first time in as long as I could remember, I was at peace.

Questions soon came my way, and I did my best to answer them. One reporter asked about my relationship with law enforcement. In a flash I thought of all the incidents I could share: being forced to stand spread-eagle over my hood for going six miles an hour over the speed limit, being asked for my ID for standing outside my apartment building. Instead, I talked about trying to set an example for my five-year-old daughter, about the times I bought meals and ice cream for police officers when we were out and about in Dallas. I wanted to model for my daughter how to show kindness and respect in a system that might view her as unworthy, or worse, a threat.

I had already broken several unspoken pacts: when we talk about tragedies, we don't talk about racism. When shootings occur, we offer thoughts and prayers and move on. We don't look at the tragedies unfolding in emergency rooms across the country as having anything to do with the tragedy of a system that privileges some and disadvantages others.

And, most importantly, the Black guy smiles, nods, and keeps his damn mouth shut.

Maybe I'd lose my job, but I would no longer hand over my dignity and self-respect pretending to be something I was not. So I took a deep breath and said to the police officers in the room and around the country: "I support you. I will defend you. And I will care for you. That doesn't mean that I do not fear you."

Finished, I pushed the microphone away, leaned back in my chair, and thought: Oh shit, what have I done?

At the gym, Kathianne was well into an elliptical machine workout when the wall of high-definition television monitors flipped from the regularly scheduled programming to the press conference. On national television was a larger-than-life image of me—crying. She hopped off her machine and recorded the soundless images with closed captioning. My unscripted comments, broadcast on media outlets around the world, soon went viral on social media, and interview requests soon overwhelmed the hospital switchboard.

Meanwhile, I was oblivious, having no idea what transpired beyond the confines of the conference room where I sat. Eager to slip out of the spotlight and ease back into anonymity, I stood from the table and turned to leave. Suddenly and without warning, Dr. Eastman wrapped me in a bear hug. Cameras from a sea of photojournalists trained on this duo, capturing an image of camaraderie that was discordant with reality. I responded with a perfunctory bro hug pat on the back and tried to inch away. But he held his embrace while whispering into my ear some platitude about brotherhood. When I finally disentangled myself, I left the conference room alone, unaware I was entering a media tempest.

"Dr. Williams, we have several reporters who would like to speak with you." It was Bret from media relations. "And they'd like some photos too, so, if you have time, we can set you up in one of the trauma bays. Do you mind doing it?"

From behind, the reply came from Dr. Eastman. "Of course, we can do it, Bret. Where do you want us?"

"Uh, they just want Dr. Williams." Bret replied.

A handful of eavesdropping nurses snickered. Some said that the most dangerous place to be is between Dr. Eastman and a camera, and I had stumbled into his spotlight.

As the media relations team arranged the trauma bay, I did a couple of interviews in the hallway outside the conference room. First came the *Dallas Morning News*, followed by the *Washington Post*, the *Daily Mail*, and the *Associated Press*. Later a well-known opinion writer from the *New York Times* who saw the press conference wrote about it as well.

And the following day, the photograph of "the hug" ran on the front page of the *Dallas Morning News* (the accompanying story was a Pulitzer Prize finalist). Here was apparent evidence of the heart-warming story many people longed for: the unique fraternal bond between two doctors, one Black and one white, forged on the front-lines of tragedy. Except it wasn't true. Eastman had not been at the hospital that night.

It wasn't the only photograph telling one story while I lived another. That same day, dressed in my white coat, shirt, and tie, I was one of dozens of mourners downtown, paying respects at the impromptu memorial that had grown over the preceding days outside of the Dallas Police Department headquarters. The centerpiece was a DPD cruiser buried beneath a mountain of flowers, photos, plac-ards, and cards. I made small talk with a pair of officers who thanked and hugged me as we shared words of comfort. I stopped to read the handwritten sentiments and study the oversized headshots of the slain officers. Media trucks with satellite antennae pointed skyward lined the street, and reporters performed visual and soundchecks with their crews. Trying not to be distracted, I noticed that where I walked, the cameras followed.

Ever since I'd cried in the hallway the night of the shooting, it was like some switch had flipped within me. Emotions leftover from the tragedy—a stew of anger and shame and grief from my inability to save Zamarripa, Krol, and Smith—overcame me, and my tears started to flow. I began to ease into a crouch to gather my thoughts and emotions as privately as I could in a public space. But I never made it to the ground.

From behind, two paws slammed onto my shoulders and whipped me around until I was face-to-face with Dr. Eastman. Now crying harder, I pushed him away. I wanted my space. I needed my space. But I sensed that he wanted something also, and he seemed determined to get it. He pulled tighter, wrapping me in his arms as I, crying convulsively, gave up the fight. What was his deal? This was supposed to be my time to pay my respects—alone. My time to grieve—alone. And there he was, once again, drawing me into another one of his photo ops.

But I would not make a scene beside a public memorial honoring dead police officers. That would be disrespectful to the them, their families, and the other mourners. I most definitely would not make a scene in front of all those cameras, several of which were now focused on this manufactured display of brotherhood. Under no circumstances could I make a scene even if I wanted to do so. Because I'm Black, and that is just not allowed.

Finally, he released me.

Simmering beneath my visible grief, my fury intensified. Twice in less than one week I allowed myself to serve as a prop in the media circus. Both times I let it happen. Both times I said nothing. And both times I emerged embarrassed and enraged. It was far from how I assessed what truly existed between us and presented what I felt was a false narrative. Dr. Eastman shared the photo widely with the caption "The Essence of Brotherhood."

Those photographs and words like this—we're all the same, we come together— became the foundation for a revisionist history with a life of its own. I suppose I could have halted the storyline as it developed. But there were dead police officers and grieving families, so I said nothing. No matter how many times I was asked, I never revealed more than necessary. When it was showtime, for the media, at speaking events, and at work, I knew how to mask my true feelings with an Oscar-worthy performance.

We, the aggrieved, become accomplices through silence and self-censorship. By not being the spokesperson for our own stories, we allow history to be rewritten. When we don't speak up—and sometimes even when we do—someone else can pose as the expert on our story. In the words of author Zora Neale Hurston: "If you are silent about your pain, they'll kill you and say you enjoyed it." Which is worse: to speak and have our truths demeaned, distorted, and dismissed, or to choose a self-imposed silence?

Looking at those photographs, you would have no idea what I actually felt. There was no way for a viewer to know how I sensed those hugs were less a symbol of interracial friendship or heroic bond and more a metaphor: for all the ways Black people get engulfed by whiteness, all the times we get wrapped in its clutches.

In the coming days I went where I was directed and did as I was asked. Reporters and producers wanted to hear from "that Black trauma surgeon from Dallas." Within twenty-four hours of the press conference, I had done interviews for local, national, and international news outlets including CNN, Fox, CBS, ABC, BBC, the *New York Times*, Associated Press, *Dallas Morning News*, and more. Then the morning after the press conference it was live interviews on CNN, Fox, and CBS with Gayle King, which placed me one degree of separation from my wife's idol, Oprah Winfrey.

That evening I did a late-night interview on CNN with Don Lemon. Since I didn't watch cable news shows, I was unaware of his reach and influence. Sitting in a local studio in my white coat and scrubs, as directed by the hospital media team, I took the earpiece from a technician, looked toward the camera, and did a sound check. That was the extent of my preparation to be interviewed by the host of one of the highest rated cable news shows in the country. I had received no media training, developed no talking points, and had no prepared remarks. I did my best to answer questions posed by this seasoned journalist about one of the defining tragedies in the history of Dallas and US law enforcement. "What do you want to say, Doctor?" Don Lemon asked. "The world is listening."

I lost it—again. A convulsive, crying mess on prime-time cable television.

Mine wasn't the only Black face of 7/7 telegraphed around the world. In addition to me there was the shooter, Dallas Chief of Police David Brown, and another Black man whose life intersected with this story: Mark Hughes.

Mark Hughes had gone to the rally with an assault rifle strapped to his back, exercising his second-amendment and state-protected right to openly carry a firearm with a license. Police officers had detained him as a possible suspect and removed his weapon. Hughes was questioned, released, then detained again. His face was broadcast everywhere, initially identified as a "cop killer." In the aftermath, Hughes received death threats, his small business disintegrated, and he had to move to another city for his own safety. Despite the fact that the real killer was dead and that Hughes had had absolutely nothing to do with the killing, he never received an apology from the city or exoneration in the press. Six years later, as I write this book, he still hasn't.

One year after the shooting, Mark and I met for lunch at a family-owned BBQ restaurant. We could have talked for hours had work not demanded his presence, and a promised trip to get ice cream with my daughter had not demanded mine. Still, as we ate, Mark and I unpacked issues of social justice, institutional racism, gun rights, and what it meant to speak truth to power.

"Yeah, I saw your press conference when it happened," Mark told me. Barbecue sauce pasted his fingers, which he sucked dry with lip-smacking satisfaction. He wagged the remnants of a pork rib at me for emphasis, his voice muffled by cheeks full of meat. "We was watching the TV, and I turned to my brother and said, 'That man right there: he's about to catch hell.'"

14 | BACKLASH

July 2016

Dear Dr. Williams,

You are a hypocrite. How many niggaz from the hood do you work on every damned week that are shot up, or beat up, by their own kind in the hood? How many have been saved because some white cops helped the paramedics get them there alive? Who do the niggaz in the hood call when they need help? Do they say, "Send Black cops only?" After I move to Texas, I pray I never need to have surgery from you. It must be very difficult to do surgery while you have your racist head up your ass.

Yours truly,

It was a letter from a midwesterner none too pleased with what I said at the press conference. There were more—many more. Letters and emails with caustic lines:

> *I can't believe they let you take care of white people.*
> *Brother, I'm glad you let those pigs die.*
> *I'm a retired cop, and you should never be allowed to treat law enforcement officers.*

I also received a surprising admonishment from one of the most respected Black surgeons in the country. He pulled me aside at a medical conference, the largest annual gathering of trauma surgeons in the country, and said, "Boy, what were you thinking at that press conference?" He said *boy* in the way some Black people do: to exert their dominance over other Black people. "You had only one job that day, and that was to represent your management."

In the months following the press conference, I rode the wave of adulation and weathered the storm of criticism without a plan. I had found a new purpose, trying to be a spokesperson for something or someone—although for what or whom, I did not yet know. In my post-traumatic state, my greatest desire was to enclose myself in a windowless, lightless, soundless room, to be forgotten.

Overnight I had gained a platform and a following. I began to explore the social media universe, at first with trepidation and then with increasing regularity. I was jetsetting around the country, sharing my personal story with thousands. I'd speak to groups about racism and violence, patriotism and service, and I'd issue a call for truth, healing, and reconciliation across racial divides. But rarely did I go too deep into the realities of structural racism, gun violence, or health equity. Despite this tragedy, or maybe because of it, we remained segregated among Black, White, and Blue. Some praised my courage. Others insisted I was a hero. Strangers asked for selfies in airports and malls and coffee shops from the Lone Star State to the Pacific Northwest to the streets of Manhattan.

In the weeks to come, I spoke to the Surgeon General, was invited to speak at the Congressional Black Caucus, and did more interviews for local, national, and international outlets. CNN flew my family to New York so I could participate in a live town hall on race and policing, hosted by Don Lemon. The following day we took the train to Washington, DC, to appear in another live town hall, this time on ABC with President Obama. Sleep-deprived and starstruck, I went mute after shaking his hand and saying, "It's a pleasure to meet you, Mr. President." Kathianne filled the void with several minutes of describing the letter she had written years earlier, to our then-unborn daughter, about growing up in a world with a Black president.

We returned home exhilarated, but my travel schedule continued to accelerate as the speaking requests multiplied. I was home even less than before, either on trauma call or traveling to speak, and Kathianne did not hesitate to express her displeasure. But I was fueled by an abundance of external affirmations, and that adrenaline kept me going. A gleeful stranger in Dallas–Fort Worth airport nearly dislocated my shoulder shaking my hand as he said, "Thank you for speaking out. What you said was powerful." A coworker stopped me in the hall on my way to the OR and said, "Dr. Williams. It's you! My brother in Nigeria saw you on the TV, and he does not believe that I know you. I need to send him a picture." There were boxes of letters, cards, and Bibles, Torahs, and Qurans that people sent. Gifts of mugs, shirts, handmade quilts, and gift cards. And enough emails to stress the limits of my inbox and surpass my ability to reply to them all.

But all the praise, accolades, and newfound purpose could not subdue what had been clawing inside me for months. I could appease it for a time, yes. But eventually all the trauma of 7/7 mated with my anger and grief. For months I had felt exhausted, spending my days trying to outmaneuver my perceived enemies and decide who was friend and who was foe, who I could trust and who I could not. After I spoke at that press conference, I felt more exposed than at any point in my medical career. Situated in the crosshairs of powerful people, who were unsympathetic and at times antagonistic, to any honest discussion connecting racism and medicine, I had begun censoring myself again. When I gave speeches around the country, I emphasized the narrative of the shooting I knew everyone wanted to hear: the hospital disaster mobilization, the gallant police officers, the professionalism of the nurses and doctors, the way a community comes together in the aftermath of tragedy. It was an inspiring message of sacrifice and service, and I received standing ovations in packed auditoriums coast-to-coast and a steady stream of media interviews. But outward appearances masked the drama, and there were few people to whom I could tell the truth.

I had the chance when I spoke at one of my alma maters. I met with an old mentor who was well past retirement age but still pulling a full schedule. He was a Black doctor who had dedicated his professional life to the work of diversity, equity, and inclusion before it became popular. As usual, he did most of the talking, dropping a stream of indisputable truths, and I took mental notes.

"Brian, you and I exist in spaces we were never meant to occupy. We know we belong, but we always have to stay vigilant. The game is different in academics, and nobody tells us the rules. Plus, they change the rules when they want to anyway."

This I knew, but I still clung to the belief that merit, service, and sacrifice mattered.

"I watched the news for about seventy hours after your press conference," he continued, "and every clip was about you. Right now, you are the most famous surgeon at your institution. People who've never heard of UT Southwestern or Parkland only know about it now for one reason: you. And that's going to be a problem."

I knew this as well.

"Because a Black man like you was never meant to be the face of Parkland," he said.

He was right: a Black man with a voice and a platform quickly becomes a threat, even when he is still towing the party line. I had a wife and daughter to feed and bills to pay, and I had already done enough at the press conference to jeopardize that. I felt a hefty amount of survivor guilt as well. Unlike the murdered police officers, at least I could be home with my family.

This was a white man's game, one I would never win. It took a while to admit to myself that I was being played. I never understood the rules, anyway. Behind the scenes of the tainted narrative, served up for public consumption, I had become the shiny token, reflecting the spotlight never meant for me. I was a walking dichotomy. Tell the truth. Don't tell the truth. Speak up. Don't speak up. The timeless truth for a Black man who forgot his place on the university plantation is that you are expendable.

Several years before 7/7, I listened with rapt attention as a colleague regaled me with his off-duty adventures, always an immersive experience replete with drama, humor, and heroism. I felt as if I were watching a movie; all I needed was popcorn. On that day, I was yet again enthralled until my storyteller wrapped his chuckle in a cocksure grin, caged his eyes upon me and said, "That nigga was crazy."

It was like a vinyl record from my youth had skipped. Time and sound looping back upon itself on endless repeat. He said it as matter of fact, like we were talking about the weather. Another supposed ally who just happened to think it was okay to drop *nigger* in casual conversation. My colleague. My friend? My brain launched into overdrive, trying to compute what had just happened and what I should do.

He hadn't called *me* a nigger, I told myself—as if that should make a difference. As I said earlier, I'd been called nigger by a lot of white people. Elementary school? Nigger. Middle school? Nigger. High school? Nigger. And it didn't stop there. I'd been called nigger as a cadet at the United States Air Force Academy and as an Air Force officer. I'd been called nigger as a medical student at the University of South Florida, as a surgery resident at Harvard Medical School, as a trauma fellow at Emory University School of Medicine, as an assistant professor of surgery at UT Southwestern Medical Center, and as a trauma surgeon at Parkland Hospital. I'd been called nigger so many times that decades ago I'd stopped counting. And as I ascended the professional ladder, I learned all the ways white people can call you a nigger without even saying the word.

So what did I do now, in my forties? I remained mute, like that eight-year-old boy on the baseball field some forty years earlier. I said nothing. I showed nothing. I did nothing. And after quelling a flash of rage, I felt nothing.

At the same time, I knew exactly what I was doing. On some conscious level I was choosing to silence myself, just as I had been doing for decades. I handed over my voice, dignity, and self-respect for acceptance and peace. But sacrificing one's truth in order to maintain external peace just fuels inner turmoil. And a lifetime of swimming in a boundless sea of racism had left me exhausted. I was tired of being the only Black face in the room and having to censor myself. Tired of having to represent for Black people everywhere, lest the door I passed through be slammed in the faces of those to follow. And damn tired of wondering who in my circle was racist and who was not.

I sat unmoving and tuned him out. He's talking about some *other* Black person, not me, I thought. He didn't *mean* it to be racist, I convinced myself. He didn't need to excuse himself or walk it back or apologize. Why would he? In my silence, I supplied every excuse he needed. I had been making excuses for white people for so long that it had become second nature.

That changed one afternoon a few months after 7/7, as Hillary Clinton and Donald Trump were in the home stretch of the 2016 presidential election, I finally stopped making excuses for white people—and for my own inaction. During a particularly fraught meeting, my mind drifted, and I was back in the emergency department on that fateful night: managing the trauma team, rushing back and forth between trauma bays, trying to save this life and then that one and then that one, as the bodies kept coming. In the context of the social issues transpiring outside the walls of the hospital, I knew this was bigger than me. And I could not remain on my current path, knowing it was a dead end.

At that moment I decided: enough. I stood, straightened my white coat, and left the meeting. I did not shake hands. I offered no explanation. I spoke not another word. I simply did an about-face and marched out of the door.

I was done with all of it: my colleagues, the institution, and, if necessary, my career. I wouldn't be the first Black doctor on an enviable trajectory to leave a career in academia, and I was certain I would not be the last. Dr. Pringl Miller writes about the continuing pattern of "Black physicians who quit or were fired after raising concerns about racism."

Weeks later, I received a message from my mentor, the one who had reminded me that becoming the public face of a predominantly white institution put me at professional risk. It was another warning: *Hi Brian. I am very proud of you, your professional accomplishments, and the stance you have taken. Be very careful. Racism runs deeply in America. In many circles it is the raison d'être. Watch your six.*

15 | BRIDGE

The night of July 7, 2016, had emerged as a tipping point, a fulcrum on which my life balanced. I had long defined racism in terms of how it directly impacted me: the names I had been called, the looks I had received, the treatment from police officers. Racism impacted me directly, but mostly as an interpersonal force. I adhered to the rules: accept, assimilate, and ascend.

The extent of my formal education in the history of Black people in America looked something like this: slavery, the Emancipation Proclamation, Jim Crow, the Civil Rights Movement, freedom. I saw it as a nice tidy timeline, progressing forward in one direction, with a storybook ending of liberty and justice for all. In the aftermath of 7/7, however, I began to talk about the broader implications of racism, especially anti-Black racism, and to discern the way systemic injustice impacts large populations of people. But I was still unprepared for the master class in something I had both endured and navigated my entire career in medicine.

For much of my life, I'd viewed healthcare as the great equalizer. Black or white, rich or poor, we all likely need to see a doctor at some point in our lives, and I thought that medical care, like education, was designed to level the playing field. Even as a doctor, who witnessed otherwise, I maintained that fallacious view for many years. But now I saw the ways institutional racism undermines our healthcare infrastructure and patient care. I had begun seeing and naming too many connections in the healthcare industry, too many complicities in my own role as doctor. My white coat was no longer protective armor; it was becoming a straitjacket—restrictive and suffocating.

So on July 15, 2017, I quit. I had actually decided to resign months earlier and began laying the groundwork for my departure. I had some measure of peace knowing the end was near, although I had no plan for what would follow. I envisioned a glorious fantasy in which, for the first time in nearly twenty years, no hospital obligations would disrupt time with my family. I wouldn't have to negotiate time off for Christmas Eve versus Christmas Day, or New Year's Eve versus New Year's Day. I could spend the entire Thanksgiving weekend with my family instead of choosing between the holiday—of inhaling turkey, stuffing, and candied yams—and the day after—of reheating the leftovers. Maybe I'd take a road trip with my wife and daughter to visit relatives, or I'd spend days binge-watching science fiction movies. Or maybe I'd do absolutely nothing.

I should have kept my plans to myself.

"Brian, you're the first Black program director for the largest residency program in the country," one of my mentors implored after I shared my plans with him in confidence. "You are a gatekeeper. Think about that. If you leave, what will happen?"

Having long been on the frontlines of diversity and inclusion efforts in academia, I had become jaded about the performative efforts that received great fanfare but little institutional support. And the implication that Black leaders were obligated to champion the efforts and be grateful—well, that was no longer enough to motivate me. I wanted to forge a new path, and I could not commit to a quixotic effort against a system resistant to change.

"Brian, we *need* you here. Think about the future and the difference you could make." His plea fell on deaf ears—mostly. And he could tell. "Well, at least, please don't leave until after the Match."

The Match is the system in which graduating medical students across the country get placed in residency programs; it's a crucial time for both soon-to-be doctors and the programs where they will train. As program director, I was responsible to recruit the next class of interns. I agreed to his request, choosing, once again, to serve someone else's agenda at the expense of myself and my family.

The mission came first.

Besides, a few extra months of salary to pad our savings would not hurt, and I'd still get to operate and teach. After a few more delays in the timeline, due to administrative issues beyond my control, I concluded my official duties one year and eight days after 7/7.

As I turned in my white coat and hospital badge, I gave little thought to my new reality. I was forty-eight-years old, had a wife and daughter to support, a six-figure medical school loan, and a rapidly depleting savings account.

No steady income, no job prospects, and no plan.

I took Abeni to school most days, recommitted to a fitness program, and traveled around the country giving keynote lectures. I met friends for lunch in shorts and sandals. And within weeks of my resignation, I learned my daughter had absorbed more about 7/7 and the legacy of racism in this country than I had appreciated.

"If I was living back in Martin Loofer King times, what would happen to me?" she asked.

We were on a daddy-daughter date for ice cream. Her kindergarten class had recently done a project on Dr. King's civil rights work, and she was enamored with his legacy.

"What do you mean?" I asked.

"I'm caramel. Part you and part Mama. So I'm curious: would I have to go with the brown people or the white people?"

I was speechless. Clearly, we were both questioning our place in the world. A few years earlier she had asked a similar question: "Would I have been a slave?" As a multiracial child, she was unable to decide to which category she belonged. Kathianne and I had always been open with her about her adoption, wanting her to understand that her birth mother made a loving choice for her to be with us. Abeni understood she had been adopted, but from her child's perspective, she still talked about Kathianne and I with no distinction between birth and adoptive parents. And she wanted to know, given her skin color, whose side must she choose: the historic oppressors or the oppressed?

I deflected, knowing my young daughter could not comprehend that society had made the choice for her long before she took her first breath. Thankfully, she hadn't been with Kathianne and I years earlier, as we sat on a worn couch across from two white women explaining the fee schedule for adoptions.

As an affluent couple, both with advanced degrees, we were clearly a desirable commodity on the adoption circuit. We also learned that our "value" skyrocketed because we were an interracial couple willing to adopt a Black or multiracial child. No adoption agency explicitly told us Black and brown children were less desirable, and I have no doubt most viewed their work as one of the highest forms of altruism. But we could not ignore the numbers in the brochure they placed before us. Adoption fees for newborn Black babies were a fraction of the adoption fees for white newborns. And Black boys were at the bottom of the list.

Abeni continued her inquisition about the history of racism.

"The mean people had white skin like Mama, right?"

"Well, Princess, not all white people were mean." I chuckled.

"And sometimes it was the police who were mean, right?" She sandwiched her hands between her thighs and the seat of her chair, and her dangling feet percussed the table leg. Before I could answer, she said, "Like the ones you couldn't fix?"

The air rushed from the room. It was one year and a few weeks since the shooting, and it was the first time Abeni had asked about the deaths of the officers. I had never explained that some of my patients arrived at the hospital beyond fixing. At that moment, I realized that in the aftermath of 7/7, everything changed not only for me but also for those closest to me. My daughter no longer saw me as infallible. At six years old, she already held a sophisticated view of the world that surprised me. She was growing up fast, and I had already missed so much. Time I had given to my career. To the hospital. To the mission. Time I could never get back.

I've heard that children are our spiritual teachers. My five-pound newborn, who was dependent on me for survival, was now a six-year-old gift saving me from myself. And this was a crucial moment I could not let slip away.

"You don't have to go with anybody, Princess. You know why?" I leaned in to be at eye level, crossed my arms on the table, and smiled like the proud father I was. "Because you're special. One of a kind. God took the best parts of everyone just to make you. You know what that means?"

"What?" She giggled as I tapped her nose.

"You don't follow anyone. You are the bridge that will bring all people together."

Soon I, too, became a bridge. Two jobs in short succession, designed to bring people together, although neither lasted very long. The mayor of Dallas appointed me to chair the Citizens Police Review Board. In that role, I could do my part outside the halls of the hospital to help the city heal. The task before me was to lead fourteen other board appointees and unite the Dallas Police Department, community activists, police unions, and the City Council in order to approve a revamping of the role Dallas civilians played in police oversight. Clearly, this was not a typical role for a frontline trauma surgeon, and I'd have to bring together a number of stakeholders with sometimes contradictory agendas for conversation.

Working together a year and a half, we achieved a milestone that had eluded Dallas for more than three decades: expanding the oversight powers, budget, and logistical support of the Citizens Police Review Board (renamed the Citizens Police Oversight Board) to ensure public safety and trust in the Dallas Police Department. It passed by a unanimous vote of the City Council.

Next came an executive role at Parkland, one they created specifically for me: medical director of a new institute focused on community health. The job was sold to me as a forward-facing role that would allow me to work in the community with patients, advocates, activists, and public officials. As one of my colleagues exclaimed on my first day, "Welcome back Dr. Williams. We need an ambassador, and you are perfect. You'll be the face of Parkland!"

But several unspoken truths became apparent. The most noble brand and most noble mission can still hide uncomfortable truths. I was given a leadership title but not leadership authority. I felt I was hired for the optics—fundraising, media, and photo ops—rather than the work itself. I felt caught in another web of diversity, equity, and inclusion initiatives that were more performative than transformative. And when I voiced my concerns, the hounds came out. I heard stories of egregious conduct by white employees swept under the rug. When I tried to raise concerns about a mission that ignored the role of structural racism, internal and external to the health system, the dismissive response left me shocked and disappointed. But I should not have been surprised.

I was experiencing in real time the phenomenon that Dr. Eugenia South, assistant professor and vice chair for inclusion, diversity, and equity at Penn Medicine, describes: "While formal human resources avenues to report racism exist, they are underutilized for reasons including fear of retaliation, uncertainty that reporting will lead to timely or meaningful change, high levels of friction impeding the process, and a sense that many experiences do not warrant HR involvement." Echoing another maxim of my mother, I received the message loud and clear: don't let the doorknob hit ya where the good Lord split ya.

Speaking of the good Lord: Reverend Joyce, a portly hospital chaplain who always had an aura of joy and serenity, glided toward me during one of my last days at Parkland. She gave me a gift: a crystal desk ornament with a touching inscription. After the standard niceties, she asked to step away from the group of people we were with.

"Dr. Williams, is it okay if I pray with you?" she asked in a soothing, yet directive, voice that left me wondering if I actually had an option to decline. I'm not sure if Reverend Joyce saw through my politeness to the suspicion and surprise that lay underneath. Maybe she did and was simply determined to pray with me no matter how I felt about the matter. Before I could answer, she had gently grasped my hands.

"Just bow your head, Dr. Williams. I'll do the talking."

Seconds seemed like hours as she asked the Almighty to "bless these hands" and "bring peace and wisdom to your servant" and "keep watch over him." Uncomfortable with this spectacle, I cracked one eye and scanned the hallway to see who might be watching. When she finished, I thanked her, but I still felt obliged to be honest.

"Reverend Joyce, I'm not so sure about God."

She didn't miss a beat.

"That's okay, Dr. Williams," she said, patting my arm. "God is sure about *you*. No matter what you believe, know that you are a vessel through which he works."

The end of my time at Parkland was unceremonious and, I felt, entirely avoidable. I now know I served as an excellent ambassador, and I still had a lot to offer the health system and to Dallas. Being a bridge can be noble work, but if you're not careful, you can become something people walk all over. Some may view you not as a bridge to cross but a barrier to be removed. If you're not careful, trying to be a bridge can break you.

With my hands at 10 and 2, I focused on the mountain road ahead. We were on a family vacation, a spring break ski trip, and heading straight into an epic winter storm. I inched our car into the thickening snow on a one-lane road snaking upwards. It was the only route to the resort, and the clock was ticking. The road was scheduled to close soon, and it would stay closed for days. Visibility was dropping, and the route became more treacherous. If we didn't summit in time, a much-needed vacation would be lost.

Impeding our glacial progress was an 18-wheeler that had jack-knifed off the road. Cars eased around the tractor clawing the side, its trailer sloping into a ravine. Rescue crews were on the way, so we needed to get past the big rig before they arrived and brought us all to a halt. As we crept along, Kathianne took advantage of the moment.

"You're always in your head. What's bothering you?" she asked.

She was right. I do spend a lot of time in my head, and the preceding two years had only convinced me of the need to fortify my defenses. Kathianne had recently taken a life coaching class and periodically practiced her burgeoning skills on me. The difference was that most clients seek out a life coach and make an appointment. Stuck on the side of a mountain in a near blinding snowstorm, I was an unwitting subject with nowhere to hide. The vacation was long overdue, and I didn't want to detract from it. But the white boys of Parkland were having a drunken party in my head, and nothing I did seemed to quell the noise. I had become the face of a major university and an iconic public hospital, a role never meant to be occupied by a Black man.

"This bullshit at work," I said in a huff. "I don't understand what the hell it's all about. I thought we were gonna do big things—actually do what most people just talk about: transform our community, uplift the people in greatest need, change the world."

"Brian, you need to stop carrying the weight of the world on your shoulders. You can't help everyone."

She was right. For years I had been emotionally detached, but now I was feeling everything, all the time, and too much. Compassion can be a burden. Sacrificing for the well-being of strangers can lead to suffering. Sometimes I missed my old self—the one who had enough defense mechanisms to work shift after shift after shift, focused on the body before him, without feeling much of anything. If I could wall myself off from the injured and dead, I'd think, my days would be less painful and my nights more restful. Then again, if I ever became that detached, I'd be no more alive than the patients I could not save.

Abeni sat in the backseat, headphones on and watching *Frozen* for the umpteenth time. Kathianne sat cross-legged in the passenger seat while she talked and knitted. All needles and wrists and fingers and yarn, she was in her element.

"Okay," she redirected. "Let's talk about this 'bullshit at work' you claim you don't understand. Let's reframe that statement. What three things actually bother you the most?"

After some thought, I answered, "One is learning that these people I liked and respected are not who I thought they were. Two is that these same people are trying to ruin my reputation and possibly my career. And three, there is nothing I can do about it."

The fuse had been lit, and she was on fire. "Now let's take the opposite of the first statement," she said, still knitting. "Is it possible that they *are* actually who you always knew they were?"

"I don't understand."

"What if they are exactly who you thought they were? What if what bothers you is not finding that out but you having to admit what you *already knew*?"

I had no response to this knitting ninja. Like my therapist, she danced around the hidden corners of my psyche as if she owned the place. At her direction, I listed all the signs they were who I always knew they were. Signs I had dismissed because of the Almighty Mission.

"Now let's skip the second one and take your third statement next: that there is nothing you can do about any of this. I find that one interesting. Is that true there is nothing you can do?"

"Well, no," I said, meekly.

"So it's not that you *can't* do anything, it's that you *choose* not to. That's on you, not them."

"Yeah, but I'm not out to scorch the earth. Just shake hands and go our separate ways. Actually, I don't want to play this game with you anymore."

Silence. Eyes ahead. Hands at 10 and 2.

She ignored that. "We're not done. Now let's take your second statement: the one where you said they are trying to ruin your career. Try taking the opposite of that statement."

"You mean, that they're *not* trying to ruin my career?" Incredulous, my voice ended three octaves higher, rivaling a teen idol pop singer.

"No. Even better: that they're actually trying to help your career."

I heaved the bullshit flag onto the field. "No way, Kats. How can trashing my reputation, shoving me out the door, and everything else they are doing be helpful to my career? They're not trying to help; they're trying to bury me."

She stopped knitting, and her implacable stare seared half my face like the midsummer Texas sun. I stayed focused, eyes front, working to keep our car from joining the 18-wheeler in the snowy ravine.

"Which brings us back to your first statement. About learning who they really are. Maybe the truth is *you* are not who *they* thought you were?"

My brain locked trying to keep up with her logic. "I don't even know how to answer that," I said. "Everything I've done has been for the hospital! I've done all their interviews. Talked to their donors. Smiled for their photographers. What more could they want?"

"Do you think they expected you to speak up for racial justice? I mean, really speak up?" she asked. "Brian, you have a national platform. People invite you to speak. You're writing op-eds. You do television and radio interviews."

Then she tossed another wrench into my mental machinery.

"For Pete's sake, Brian, did you ever consider that this is not happening *to* you—that maybe it's actually happening *for* you?"

"What? That makes no sense." My track superstar wife was already leaning into her turn before I'd even left the starting block.

"Think about it. How many times have you tried to leave Parkland?"

It was true: I tried to leave many times before. Hawaii, Georgia, California, Arizona, Illinois, Texas: every time another opportunity presented itself, I had chosen to stay. Sometimes, with a pen in hand dangling over a generous contract, I'd change my mind at the eleventh hour. I knew the institution was imperfect, but I believed in the mission. Serving the greater good. Helping those who would otherwise fall through the cracks. Suddenly I wondered how many bridges I had burned on my way to serve the mission.

"You even gave up your surgical practice for this executive job you now have at Parkland. I mean, you haven't done trauma surgery in two years."

That *was* crazy. A surgeon at my stage, choosing to no longer operate?

"Maybe this is another sign that you need to let go," she said.

She turned from me and kept knitting. I drove in silence while my brain twisted to knots. In fifteen minutes, she had demolished my self-serving, self-pitying story and handed me the pieces to put back together. I didn't leave under positive circumstances, but I left a positive legacy. One that may never be acknowledged but is impossible to erase. Some habits are hard to break, such as blind adherence to hierarchy and mission.

"Maybe this is the Universe telling you it's time to go," she said.

"Or God," I replied absentmindedly.

"Call it what you want. The point is, you don't get to choose the message or how it's delivered. And you may not like either. Your only choice is whether you'll listen to the message, no matter what form, when received."

Kathianne's wisdom and logic are often powerful, shocking. Our discussions about racism have deepened, and she continues to endure the challenging life of being married to a trauma surgeon after nearly twenty years. We remain a team that always rebounds, sometimes when the rubber band binding us seems stretched to the point of breakage. Sometimes when she has needed me, I have been, well, working. When I have needed her, though, she is right there, with her annoyingly accurate diagnoses and palpable moral support. Others have been supportive too: people who knew what was happening sent supportive cards, letters, and emails. But on that snowy road, when I felt like my life was unraveling once again, it was Kathianne who used her superhuman strength to pull me from the depths.

I am still working to accept Kathianne's "God put you there that night for a reason" logic and Reverend Joyce's claim that "you're a vessel through which God works." Yet sometimes I do wonder about God and sprituality and religion. About rituals and prayers and dogma. And how would God communicate with me? Through my wife? My daughter? My tragedies? My triumphs? Maybe, at times, it's even by old-fashioned email.

A few weeks after the ski trip, an old mentor reached out to me. He was recruiting me to join the team at a state-of-the-art Level 1 trauma center on the South Side of Chicago. I interviewed for the position, and in April I received an email confirming I had been appointed to the faculty. To be a Black trauma surgeon serving on Chicago's South Side, a community well-known for racial segregation, endemic violence, and healthcare inequity: well, it felt like I'd been preparing for that role my entire life.

Another therapy session. Another bowl of chocolates. The same cannibalistic couch. It's three years after 7/7, a few months after the ski trip, and my last session before the move to Chicago. Today during the session, I break routine and leave my phone on.

"It's been a while," my therapist says.

"I know. That's why I scheduled ninety minutes." I give her the same tired reasons for having not made a therapy appointment for a while: work, family, an impending move. The proper response should have been, "No excuse."

"So, why don't you catch me up," she says.

I shift on the couch. "Well, I have my trauma narrative." I had finally done what she had assigned me to do years earlier.

"How was the experience?" she asks. "Writing it, I mean."

Like vomiting after a weekend bender, I tell her. Prolonged retching. You know you'll feel better after it's all out, but first you have to bury your head in a toilet.

"Do you want to read it?" I said.

"I think it's better if you read it to me."

I should have expected that. I open the file on my phone and begin to read aloud: "Everything happened all at once, and much of it was a blur. But I remember the blood. Lots of blood . . ."

Crying, I finish reading the story and set my phone down. We sit in silence.

"Can you name your feelings?" she finally asks.

"Guilt. Shame."

"Tell me more about that."

"It was my watch. My responsibility."

"Guilt is I *did* bad. Shame is I *am* bad," she says, enunciating each word for clarity to make sure I understand the distinction. "Do you think you're a bad person?"

"Well, no."

"What do you feel you did wrong that you feel guilty about?"

Dead air fills the space between us. Leaning back, I sink deeper into her couch and say nothing.

"Sometimes people just die," she says quietly. "With the work you do, you should know that better than anybody else."

More silence. I don't understand how this white woman half my age has helped, but she has. In therapy, she kept finding secrets I squirreled away. Over several sessions, I have found the strength to turn over a few rocks myself, expecting to find one thing here and another there. She helped me see how I spent my life assimilating into a majority-white world at the expense of being true to myself. To be able, affable, and approachable was the path I had chosen. Along the way to career success, I had allowed my anger to simmer until I could no longer ignore how doing so prevented genuine human connection.

The era of assimilation is over now. Getting better, for me, begins with forgiveness. There are others I have to forgive, yes, and I'm still working on that. But forgiveness is a gift, my therapist has helped me to see—one we sometimes have to give to ourselves.

And she isn't done.

"Have you written those letters to the families of the police officers yet?"

"Not yet."

I've always been a superb student, but I can procrastinate when the homework involves emotions. But several weeks later, I close the door of my home office, sit down, and stare at my laptop. I decide I'll start with a letter to the family of Officer Patrick Zamarripa, the first officer who died, and then Officer Krol, and then Officer Smith. Inhaling deeply, I slide my thumb under the lip of the laptop and open its jaw. I know unwelcome memories await, lying in ambush.

I begin to type. Select all. Delete. Begin typing again. Repeat. I can't get any further than the opening line.

I wait.

And wait.

And wait.

Leaning back, I cross my arms, bow my head, and close my eyes. My breath deepens. Seconds seem like minutes. Minutes seem like hours. Suddenly I relax, as the realization washes over me: it is not the families to whom I need to write letters. It's not the families of the officers to whom I long to speak. I see their faces clearly now, as clearly as I saw them on July 7, 2016.

I open my eyes as the words coalesce, rest my fingers upon the keyboard, and begin to type.

Dear Officer . . .

PART IV

Awakening

You have to act as if it were possible to radically transform the world. And you have to do it all the time.

—Angela Davis

16 | FAILURE BY DESIGN

One night, in the weeks leading up to our move to Chicago, Kathianne and I nestled in bed like two spoons, contemplating our impending departure from Dallas. Three years had passed since the shooting, and we savored the nightly peace that came after wrangling our strong-willed, eight-year-old daughter to bed. Abeni slept soundly in her room across the hall, and Disco, our Goldendoodle, curled on the hardwood floor at our feet.

"Are you worried?" she asked.

"About what?"

As I floated to unconsciousness, Kathianne began a discussion that now required my full attention. I refused to open my eyes, hoping that sleep would come quickly. But I knew from the tone of her voice that it wouldn't. Couples therapy helped us get on the same page about communicating better, but not always the same schedule.

"Taking trauma call again," she continued.

"I'm not following you."

"Well, you haven't done it in a long time."

It was true: I had not taken any trauma call in a while. After more than two decades in medicine and tens of thousands of hours mastering my craft, I had not done any operations for two years. No patient examinations. No teaching residents. No research publications. Still, I bristled a bit.

"Listen to you. You're starting to sound like the rest of them. Waiting for me to fail. You do realize some of them actually want me to fail, right?" The space between us chilled. I knew my ire was misdirected and that I was probably sounding paranoid. "Seriously, do you think I just forgot everything I learned? I've been doing this for a long time. Remember?"

"I know, Honey. But you'll have to deal with all that death again." She spoke soberly, with a maternal concern. We lay silent, knowing the freight her words carried. My defensiveness dissolved, and I didn't know what to say.

But she did.

"I mean, all those Black men dying. And you telling their families. I just wonder how that will affect you."

Kathianne was right to be concerned about my psychological well-being, which I had a long history of ignoring. Therapy helped, but I still underestimated the role emotions, and my suppression of them, played in every aspect of my life.

And it's true: most of my patients in Chicago would be Black. Also true is the fact that trauma surgeons make a living off the death and dismemberment of strangers. It is written into our job description, and it is the reason we get paid. If most of my patients were Black, well, so be it. If I hadn't made peace with that by this point in my career, I wasn't sure I ever would. No matter what, I still had to continue trying to make a difference.

Besides, the majority of my patients being Black and medically underserved was the prime reason I wanted the job. I chose my work not to make the most money (although it did pay well), but to help the most people. This role was an opportunity for me to be more than a trauma surgeon. Maybe I could finally work in the role to which I aspired: bridging work inside and outside of the hospital and serving as a champion for community transformation. To be a Black trauma surgeon serving on Chicago's South Side—a neighborhood well-known for racial segregation, endemic violence, and healthcare inequity—was a role tailor-made for me.

"I'll be fine," I assured her. "I'm ready. I've been ready,"

And in one way, I was. Coming out on the back end of an experience like the one I had in Dallas, you become liberated from the opinions of others, no longer beholden to external approval. The storm clouds had begun to part, and I could see my north star burning brightly and guiding my way. Finally, I could better articulate what that north star was: Advancing racial justice, ending the epidemic of gun violence, and creating health equity—three seemingly separate yet unified ideals. They were audacious in scope, but I couldn't imagine three issues more critical to our healing as a nation.

"I guess I just worry about you," Kathianne said. "With all that you've been through— we've all been through. And Abeni . . ." Her voice quieted without finishing her thought.

"I appreciate your concern," I demurred. "But we are the Williams, and we will get through this. And don't worry about me. Like you always say: everything happened *for* me, not *to* me, right?" I locked eyes with her in a dead serious gaze as the corner of my mouth slithered into a cocksure grin. "Besides, the moment I walk into the trauma hall, trust me: I'll still be the baddest motherfucker in the room."

Rolling her eyes, she peeled away. "Oh, dear God. Just go to sleep."

The University of Chicago Trauma Center opened in May 2018 as the city's newest Level 1 center. Located on Chicago's South Side, it is proximal to some of the worst gun violence in the country. Nearly 50 percent of the gun violence in Chicago occurs within a five-mile radius of the trauma center. Black people are less than one-third of the city population but more than 80 percent of the gun homicides, 86 percent of gun homicide victims are male, and most of the gun violence is hyper-concentrated in racially segregated neighborhoods.

Lakeshore Drive, a major multilane highway, extends from the wealthy northern suburbs to the impoverished neighborhoods on the South Side. It's a main vein connecting two opposing manifestations of economic mobility—or immobility. An eight-mile southerly drive—from the predominantly white neighborhood of Streeterville, which abuts the high-end shopping district known as the Magnificent Mile, to the majority-Black neighborhood of Englewood—means a thirty-year decrease in life expectancy. In other words, if you are born in Englewood, your average lifespan is thirty years shorter than if you'd been born eight miles north.

Similar disparities exist where I worked in Dallas, where two miles' distance could mean a twenty-six-year difference in life expectancy, Atlanta (5.5 miles = 25 years gap), Boston (0.5 mile = 33 years), and Tampa (2 miles = 15 years gap). "Your neighborhood shouldn't influence your odds of seeing your grandchildren grow up," says professor Mark N. Gourevitch, a creator of City Health Dashboard, which offers data on communities. But clearly it does.

The hospital where I work is located in a former "trauma desert," an area where no trauma services are geographically close to the neighborhood. If you live in a trauma desert and suffer life-threatening injuries, such as traumatic brain injury or a gunshot wound, you will not have rapid access to the advanced hospital resources and experts necessary to save your life. A study published by my colleagues at the University of Chicago, using census tract data from several US cities, found that "black majority census tracts were the only racial/ethnic group that appeared to be associated with disparities in geographic access to trauma centers." Another study by some of the same colleagues found that in Chicago, communities that are majority Black are much more likely to be located in a trauma desert than majority-white communities. Why are life-saving resources notably absent from Black neighborhoods?

In the same way that food deserts—areas where there are not enough grocery stores per capita—increase health and nutritional disparities between poor and rich, and Black and white, trauma deserts also worsen healthcare disparities. Longer transport times can mean the difference between life and death—literally. If you are bleeding out from a gunshot wound, the longer it takes to get you to a well-resourced trauma center, the less chance you will arrive alive.

But the term "trauma deserts" is a misnomer because deserts are a naturally occurring phenomenon. We now know that resources in these racially segregated areas—such as food, education, and healthcare—are frequently absent by intent, not accident. Between 1990 and 2005, 339 trauma centers closed across the country, a higher rate of closure than in previous decades, and the authors of one study found that "hospitals in areas with higher shares of minorities face a higher risk of trauma center closure."

In other words, the neighborhoods most in need of a trauma center were also the most likely to have theirs taken away. As part of a wave of such closings, the previous trauma center on the South Side shuttered in 1991, the year I graduated from the Academy (and a half a decade before I committed to a career in medicine). The closing of that hospital left another racially segregated community to fend for itself. For three decades, gunshot victims died from survivable injuries because they had no place close enough to go. When seconds mattered, they spent minutes in ambulances racing to the north side of town, many dying during transport. I had witnessed endemic healthcare inequity while working in Dallas, Atlanta, Boston, and Tampa, and had become numb to what I saw. In those early days I was an eager participant in the healthcare system, ignoring the ways my actions perpetuated the inequities we must eliminate.

Now, not a day passed that I didn't notice all the ways healthcare and health equity were malaligned. Like a broken bone that heals but is not set right, the system may function but will always be weak. Within a year of my move to Chicago, the coronavirus pandemic began ravaging the Southside Chicago neighborhood I served. Nationwide, the COVID-19 mortality rate for Black people was more than double that of white and Asian people, and a third higher than that of Latino people. In Chicago, more research by my colleagues found that "patients living in Black majority neighborhoods had two times higher odds of COVID-19 positivity relative to those in White majority neighborhoods." Once again, I had a front row seat to death and healthcare inequity, replicated in impoverished Black communities across America, being accepted as business as usual.

The crescendo of 2020 tragedies included not only COVID-19 but record-breaking gun violence, a contentious presidential election, and headline-making killings of Black people. Breonna Taylor was shot and killed in her home during a nighttime, no-knock raid. Years later we'd learn that law enforcement fabricated information to get the search warrant approved. In Georgia, avid runner Ahmaud Arbery was pursued by three white men, two of whom instigated an altercation before fatally shooting him. One of the killers was a former police officer. A third man recorded the encounter, which was later used as evidence to convict all three men, but not before local authorities had worked to cover up the murder. These were merely a prelude to May 25, 2020, when Minneapolis police officer Derek Chauvin murdered George Floyd by kneeling on his neck for eight minutes and forty-six seconds.

An international uprising for racial justice ensued.

The end of the first year of the pandemic, then, saw firearm homicides eclipse the highest level in more than twenty-five years. On Chicago's South Side, we were seeing record numbers of bullet-ridden bodies. Even as these tragedies unfolded, I awakened each day energized, knowing my job had purpose. I was part of a team saving lives, comforting families, and teaching trainees. For a trauma surgeon like me, who thrives on adrenaline, it was a dream job. Yet questions continued to plague me.

Did my work have a sustainable impact? How could I participate in an unjust healthcare system that was part of the problem? Were my patients better off after I cared for them than they were before?

During the early years of my career, saving the life of a gunshot victim—or trying to—was exhilarating. And the more gunshot victims the better. But now I kept thinking: by the time patients are lying on the gurney in front of me, it's too late. I might be able to save them from immediate death, yes. But what about the circumstances that led them to my trauma bay? What about the forces that shape where they live, work, learn, worship, and play? What access to transportation and banks and grocery stores and parks do they have—or not have? Did my work as a trauma surgeon truly help transform the communities I served?

The answer I felt was a resounding no. At times I felt the despair I'd felt on 7/7, and in the months afterward as I replayed that night in my head, and then again when I wrote my trauma narrative. Sometimes my work felt like an exercise in futility: trying and failing, over and over again, to save lives one at a time. Now I saw, in more vivid detail than ever before, that the Black bodies on which I worked were imprisoned within transgenerational systems designed, from the start, to *restrict* the pursuit of life, liberty, and happiness. In fact, I saw that the systems around us—of healthcare, housing, education, economic opportunity—weren't actually *failing*. It only seemed like they were. In fact, they were working exactly as they had been designed: to advantage some people and disadvantage others.

I still didn't know exactly how those systems functioned, but I knew I had to learn. I had to understand how they interacted with the healthcare my colleagues and I provided. And the idea gave me a modicum of hope, which is sometimes just enough to get through the day. If systems like healthcare and housing policy and economic opportunity could "succeed" at replicating and even profiting from racism and inequality, what if we changed the intent written into their design? What if we rewrote the code that made them run in certain ways? Could they begin to succeed at creating healthcare justice?

America was founded on the genocide of Indigenous peoples and made wealthy on the labor of enslaved Black people. These facts are indisputable. From our nation's founding until after the Civil War, more than 1,800 elected lawmakers owned Black people. Twelve of the first eighteen presidents were enslavers. Some, like George Washington and Thomas Jefferson, contracted out the people they enslaved to help build the US Capitol Building, the international symbol of democracy and freedom sitting atop "The Hill" at the center of Washington, DC.

Beginning in 1619, over the course of nearly two centuries, eleven million Africans were kidnapped and forced into chattel slavery in the American colonies to produce crops such as cotton and tobacco. Congress abolished the transatlantic slave trade in 1808, but the domestic trade continued until the Emancipation Proclamation of 1863, which ostensibly freed the slaves and was a catalyst to the Civil War. That period of our nation's history made America an economic powerhouse—one whose riches have been denied to the ancestors of enslaved people, and still sculpts our sociopolitical landscape. Do you think these individuals who held the most powerful policy-making positions in the country simply set aside their white supremacist beliefs when enacting laws that govern the nation?

"America began with a great paradox: the same men who came up with the radical idea of constructing a nation on the principle of equality also owned slaves, thought Indians were savages, and considered women inferior," writes historian Heather Cox Richardson in

How the South Won the Civil War. "This apparent contradiction was not a flaw, though; it was a key feature of the new democratic republic."

Richardson's point—that sometimes what we believe to be *flaws* of a system are actually *features*—now informed my perception of healthcare in the United States. It informed my view of everything, really. The reality that systems produce the results they've been designed to create illuminates so much about our country. If racism is not a bug, but a feature of our common life, I knew we had to do more than nibble at the edges. As imperfect as our shared history is, we can use the knowledge of our past to understand our present and create a better future. Despite the flaws of the authors, the words in our Declaration of Independence and Constitution are still ideals toward which we can, and should, strive.

But to achieve this, we must hold these dichotomous truths to be self-evident. America is a great nation born from genocide and chattel slavery. Many of our founding fathers championed both racism *and* equality, slavery *and* freedom. And the seeds of our history, while creating the greatest democracy the world has ever known, grew roots that permeate all aspects of our society: seen and unseen, good and bad, triumphs we praise and mistakes we ignore.

At some point the past has to be the past, yes. But any future greatness America attains will not happen by ignoring, rewriting, and excusing our shared history—but by affirming it. What I began learning about the systems that structure our lives as Americans was sobering. One of those systems, I was beginning to see, is an almost insatiable beast, one that consumes 20 percent of our Gross Domestic Product (GDP) and hungers for more: our healthcare system.

The US is the only high-wealth country that treats healthcare as a for-profit commodity. A nation that accounts for 5 percent of the world's population consumes 50 percent of its healthcare resources—and still ranks near the bottom for most objective measures of health. On average, compared to other high-wealth nations, the US has higher infant mortality, lower life expectancy, and higher healthcare expenditures. In short, we spend more than other countries—much more—and get worse outcomes.

Some might say we do not actually have a healthcare system that provides value; instead, we have a revenue-generating system that provides healthcare. We could look in more detail at some of the reasons: a for-profit insurance industry with extortionary pricing for pharmaceuticals. Employee-based insurance plans that, in many ways, do more to serve the bottom line of the employer than provide choice and value to the employee. Federally funded insurance for the elderly and the poor built upon the rickety foundation of our strained healthcare infrastructure.

In the United States, we spend 90 percent of our healthcare dollars as a country to improve access to care. The US Agency for Healthcare Research and Quality (AHRQ) defines access as having "the timely use of personal health services to achieve the best health outcomes." In other words, you must have the ability to take time off from work, insurance or cash to pay, and ready access to a facility with qualified healthcare workers. But access only accounts for 6 percent of what makes us healthy. The remainder of the equation with regard to physical health is deeply tied to where we live, work, learn, worship, and play. As a country, to maximize health and eliminate inequities, we must be more strategic about how we spend our money.

Make no mistake: health inequity is a national crisis. The United States ranks last among high-wealth nations for maternal mortality, and Black women, regardless of education or income, have a maternal death rate 2.5 times higher than white women and three times higher than Hispanic women. Our country commits 20 percent of our gross domestic product to healthcare, which is 7 percent more than the next highest nation. That 7 percent is twice what we spend on the Department of Defense and could fund primary and secondary education for the entire country. Yet we still underperform on nearly every metric of health, ranking last in access, equity, and outcomes. Nelson Mandela, anti-apartheid activist and the first Black president of South Africa, said, "Health cannot be a question of income. It is a fundamental human right." Yet here, an ocean away, in the crown jewel of democracy, wealth equals health.

The history of healthcare in the United States is one of incessant tension between coverage and cost in what appears to be a zero-sum game. The more people we cover, the more we have to pay. The less we cover, the less we pay. And for much of the twentieth century, some of the most forceful and effective opposition to healthcare reform came from physicians and surgeons. The influential American Medical Association (AMA) has at times wielded its power on behalf of doctors' interests at the expense of patients' interests.

In the early 1900s, the AMA and state physician groups organized and resisted attempts at government-sponsored health insurance, describing it as "an incitement to revolution," and that "no third party must be permitted to come between the patient and his physician in any medical relation." Dr. Cushing, the famed neurosurgeon whose portrait hung in our conference room at Brigham and Women's Hospital, had the ear of FDR and opposed government-sponsored health insurance. Physician opposition, allied with the 1910 Flexner Report recommending the closure of several predominantly Black medical training institutions, fueled the perpetuation of health inequity stretching across generations. As Shirley Chisolm, the first Black woman elected to Congress (who also ran for president), said, "We have never seen health as a right, it has been conceived as a privilege, available only to those who can afford it. This is the real reason the American healthcare system is in such a scandalous state."

Ironically, the only population with a constitutional right to receive healthcare, as guaranteed by the eighth amendment's prohibition against cruel and unusual punishment, are those who are incarcerated. The healthcare prisoners receive is often exceedingly substandard; access does not guarantee quality. Considering the devastation that mass incarceration has levied on Black men and their families, it is a cruel, twisted irony indeed.

As a presidential candidate, Shirley Chisolm highlighted healthcare injustice. Interestingly enough, sitting presidents from both major political parties have championed universal healthcare. Teddy Roosevelt, a two-term Republican who ran for a third term, called for a national health service that would provide for the "protection of home life against the hazards of sickness, irregular employment and old age through the adoption of a system of social insurance adapted to American use." He believed it was vital to the health of America, stating that "the health and vitality of our people are at least as well worth conserving as their forests, waters, lands, and minerals, and in this great work the national government must bear a most important part."

A distant cousin of his, four-term President and Democratic icon Franklin Delano Roosevelt, was also initially a proponent of universal healthcare. But political realities forced him to shepherd the Social Security Act of 1935 and other New Deal programs instead, thus leaving healthcare for future administrations. Presidents Truman, Eisenhower, and Kennedy all pushed for universal healthcare, whether it was government, private, or some hybrid. White Americans, comprising 90 percent of the US population in the post-World War II era, would have been the major beneficiaries of universal coverage. But, as author Heather McGhee writes, "the threat of sharing [universal coverage] with even a small number of Black and brown Americans helped doom the entire plan from the start."

The assassination of JFK propelled Lyndon Baines Johnson (LBJ) to the Oval office, resulting in some of the most consequential legislative accomplishments in presidential history. His Great Society programs included the Voting Rights Act, the Civil Rights Act, and the two programs that transformed US healthcare: Medicare and Medicaid.

Two decades earlier, Congress passed the Hill-Burton Act of 1946, which gave health facilities loans and grants for construction and modernization, thus creating a network of safety-net hospitals to provide free or reduced-cost care. This network of safety-net hospitals has been foundational in my training as a medical student, surgical resident, and trauma fellow, and the mission of serving the under-served is why I choose to continue working at safety-net hospitals as an attending. Under LBJ, the introduction of Medicare and Medicaid further transformed the role of government in healthcare.

Medicare is a federal insurance program for the elderly, people with end-stage renal disease, and certain younger individuals with disabilities. Medicaid provides coverage for low-income children and their families, low-income seniors, and low-income people with disabilities. Put simply, Medicare provides coverage for the elderly and Medicaid for the poor. In their book, *The Heart of Power: Health and Politics in the Oval Office*, authors David Blumenthal and James Morone write that Medicare and Medicaid are "among Johnson's proudest legacies—two sections of the single most important piece of health-care legislation in American history. Taken together, the programs weigh in as one of the three largest items on the federal budget after Social Security and (in some years) military spending. LBJ was the most important healthcare president the United States has ever had."

LBJ's initial goal was universal coverage for every American, regardless of age, wealth, or race, however public policy collided with segregationist politics. As a result of Johnson's signing of the Medicare and Medicaid Act of 1965, hospitals desegregated. While Medicare is administered by the federal government, Medicaid is administered primarily by the states, each with their own rules for eligibility. Therefore, to truly understand health inequity in America, we must understand Medicaid.

Today, some 60 percent of Medicaid recipients are people of color. The program, along with the Children's Health Insurance Program (CHIP), which is essentially Medicaid for children, is the largest insurer covering mental health services, childbirths, and children eighteen and younger in the US. Medicaid is actually a joint health insurance program between the federal government and the states—one that began as a grand bargain the federal government made with segregationist southern states to get Medicare, a program of universal coverage for seniors, passed.

Southern Democrats, the "Dixiecrats," feared that federal intrusion on state healthcare would further erode Jim-Crow-era segregation, and they had enough votes to derail LBJ's entire Great Society legislative agenda—voting rights, housing rights, and healthcare. Segregationists were right to be concerned: Medicare had led to desegregation of hospitals, a result they found untenable. But Medicaid still allowed the states to retain power over how they would deliver care to the poor—a category that was, and still is, a proxy for being Black. The result is tremendous variability in Medicaid across fifty states. As one nonpartisan report says: "States establish their own eligibility standards, benefit packages, provider payment policies, and administrative structures under broad federal guidelines, effectively creating fifty-six different Medicaid programs—one for each state, territory, and the District of Columbia."

Most of my patients, both in Chicago and the other cities where I've worked, are uninsured, underinsured, or on Medicaid. They are also poor, Black, and many are chronically ill. As of May 2022, 81.9 million people across the United States, or 24 percent of the population based on the 2022 census, are enrolled in Medicaid. The majority reside in southern states that did not accept Medicaid subsidies under the Affordable Care Act, which expanded healthcare coverage to millions of previously uninsured Americans; it was President Obama's signature legislative achievement. Those states are essentially refusing free money from the federal government that would help keep their constituents healthy. Why states that rank near the bottom for life expectancy, fetal mortality, and rates of uninsured citizens would refuse funding allocated to benefit their citizens is hard to fathom.

LBJ was the first of only four presidents who passed major healthcare legislation. The second was George W. Bush, who signed the Medicare Prescription Drug, Improvement, and Modernization Act of 2003, allowing private health plans and prescription drug benefits to be covered under Medicare. In 2010, President Obama signed the Patient Protection and Affordable Care Act, which, despite its political divisiveness, was simply a federal version of the universal coverage long championed by Republicans. In 2022, President Biden signed the Inflation Reduction Act which, for the first time, allowed Medicare to negotiate prescription drug prices, which is estimated to reduce the deficit by more than $230 billion over ten years. Donald Trump was the first and only president to attempt to take away health benefits. The effort to repeal failed in a 51–49 vote in the Senate.

Today, states that refuse Medicaid expansion have the highest rates of healthcare disparities across all demographics. Since the Supreme Court made Medicaid expansion optional, many states refused. State governments did this for a number of reasons, but no matter how you look at it, fear of the slippery slope toward a government-run healthcare system ranks high on the list. "The long-term impact of policies that perpetuate disparities in health outcomes varies widely by state and even community, depending on whether elected officials have taken action to mitigate the consequences of such policy decisions," writes Adina Marx, a staffer at Families USA, a nonpartisan group working on healthcare issues. "This in and of itself is another social determinant of health: where you were born, where you grow up and where you live now. Because states have so much discretion in what policies they enact (just look at how twelve states have still refused to expand Medicaid) access to affordable, high-quality healthcare varies widely and unjustly across the country."

In 2002, the National Academy of Medicine published the first systematic review of racial and ethnic healthcare disparities in the United States. The landmark report found that, even after correcting for socioeconomic conditions, "race and ethnicity remain significant predictors of the quality of health care received." Healthcare systems and providers contribute to these disparities, the report said, and it provided a framework to correct the inequities. This included increasing the number of underrepresented minorities in medicine; educating society at large about racial and ethnic disparities; and collecting better data to guide interventions and resource allocation. Two decades after the report's publication, during the worst of the coronavirus pandemic, not much had improved. Black Americans continue to die at rates higher than white Americans, and the healthcare system was clearly part of the problem.

The problems of healthcare disparities and racism in medicine are not limited to a once-in-a-century pandemic. When admitted to a hospital, Black patients experience more adverse events than white patients. In reviewing patient safety according to eleven different indicators, a report by the Urban Institute and Robert Wood Johnson Foundation found that "Black adult patients experienced significantly worse patient safety in six indicators when compared to White adult patients who were in the same age group, of the same gender, and treated in the same hospital." These disparities occur more frequently in surgery, my specialty, than in some others.

By underinvesting in the health of poor and Black citizens, the infrastructure of the entire state suffers—which, in some way, impacts all of its citizens. And these healthcare inequities are connected to other types of injustice. But here's the thing: history is not inevitable. People in power make choices, and just because the United States now has massive health disparities does not mean that it had to be that way. Nor does it have to continue.

That is why we must talk about structural racism and how it binds us all.

17 | RACE IS NOT A RISK FACTOR

Over the years I have performed numerous below-knee amputations for patients with uncontrolled diabetes. Amputations are dramatic procedures, but many of them actually unfold gradually, in slow motion, over the course of years. It's a process that we surgeons sometimes pejoratively call "whittling."

Let me illustrate with the story of my patient Mr. Reed. He was a middle-aged Black handyman who made money doing odd jobs for his neighbors: installing fences, painting houses, and changing door locks. He got his contracts by word of mouth, and the work kept him mobile and with a semi-reliable stream of income. Still, he had diabetes, no health insurance, no primary care doctor, and no access to a steady supply of insulin. The result: microvascular disease that slowly choked off the blood supply to his feet.

The first time I cared for Mr. Reed, we debrided his superficial diabetic infection—that is, using a scalpel to shave the dead skin off the pressure point on the side of his foot. Then we cleaned the wound and applied a sterile dressing to protect it while it healed. Within a few months he came back to the emergency department with a right pinky toe that was black, puffy, and spewing pus. To prevent the infection from spreading further up his foot, I amputated the toe that night. He spent a few days in the hospital recovering before we again discharged him home. Within a year, Mr. Reed returned with three more toes looking as bad as the first on a foot that was purple and puffy like an eggplant. This required another trip to the operating room, his third with me. This time I had to perform a transmetatarsal amputation: saw off the front half of his foot to prevent the infection from spreading. Again, he spent a few days in the hospital recovering, followed by discharge home.

Still, Mr. Reed had the same problems: No steady income. No health insurance. No reliable supply of insulin. He also had a new problem of impaired mobility, which led to less work and lower wages.

Within a year after the third operation, Mr. Reed returned, near death from septic shock. A new infection from his foot had entered his bloodstream and coursed throughout his body—a life-threatening condition requiring an emergency operation and admission to the intensive care unit. On that hospital admission, I performed a BKA: a below-knee amputation. It was the only means to save his life.

Over the course of two years of whittling from a small toe to half of the foot to the lower portion of his leg, I progressively impaired Mr. Reed's ability to function independently. He still had no access to a steady supply of insulin, nor could he afford a prosthesis or a wheelchair after the amputation. And worse, he could no longer work. None of those surgical procedures cured Mr. Reed, because the root of his problem was uncontrolled diabetes. My scalpel saved his life but did not cure his underlying disease.

I don't know what happened to Mr. Reed because, like many of my uninsured patients, he was "lost to follow-up." He may not have received follow-up care due to lack of insurance or lack of transportation to a healthcare facility. He may have moved to another city or state. Or he may have died from his progressive disease, which can lead to a heart attack or stroke. I may never know, and I sometimes wonder how many of my past patients "lost to follow-up" are still alive.

Treating disease is not the same as creating health, and in many ways, the fate of Mr. Reed was preordained centuries before his birth.

If a patient cannot afford insulin or pay for a doctor, how can they buy a prosthetic limb or a wheelchair? And once surgically disabled, how can they work to qualify for employee-based insurance? I had learned in medical school that race is a risk factor for not only diabetes, but also hypertension, heart attacks, and strokes. Basically, that idea—race is a risk factor—states that if you're Black, you are at more risk for debilitating or life-threatening disease than people of other racial and ethnic groups.

The idea that the bodies of Black people place them at risk for certain diseases or conditions has held such power in the medical community that as late as the 1960s, Black patients received higher doses of radiation for routine x-rays because researchers thought Black people had denser skin, muscle, and bones (remember the Pentagon study from chapter 6). And of course, excessive radiation increases your risk for developing certain types of cancer, which is why we shield body parts, when possible, to avoid unnecessary exposure (especially the ovaries of women of child-bearing age). In medical school, I was taught that race is a risk factor for kidney disease, and we even learned a special formula to compute kidney function in Black patients. And today at medical conferences, I still hear respected physicians say "race is a risk factor," for everything from diabetes to heart disease to gun violence. I cringe every time I hear it.

Such erroneous beliefs in medicine have wide-ranging implications on everything from medication dosages, eligibility for kidney transplants, implicit racial bias in practitioners, and exposure to cancer-causing radiation. Racialized assumptions in medicine can influence diagnosis, treatment, follow-up care, and even the design of medical technologies. In an article about the history of race classifications published in the *New England Journal of Medicine*, the authors wrote, "Psychologists used race-specific norms to interpret neuropsychological tests of retired football players who had had concussions. They have exhibited bias in the assessment and management of pain.

Some widely used technologies underperform in Black and Brown people: pulse oximeters, for instance, can overestimate blood oxygen levels in patients with darker complexions and delay identification of patients in need of treatment."

In chapter 6, we learned how Black people have been used in harmful medical experiments without consent. We also learned how Black people have endured mutilating operations without their consent. How many Black people, treated by a seemingly "color-blind" profession, have received harmful treatment or been denied the necessary one because of faulty truisms like "race is a risk factor"?

Learning about the root causes of health disparities was a first step for me in understanding how race, violence, and medicine are linked. But it was only a first step. "The movement to bolster health equity has heavily focused on health disparities, which are differences in health outcomes among population groups," writes health policy expert Daniel Dawes. "However, not as much attention has been given to understanding the factors, systems, or structures (laws and policies) that create, perpetuate, or exacerbate these differences, many of which are unfair, avoidable, and remediable."

I needed to understand the factors, systems, and structures. I was finally beginning to understand that, unlike what I internalized in medical school, race itself is not a risk factor for health disparities. Race is not a risk factor in chronic diseases, medical errors, and life expectancy.

It's racism.

Physical violence is the easiest form of violence for us to understand. When one individual exerts injurious force upon another—a punch, slap, or gunshot—that is an undeniable violent act. We can see the injury, imagine the physical pain, and understand the sequence of cause and effect.

Structural violence is different because it exists in the air around us. We cannot identify one perpetrator, one act of force that caused injury. Yet the effects are no less destructive, and structural violence is the link to structural racism.

Structural racism is a form of violence, one that researcher Johan Galtung, the first to use the term, described as being "built into the structure and shows up as unequal power and subsequently as unequal life chances." Structural racism can appear—especially to those who benefit from it—to be part of the natural order of things. It's just how society functions. I appreciate that structural racism remains a vexing term for many. Those of us who understand it see the way it connects the dots, from historical policy decisions to the racial disparities in health-care, education, housing, income, and wealth manifesting today. Others may not understand the term but remain curious and willing to learn. Still others continue to deny that racism in any form—interpersonal or structural—remains an issue in the twenty-first century.

Because structural racism is often invisible, especially to those advantaged by it, its effects can be difficult to understand and accept. But the harm is undeniable, entrenched, and long-lasting. One review of 293 studies found that racism contributes to worse mental and physical health. Simply put, "being black is bad for your health," the Pew Research Center recently declared, with the critical addition: "And pervasive racism is the cause."

When we talk about physical health, we usually focus on choices, habits, cause, and effect. A lack of sleep, no exercise, and an unhealthy diet lead to poor health—in other words, poor individual choices. And healthy choices *do* matter. But health is more than just exercising, eating right, getting regular checkups, taking your medications, and visiting the doctor when sick. Health is shaped by the context in which we live. And the context in which we live binds together every sector of American life: housing, education, employment, and more. We may not live in the same neighborhoods, our children may not attend the same schools, and we may not shop at the same grocery stores, but we can all appreciate how much our lives, and our health, would suffer if any were absent or compromised. You don't have to believe that the systems in which we live are explicitly rigged to see that a system negatively impacts some groups more than others.

Over the years, as I amputated limbs, removed necrotic gallbladders, and excised pounds of dead skin and muscle for necrotizing fasciitis (colloquially known as the "flesh-eating disease"), I began to wonder: Do hospitals eliminate health inequity or perpetuate it? Were Tampa General, The Gradys, Parkland, and the wider safety-net hospital system a part of the solution or emblematic of a larger problem? The term *safety-net hospital* implies a backup: a stopgap system that can catch people who would otherwise fall through the cracks of the healthcare system, the last resort to keep people from getting sicker and dying.

But what happens when the backup doesn't function like a backup? When the last resort becomes the frontline? The safety-net hospital system has become integral to our national healthcare infrastructure. It exists not because people are falling through the cracks but because we, as a nation, have abandoned millions of people to fend for themselves. It's like a deflated life raft adrift in a sea of injustice: it might work to rescue a few people, but there is no way it can save everyone.

I was starting to connect the dots between the health inequities I had seen in Tampa, Boston, Atlanta, Dallas, and now Chicago. Fifteen years after graduating from medical school, I could see my role in perpetuating disparate streams of medical care. My work had impact in the one-on-one interactions with patients, but systemic transformation remained elusive. I still believe that our model, democratic republic, makes America respected around the world. But I now see all the ways that structural racism prevents us from achieving greater heights.

Persistent healthcare injustice is a prime example. Racism manifests in healthcare not only in the way that Black people are treated when they arrive in the emergency room (if they arrive); it's the conditions that shape the lives of Black people in America that influence their life chances in the first place. There is no individual to hold accountable, no individual threat we can lock up to prevent the violence from happening, so change requires systemic transformation. Yes, asthma and diabetes put one at more risk of dying of COVID-19, both of which occur at higher rates in Black communities; but so do environmental injustices like exposure to hazardous waste and air pollution, housing inequality, and food deserts.

Structural racism, figuratively and literally, exists in the air we breathe.

Public policy is the scaffolding upon which structural racism rests. One such policy was the discriminatory practice of redlining—in which mortgage brokers and government officials marked Black and brown neighborhoods as "risky investments" and refused loans and services in those areas. It spawned nearly one century ago when the Great Depression threatened the financial security of families who, supported by federal programs to encourage home ownership, faced foreclosure. To remedy the pending crisis, the Roosevelt administration created the Home Owners' Loan Corporation (HOLC) to rescue homeowners at risk of default. But the program was not race-neutral, as Richard Rothstein has so expertly documented in *The Color of Law*: "The HOLC created color-coded maps of every metropolitan area in the nation, with the safest neighborhoods colored green and the riskiest colored red. A neighborhood earned a red color if African Americans lived in it, even if it was a solid middle-class neighborhood of single-family homes." In short, the federal government went on record that skin color determined financial risk. Again, according to Rothstein: "Today's residential segregation in the North, South, Midwest, and West is not the unintended consequence of individual choices and of otherwise well-meaning law or regulation but of unhidden public policy that explicitly segregated every metropolitan area in the United States."

Today 75 percent of formerly redlined neighborhoods remain impoverished and populated by racial minorities, while 91 percent of the communities identified as "best" by the HOLC have majority white populations. Redlining led to economic divestment, resulting in depressed home values and poor public education. It also created health disparities that continue to this day—including gun violence. Matthew Desmond, who won the Pulitzer Prize for *Evicted*, his book on housing injustice, writes: "Concentrated poverty and violence inflict their own wounds, since neighborhoods determine so much about your life, from the kinds of job opportunities you have to the kinds of schools your children attend."

What does redlining have to do with health disparities? More than you might think. Residents of formerly redlined neighborhoods today still experience racial segregation, concentrated poverty, endemic gun violence, worse life expectancy, higher infant mortality, and more late-stage cancer diagnoses than other communities. Put simply, inequity persists in neighborhoods segregated by race through federal, state, and local policies. Today, the majority of poor families in America who rent spend over half of their income on housing, and at least one in four dedicates over 70 percent off their income to paying the rent and keeping the lights on. That leaves little left over for healthy foods, medications, and visits to the doctor.

In chapter 3, we saw how Black World War II veterans were excluded from GI bill housing stipends, educational grants, and other benefits that helped create a white middle-class. Government assistance to purchase a home and get a college degree, assistance denied to many Black Americans, is a major contributor to the wealth and education gaps existing today. Ongoing segregation and underfunding of public schools in Black neighborhoods contribute to diminished economic status and education levels. The result is recalcitrant poverty, which fuels violence. "As a society, we must establish goals, strategies, and programs to reduce poverty and racial segregation," wrote Diane Ravitch, former US Assistant Secretary of Education. "Only by eliminating opportunity gaps can we eliminate achievement gaps."

Housing is health. Education is health. Wealth is health. Collectively, these go by another name: social determinants of health. The CDC lists five social determinants of health that "affect a wide range of health outcomes." Neighborhood, education, and economic stability are three domains that influence health status in communities and individuals. The remaining two, according to the CDC, are healthcare access and quality, and social and community context.

We now know that reducing health disparities requires more than focusing on an individual's nutrition, exercise, and regular visits to the doctor. Health disparities do not appear out of nowhere, and they are not caused by someone's race. Again: race, a construct of society not genetics, does not put you at risk for certain illness, disease, and death. Medical educators, journalists, and politicians are finally making connections between the conditions in which people live—conditions often the legacy of antecedent racist policies—and the conditions of our bodies. But it's hardly a new idea.

More than a century before the term "social determinants of health" entered the medical lexicon, W. E. B. Du Bois published his seminal study, *The Philadelphia Negro*, which used statistical analysis and ethnographic observation to show racial and gender disparities for Black men and women—disparities that persist to this day. His work was groundbreaking and, since he was a sociologist instead of a healthcare worker, it showed the important role non-clinicians could play in addressing health disparities. In 1899 Du Bois recognized that social structures—such as where we live, learn, work, and play—are factors as important to health as affordability and access to healthcare. "The most difficult social problem in the matter of Negro health is the peculiar attitude of the nation toward the well-being of the race," Du Bois wrote. "There have . . . been few other cases in the history of civilized peoples where human suffering has been viewed with such peculiar indifference."

But it does not have to be this way; America can choose to invest in communities and embody the ideals we profess about liberty and justice for all. We can evaluate our past to understand our present and transform our future. Since our country has evolved from a period of explicitly racist policies in housing, education, and employment over generations, reversing the negative outcomes requires more than eliminating the policies. It requires active, consistent, durable investment to promote equity.

So how do we transform systems resistant to transformation—systems that are actually functioning exactly as they were intended?

First, we begin by asking different questions. As John Maynard Keyes said, "The difficulty lies not so much in developing new ideas as in escaping from old ones." Our healthcare and social safety-net systems are replete with old ideas. Changing hearts and minds through education is one step, but another is enacting public policy to undo centuries of discriminatory practices. Through public policy we can achieve transformation that benefits everyone. It is the essence of democracy: the belief that our shared history binds us, and that we are all in this together. And escaping from old ideas begins with naming them in the first place.

One old idea we must discard is the dominant narrative about the lack of leadership in Black communities, which have been systematically disadvantaged for centuries, and actually watch, listen, and learn from the amazing solutions emerging from them. I spent much of my career referring to communities I served with terms I now consciously avoid: underserved, urban poor, at risk, marginalized. We must push back against multiple narratives that are false and destructive. Carol Anderson writes about their power, including the one "about a culture of black poverty that devalues education, hard work, family, and ambition. It's a mantra told so often that some African Americans themselves have come to believe it. Few even think anymore to question the stories, the 'studies' of black fathers abandoning their children, of rampant drug use in black neighborhoods, of African American children hating education because school is 'acting white'—all of which have been disproved but remain foundational in American lore."

I now refer to the communities in which I work as "communities of opportunity." Colloquialisms like "urban poor" and "at-risk communities" diminish the humanity of my neighbors and tend to erase the creativity and agency of the communities themselves. The residents, activists, and leaders know better than any of us what their communities need and how to achieve transformation. Helping communities of opportunity thrive will take collaboration between academics like myself and those living within them. Those closest to the problem are often closest to the solution. Therefore, it is time for us to listen.

I have witnessed amazing work to reduce violence and healthcare inequity, led by the community surrounding the trauma centers where I've worked, across the country. High schoolers organizing themselves to lead anti-violence efforts. Former gang members serving to interrupt the cycle of violence and providing support to gun violence survivors and their families. And faith leaders creating programs to expand access to preventative healthcare. All of these efforts are led by the community, for the community. When people ask me, "Why don't they take care of their neighborhood," I respond: *How do you know they are not?*

Another important step is to enact local, state, and federal laws and policies to dismantle structural racism. First, these policies must dismantle de facto barriers intended to exclude Black Americans from mainstream society. Second, they must promote economic reinvestment in communities through federal collaboration with local businesses, public officials, and community leaders. Last, they must acknowledge the role systemic racism plays in our society. Name it. Demystify it. Eliminate it. Radical inclusion through economic reinvestment is needed to ensure every American, regardless of race or ethnicity, has the opportunity to live safely, and thrive, within their communities. Criminology professor Elliot Currie writes, "The cornerstone of any serious effort to reduce the burden of endemic violence must be a guarantee of meaningful employment for everyone able to work, at wages that can support a decent standard of living."

The good news is that, while the nature of the structures leading to harm is complex, finding solutions is not impossible. Imagine a nation where we promote health as its own form of currency. When individuals are healthy, communities are uplifted. When communities are uplifted, society thrives. When society thrives, we all win.

Times are changing, and the idea that racism, not race, is a risk factor is gaining momentum. For example, COVID-19, which disproportionately infected and killed people of color, helped pull back the curtain on racism as a public health threat. In 2022, the United Network of Organ Sharing stopped the practice of race-based calculation for kidney transplants. And many professional societies are now highlighting racism as a health risk factor.

In 2019, recognizing its role in perpetuating systemic healthcare disparities, the AMA created a Center for Health Equity to "embed health equity across the AMA organization so that health equity becomes part of the practice, process, action, innovation, and organizational performance and outcomes." Similarly, the Association of American Medical Colleges created a Center for Health Equity to "look beyond medical care to the other factors that create opportunities for communities to thrive." And the American Public Health Association reported in 2022 that more than 250 states, counties, and cities across the country had declared racism a public health crisis. Even my profession of trauma surgery, which I believe has too long minimized the role structural racism plays in the prevalence of gun violence in the communities we serve, is course correcting, guided by a generation of socially conscious, rising leaders in the field. These are but a few examples of trade organizations moving in the right direction.

The federal government is also taking a leading role to advance racial equity and justice. In 2021 President Biden signed Executive Order 13985, committing the executive branch to make racial equity foundational in its quest to advance healthcare justice. It called for a "whole-of-government equity agenda that matches the scale of the opportunities and challenges that we face." The House Ways and Means Committee, the oldest and most powerful committee in Congress, released a report in 2020 that analyzed state-by-state racial and economic disparities in healthcare. And the Supreme Court has denied repeated challenges to overturn President Obama's Affordable Care Act.

The rise of prepaid group health plans for Texas teachers became the model for Blue Cross. Wage and price controls during World War II prevented employers from attracting workers with higher salaries, which led to non-taxable employer-paid health benefits as a substitute. What was meant to be a temporary, wartime exemption is now a permanent fixture of American healthcare. These types of successes, historic and recent, can give us hope for future actions to invest in promoting healthcare equity. One could argue that these efforts were the prologue to a historic achievement in 2022 when the Census

Bureau reported that the United States had reached record lows in the number of children living in poverty and the number of children who were uninsured. Securing the health and safety of our most vulnerable is indeed a cause for celebration.

The Centers for Medicare & Medicaid Services defines health equity as "the attainment of the highest level of health for all people, where everyone has a fair and just opportunity to attain their optimal health regardless of race, ethnicity, disability, sexual orientation, gender identity, socioeconomic status, geography, preferred language, or other factors that affect access to care and health outcomes." Policy makers did, and can continue to, make a difference.

Community leaders, academics, politicians, activists, and more are working together to create health equity. And it is important to understand that the root causes of health inequity are the same root causes of endemic violence, which means that the solutions are similar.

Another of my mother's favorite maxims was, "Brian, when you know better, *do* better." What will we do with what we know?

18 | ANATOMY OF A GUNSHOT WOUND

If you've ever wondered what a speeding bullet can do to your insides, recall the law of conservation of energy from high school physics class. Remember that energy cannot be created or destroyed; it can only be transformed, from one form to another. Within this scientific principle resides the answer to the question: How does a bullet devastate a body?

When a shooter pulls the trigger, the chemical energy of the explosive within the cartridge is transformed into kinetic energy, and the bullet discharges from the barrel at one thousand feet per second: a heated missile that covers the length of a football field in less than one second. The amount of kinetic energy transferred from the bullet to the body will determine the amount of damage. Higher velocity means more energy, which results in greater bodily damage. Having never been shot, I cannot describe how it feels. But having operated on countless gunshot victims, I can describe the damage.

No matter how many bullets penetrate your body, only one matters. It's that single bullet, hidden in the crowd of wounds, that makes the difference. Only one bullet needs to find a path to transect the aorta, shred the heart, or penetrate the skull, leaving a mass of pulverized gelatin. And the damage done by a bullet extends far beyond the direct path it takes through the human body. We trauma surgeons worry not only about bodily structures in the direct line of the bullet trajectory but also about cavitary injuries. Bystanders may see the wound at the point of entry. What you will not see, unless you are the surgeon doing the operation, is the damage done to internal organs along the path, as well as surrounding structures.

Beyond gunshot wounds to the chest and abdomen, I've treated gunshot injuries to the arms and legs that damage major blood vessels and nerves and shatter bones. The fortunate patients will only have a tangential injury, what most call a flesh wound, which only needs a bedside washout and a clean dressing. I've also treated gunshot wounds to the head, which, as we've seen, are almost uniformly fatal.

None of this encapsulates, however, the bodily devastation from an AR-15, the civilian version of the M-16 I fired as an Air Force Academy cadet, and the weapon of choice for mass shooters since Columbine. It is in a destructive class all its own, creating wounds beyond the skill of even the best trauma surgeons to repair. Gunshot wounds from an AR-15 frequently leave victims unidentifiable without analyzing DNA. Imagine what would happen to your body if you laid on a grenade: that's the AR-15.

But we exist in a sanitized world, one scrubbed of the reality of what bullets do to bodies. Living in a country in which there are more guns than people, we still manage to maintain a certain naivete about bullets and bodies. We might watch Hollywood heroes grimace while some untrained sidekick or well-trained doctor grabs a pair of fancy pliers and goes digging to retrieve a bullet inside them, but that's about it. Let me set the record straight: we never do that. Trauma surgeons don't go digging for the bullet. We will leave the bullet embedded in your body, wherever it is, unless it is lying in plain sight. Trying to retrieve it would simply cause more internal damage to blood vessels, soft tissue, and nerves. It is much safer to leave the bullet wherever it has come to rest.

That means that while you will hopefully recover, go home, and keep living your life, the bullet, and the memory, will remain.

No amount of gross anatomy, ballistic analysis, or forensic pathology explains the injuries I cannot treat with a scalpel. The psychological trauma to the survivor, friends, family, and community can remain for a lifetime. More than half of survivors suffer from post-traumatic stress years after a non-fatal injury. Many remain unemployed, while others develop substance use disorders. The psychological effects can traumatize neighborhoods, and, for highly publicized mass shootings, people thousands of miles away from where the shootings occur. These are the ripple effects of gun violence we ignore, particularly in racially segregated neighborhoods with endemic violence.

The annual economic toll of gun violence is estimated to be $1 billion in direct medical costs, according to a report by the Senate Joint Economic Committee. This figure does not account for indirect costs, such as increased security measures at public places (schools, shopping malls, and concerts are but a few examples), depressed housing values in some neighborhoods, and reduced productive years in the workforce for victims and survivors who would otherwise contribute to the national economy. The human toll is forty-nine thousand lives lost per year and continues to rise year over year. I would not be surprised if, by the time this book is published, that figure exceeds fifty thousand annual deaths—the equivalent of a passenger aircraft, filled to capacity, crashing every day for eight consecutive months.

When discussing gun violence, we tend to focus on what's tangible: the number dead, ages of the victims, weapons used, and venue of the shootings. But the intangibles can be just as lethal. Like the cavitary destruction a single bullet causes, the epidemic of gun violence creates damage far beyond the location of the violence. Whether it be the gun violence in areas of concentrated poverty, or the random mass shootings at schools, malls, and places of worship, the cavitary injury to society extends far beyond any geographic or physical boundary.

For a gunshot wound is more than a life-threatening hole in the body, as graphic as that is. Peel back the layers and you will find a complex system of upstream social ills: community divestment, income inequality, failing infrastructure. We have already looked at some of the social determinants of health. We saw how talking about individual health is only part of the equation. Similarly, gun violence isn't the only kind of violence we need to talk about; structural racism enacts its own variety of state-supported violence. We can't discuss interpersonal violence without discussing structural violence. Put simply, you don't need to pull the trigger of a gun to cause harm because silence is its own form of violence, too.

To say nothing when one sees injustice and suffering is giving tacit approval of its existence. Holocaust survivor Elie Wiesel wrote that, "Silence encourages the tormentor, never the tormented." Dr. Martin Luther King, Jr. said, "In the end, we will remember not the words of our enemies, but the silence of our friends." In America, racialized gun violence is the enemy. It affects us all, so we must not remain silent.

I've saved this chapter on gun violence, policy, and possible solutions until almost the end of the book because you must understand racism before you understand guns in America. Gun policy has evolved, as we will see, but the racially biased impact has not. We must view the gun debate through the prism of race and ask: Who has access to guns? Who is harmed by them? Who is protected? Who is expendable? Ending the epidemic of gun violence will be difficult because politics, policy, and race are tightly bound together. Pulling on one strand disrupts the others. Tugging on the thread of race results in resistance from the other two. But it is simply impossible to decouple the issue of gun violence from issues of systemic racism.

To understand gun violence in America, it's important to look at the demographic that owns more guns than anyone else. Owning a gun is not the same as killing someone, and many gun owners use them legally and safely. Still, gun violence happens because people own guns—a trite but true statement. Gun ownership is more prevalent among men than among women, and most gun-owners are white. About half of white men (48 percent) say they own a gun, compared to about a quarter (24 percent) of men of color.

In other words, when we are talking about guns in America, it's important to start not with Black and brown men, but with white men.

The melon-sized, swastika tattoo on his belly was impossible to miss but easy to ignore. The white man on the gurney before me was a gunshot victim. He was not my first patient to bear the symbol, and the story behind his body art was irrelevant to the job I was trained to do. My role was to heal, not judge.

Writhing in misery, he squirmed to resist the trauma team doing the primary survey, but was easily restrained by two nurses and a resident. His partner, wearing a tank top T-shirt, had the same swastika tattoo on his deltoid. He was DOA.

"Shit," he slurred. "I can't believe they shot us."

I surveyed the scene from my usual perch, a body's length from the foot of the bed. His speech was garbled, impaired by a night of hard drinking. Thoroughly intoxicated, he spoke to nobody in particular, and never explained who *they* were, the ones who had shot him and the DOA, the first to arrive and who I later learned was his brother. He had been wheeled into an adjacent trauma bay minutes earlier while receiving chest compressions. I called his death before moving to my current gunshot victim.

It was nearly 1:00 a.m., less than one year after 7/7 and I was back into my routine at Parkland: taking trauma call. The Muslim travel ban dominated the news cycle, which did not portend well for the new administration's immigration policy. My patients, many of whom were undocumented immigrants, would likely suffer. From across the room, the smell emanating from our patient meant he spent an evening consuming industrial amounts of liquor. Glassy-eyed, he'd raise his head from the stretcher to look at the team members working on his body. He weakly fought the removal of his clothes and the placement of the intravenous lines and the rolling of his body from side to side to check for bullet wounds. He finally lay back and drunkenly accepted his fate: receiving top-notch care from a team of seasoned professionals at a premier trauma center.

"What's your name, sir?" the emergency medicine resident at the head of the bed asked.

"Jared." Given the copious amount of intoxicants in his system, he slurred his two-syllable name into one: *Jerd*. "Motherfucker. You believe that sumbitch shot us?" he queried the resident, who simply announced "Airway intact" and continued her assessment.

"Clear breath sounds bilaterally."

"2+ femoral pulse."

"Aaaarrrrghhh! Stop!" The resident had given a few syncopated taps on his abdomen.

"He's got diffuse peritonitis."

"Do the usual," I said. "I'll call the OR."

White men, who make up one-third of the US population, possess the majority of privately owned firearms according to multiple reports. I have chosen to work at centers in close proximity to majority-Black neighborhoods, so the majority of my patients have been Black. It is an example of the multidimensional nature of gun violence and the demographic of patients I treat as an urban trauma surgeon. Jared was an outlier. Curiously, regarding gun ownership, research suggests that Black and white men are in fact united. Both are motivated by the need for self-protection.

The "well-regulated militia," deified in the Second Amendment, has energized a confluence of white nationalists and anti-government entities that the Department of Homeland Security described as "the most significant terror-related threat facing the US today." No longer hidden beneath white hoods, but wrapped in Old Glory with rhetoric about making America great again, the armed, white male is the representative model of this movement. "Whiteness and masculinity are central features—though often not clearly obvious ones—in the rearview nationalism of militia members' values," writes sociologist Dr. Amy Cooter, an expert on militias in the US. "Their nostalgic stories hinge on archetypes of independent, brave men whose heroic efforts were responsible for establishing a nation as these groups wish it to be again. Those men are always white."

In 2015, twenty-eight years after I completed basic training, a white supremacist walked into Mother Emanuel AME Church in Charleston and killed nine Black people during Bible study. Three of the victims were relatives of one of my coworkers, who is now a renowned gun safety advocate. Seven years later, another teenager bought an AR-15 style weapon on credit, wrote "Die Nigger" on the barrel, and livestreamed his mass murder of elderly shoppers at a grocery store in a predominantly Black neighborhood in Buffalo, New York. As Dr. Anthea Butler pointed out in the *Washington Post* after the Charleston shooting, the typical media narrative about white shooters is that they are "lone, disturbed, mentally ill young men failed by society." It's a convenient narrative, one that minimizes the causes of gun violence by scapegoating mental health to distract from the confluence of easy access to guns and white nationalist extremism.

There are signs that domestic, racist terrorism is finally being taken seriously. In 2021, a White House strategy document, focused on countering domestic terrorism, suggests that while domestic terror threats are wide-ranging, "racially or ethnically motivated violent extremists (principally those who promote the superiority of the white race) and militia violent extremists are assessed as presenting the most persistent and lethal threats." One report published in 2021, titled *Armed Assembly: Guns, Demonstrations, and Political Violence in America*, showed that the majority of armed demonstrations were driven by far-right activists responding to left-wing activism, particularly those advocating for racial justice.

Yet, to admit that America needs to protect herself from domestic terrorism means admitting that America must protect herself from white supremacy. And that is a reality that we as a nation have never been willing to fully confront. The Domestic Terrorism Prevention Act of 2021, which passed the House of Representatives, would have authorized "dedicated domestic terrorism offices within the Department of Homeland Security, the Department of Justice, and the Federal Bureau of Investigation to analyze and monitor domestic terrorist activity and require the Federal Government to take steps to prevent domestic terrorism." The bill died in the Senate due to the filibuster.

Indeed, white gun owners are celebrated in ways that elude their Black counterparts: idolized as patriots and revered as protectors. This mythology persists, and no amount of evidence to the contrary seems to matter much.

I don't know who shot Jared or why, nor whether he was involved in any organized militia. I left those details to the detectives, who would likely visit the hospital to take his statement. Unfortunately, by the time they arrived, Jared was under general anesthesia with his abdomen splayed open for an exploratory laparotomy, the classic emergency operation for a gunshot wound to the abdomen.

I've treated patients injured by shotguns, rifles, and assault weapons. But handguns, which account for nearly two-thirds of firearm homicides in the United States, are the bulk of my work. Handguns may not be as powerful as assault weapons, but they are more prolific. I supervised the trauma fellow who made a midline abdominal incision, whereupon entry into the abdomen released the acrid concoction of partially digested alcohol, food, and stomach acid that would curl the hair in your nostrils. A bullet had caused a tangential wound on the front of his stomach and the contents of the night—beer, tequila, and an assortment of Mexican food—floated freely in his abdomen.

First, we controlled active hemorrhage and checked for retroperitoneal hematomas (he had none). Second, we controlled spillage of gastrointestinal contents (he had a lot). We then placed several temporary clamps along the stomach wound, four on wounds to his small intestine leaking milky green contents that looked like dark radiator fluid, and two on injuries to his large intestine which leaked stool like brown toothpaste. Next, we performed a thorough exploration of the abdomen, searching for injuries to solid organs like the kidneys, liver, and diaphragm. We repaired the colon wound without giving him a colostomy, repaired the linear tear in the stomach, and resected the injured segment of small intestine, repairing it with a primary stapled anastomosis. We conducted another thorough exploration to double-check for injuries we may have overlooked, confirmed our repairs were sturdy, and washed out the abdomen with several liters of warm sterile saline.

Usually after closing the fascia, the leathery tissue that holds your abdominal muscles together, I'd scrub out and allow the trainees to finish the closure. On that night, I chose to close the swastika-branded skin myself. As team members, Black and white, joked about purposely defacing the patient's body art, I dismissed everyone except the scrub nurse, circulator, and the anesthesiologist. I carefully aligned the edges of that swastika to ensure that his skin would heal properly. How easy it would have been to staple the skin off-center, knowing it would heal askew. Yet I aligned the inked edges with the same attention to detail I used to prepare my Air Force blues for inspection, attending to small imperfections that might escape the untrained eye.

I felt something akin to compassion mixed with pity for this stranger, who was clearly consumed by such hate. Had he learned it from his parents? His friends? Somewhere along his way from child-hood to adulthood, something had corrupted his sense of shared humanity. I intended to hold on to my own.

After the closure we covered the wound with a sterile dressing, awakened him from general anesthesia, and transported him to the recovery room. Jared would leave the hospital six days later, with a well-healed midline abdominal scar bisecting his perfectly aligned swastika tattoo. Since I checked on him daily until he was well enough for discharge, I was a routine presence in his hospital room with him and his family. Every day they were reminded that I was the one who had saved both his tattoo and his life.

No matter where you live, work, play, or worship, you should prob-ably have an active shooter plan. It's simply the reality of our time in history. For many Americans, the real threat of random gun violence is probably a new phenomenon, one that has taken hold of the collec-tive American consciousness only within the last few decades. I include myself in that group.

Since the Columbine High School shooting in 1999, and several headline-grabbing mass shootings after expiration of the assault weapons ban in 2005, many Americans have become fearful that gun violence will affect them. These days, according to the American Psychological Association, "Sixty-two percent of parents said they lived in fear of their children becoming victims of a mass shooting, and 71 percent said the possibility of mass violence was adding stress to their lives."

But for Black people, the threat of random gun violence goes back centuries. Fear of our children becoming victims of gun violence is nothing new (remember: my mother forbade me playing with toy guns as a child). Long before the Bill of Rights enshrined the right to bear arms, anti-Black racism was foundational in American gun policy. In antebellum Louisiana, colonists were legally obligated to stop Black people who carried any potential weapon, such as a cane, and "shoot to kill" if necessary. It was the eighteenth-century version of modern stand-your-ground laws, which we will look at in more detail later in this chapter—and which do little to reduce violent crime but do increase the number of lethal shootings of Black people by white people.

After the Civil War, enthusiasm for open-carry rights waned as states narrowed the definition of who possessed those rights. On Christmas Eve in 1865, the Ku Klux Klan was founded in Pulaski, Tennessee, launching a century of intensified racial terror and extra-judicial enforcement of disarming Black people. The legacy of Jim Crow, racist policing, and a rigid racial caste system reverberates today. It is the reason thousands of people can feel entitled to storm the US Capitol in a frenzied effort to eradicate a perceived threat to their privilege.

Guns, and by extension gun policy, have been a symbol of racialized terror for centuries. Racialized gun policy was the means of maintaining a racial caste system. It is why so many federal, state, and local laws have been passed to disarm Black people, to make it difficult for Black people to legally obtain firearms, and to minimize the consequences of using firearms to dispose of Black people. And the end result of those same laws contributes to devastating countless lives in impoverished communities where gun violence is endemic.

Many attributed the perceived rise in gun violence to the ready accessibility of AR-15s. But when we analyze the data during the decade following the Public Safety and Recreational Firearms Use Protection Act of 1994, also known as the assault weapons ban, we find that it is inconclusive. The assault weapons ban did have an effect in reducing mass shootings, particularly in large, public gatherings.

But mass shootings account for less than 1 percent of gun violence deaths, and, despite the proclamations of media, politicians, and gun rights advocates, most mass shootings are committed with handguns in racially segregated neighborhoods.

Still, the AR-15 has become the dominant symbol of the US gun violence debate. However, there is a single policy that resides at the confluence of politics, gun violence, public health, criminal justice, and race. Let's look at this policy, which is responsible for more deaths each year than a decade's worth of deaths from AR-15s.

There are few more egregious examples of racialized gun legislation than defensive gun laws, also known as Stand Your Ground laws. These laws are a public health threat, rooted in structural racism, that endanger us all. Elevated to public awareness in 2012 following the murder of Trayvon Martin by George Zimmerman, Stand Your Ground laws have not been proven to deter crime. They do lead to an increase in gun-related deaths, and the disproportionate incarceration and deaths of Black people.

Stand Your Ground laws are rooted in a legal concept called the Castle Doctrine, which empowers individuals to use lethal force when in their home—in other words their "castle." If there is a threat to your life or your property, you have the right to kill in self-defense, even if you can safely retreat. What Stand Your Ground laws do is extend the geography of what is considered to be one's "castle" to any public space. That means individuals have no duty to retreat from a threat, even when they can safely do so. In essence, Stand Your Ground laws promote vigilante justice through a culture of "shoot first, ask questions later."

The resulting impact was predictable. Stand Your Ground laws have *increased* deaths due to firearms by an additional 700 to 800 deaths each year. That is approximately two years of mass shootings combined.

Not surprisingly, these laws also worsen racial disparities in gun violence. Studies suggest that the race of the shooter and the race of the victim influence the outcome of legal cases in which Stand Your Ground is a defense. The Department of Justice analyzed statistics by the Urban Institute and found that if the shooter is white and the victim is Black, that shooting is deemed "justified" by judges and juries five times more often than if the situation is reversed. And if the victim is Black, no matter the race of the shooter, that shooting is deemed justified two times more often than if the victim is white. So whether the Black person is shooter or victim, Stand Your Ground laws place Black Americans at increased risk of violence, death, and criminality due to firearms.

When a white shooter murders a Black victim, that shooting is more likely to be deemed justified. The odds of a white person killing a Black person and it being deemed justified is 281 percent greater than a white person killing another white person. And no matter the race of the shooter, they were two times more likely to be convicted if the victim is white than a person of color. Stand Your Ground laws are so protective of white men that a woman who shoots and kills her male, domestic abuser is *more* likely to be convicted of a crime than a white man who shoots an unarmed civilian in public.

Since the time of our founding, the right to bear arms has been used, explicitly and implicitly, to disarm and control Black people. Stand Your Ground laws are the legalized means of continuing that lethal tradition. And since gun violence and gun policy are linked, reducing preventable firearm-related deaths requires addressing racialized gun policy.

Interestingly enough, the same Second Amendment that white gun owners defend often doesn't mean much with regard to protecting Black gun owners. Emantic Fitzgerald Bradford Jr., a legally licensed gun owner directing panicked shoppers to safety during a mall shooting in Alabama, was shot in the back and killed by a responding police officer. Philando Castile, also legally licensed, was shot and killed in the driver's seat of his car during a traffic stop. And remember, the day prior to Castile's death, Alton Sterling was shot and killed in Louisiana. As writer David Graham noted in the *Atlantic*, the shooting deaths of Alton Sterling and Philando Castile "give a strong sense that the Second Amendment does not apply to Black Americans."

In May 2016, nearly four years after George Zimmerman murdered Trayvon Martin and three years after his acquittal, Zimmerman auctioned the weapon he used to kill Trayvon. Reportedly, a woman purchased the murder weapon as a present for her son for $250,000.

Since policy, politics, and race are interwoven, how do we choose what voices to elevate in the gun violence debate? A mass shooting becomes national news, while most shootings barely become local stories. We usually hear from advocates of gun rights and gun control, from healthcare professionals on the front lines of gun violence, and from the families and friends of school children killed in mass shootings. And we must not diminish the loss and grief following those tragedies.

But what about the mothers of Black children and teens? Of the Black youth who die during their teenage years, more than half of whom die from gun violence. What about community violence interrupters, who work in neighborhoods to prevent further violence and who relive this trauma repeatedly as a result of the work? Or community leaders who deal with the effects of community-level trauma that come from living within areas of endemic violence? These are the voices we must promote in the discussion about solutions to ending gun violence.

The likelihood of a white man being killed with a gun remains less than a Black man being killed without one. In fact, homicide is the leading cause of death for Black men from the first year of life until forty-four years of age. For white men it is fourth until age twenty, at which time it becomes the fifth most common cause of death. Nearly 80 percent of homicides are due to firearms. The public narrative about fatal shootings of Black people tends to pivot toward our presumed criminality. That is misleading because violent crime in the US is at record lows, continuing a downtrend since its peak in the early 1990s. Still, for nearly a decade, fatal shootings of civilians by law enforcement remain constant, at about one thousand victims per year. Decreasing violent crime has not resulted in a proportionate decrease in police shootings; and Black people, who are less likely to have a gun, are more likely to be shot and killed. Given the choice, would you feel safer being Black or white in an encounter with the police?

The idea of "Black-on-Black crime," implying that Black people are prone to criminality and violence, is another false narrative we must debunk. As we saw earlier, it is a misnomer. It is true that the majority of Black homicides are committed by Black people; however, the same is true for white people. That's because violent crime, and by extension gun violence, is a byproduct of proximity and economic divestment. According to the Department of Justice, people living below the federal poverty level are twice as likely to commit violent crimes. That's true across racial demographics. Since rigid racial segregation still defines American society—with redlining a major contributor—poor Black people live in neighborhoods with majority Black populations, and poor white people live in neighborhoods with majority white populations. One result of this geographic isolation is that Black people kill Black people, and white people kill white people.

And a report from the Robert Wood Johnson Foundation concluded that "the same social factors that shape health—including education, income and wealth, and related conditions where we live, learn, work and play—also are strongly linked to violence, and considering those links can contribute to understanding why some groups of Americans are more affected by violence than others." In short, investing in communities—in housing, education, and jobs—is the key to reducing gun violence.

I benefited from my father's military service, which helped remove many of these systemic barriers. My sister and I had reliable housing, a quality public education, a steady income, and, most importantly, ready access to affordable healthcare. Yes, we pulled ourselves up by our bootstraps to keep climbing, in a sense, but we also had one less boot on our neck to fight against.

Proximity is essential to developing empathy for those whose lives are otherwise disconnected from our own. Through treating patients who had attempted suicide with a gun, unsupervised children injured by unsecured weapons, and women shot by their abusive partners, I have learned the complex relationship between fear, grief, violence, and harm.

Reducing gun violence is not only a matter of life or death; it is a matter of racial justice. Racialized violence is inherent in the statistics. Black women are three times more likely than white women to be shot and killed by an intimate partner. Black men comprise more than half of gun homicide victims. As previously mentioned, Black people are less likely to be armed than their white counterparts during police encounters—but nearly three times more likely to be fatally shot. The one outlier is suicides, which is the leading cause of firearm-related deaths; white men suffer the most gun deaths by suicide.

We must broaden the discussion about gun violence prevention because gun violence is not monolithic or singular. The United States does not have only one gun violence problem, we have multiple types of gun violence: suicides, intimate partner violence, urban gun violence, unintentional shootings, and mass shootings. Some experts call for another class of gun violence: police shootings of civilians. More people are shot and killed by police each year than in all mass shootings combined, and Black people are overrepresented in the victim pool. Therefore, when we talk about gun violence, we must include police shootings. Ending the epidemic of gun violence will require a multilevel effort. We see different root causes, different populations impacted, and thus different solutions are needed. Some problems require a hammer, while others require a screwdriver.

Most importantly, we must accept ideas championed by communities because those closest to the problem most often have the best solutions. And the government must bolster those solutions because it is our policy makers who have the power to implement transformative public policy. Policies such as extreme risk protection orders, child safety devices, and better mental health services can help reduce firearm-related injuries and death due to suicides, intimate partner violence, unintentional shootings, and high-profile mass shootings. To reduce urban gun violence, the type that dominates my experience as a trauma surgeon, requires eliminating poverty and lack of opportunities by investing in stable housing, high-quality education, and employment. Each may seem like separate issues, but all have roots in disparities created by our history of redlining.

So what can you do? We can help break the cycle of violence by mentoring youth, for example, or voting for politicians committed to radical economic investment in communities with endemic violence. We can highlight and learn from the heroic gun violence prevention that Black women and girls are doing, all without accolades and little acknowledgment. I think of my mother who would not allow me to play with toy guns as a child. I wonder if the mother of Malik, from the opening scene of this book, became an activist herself. I think of my coworker who lost family members in the shooting at Mother

Emanuel AME in Charleston, who has become a leading gun violence prevention advocate. There are many examples of Black mothers organizing, educating, and advocating for the safety of their children and their neighborhoods. These are some of the unsung heroes working to end the epidemic of gun violence: Mothers of the Movement, Mothers Against Senseless Killings in Chicago, Mothers in Charge in Philadelphia, and the Community Justice Action Fund, to name a few. Journalist and professor Arionne Nettles interviewed Black mothers about gun violence for a piece she wrote for the *New York Times.* They are the "true experts on the issue," she writes. As the epidemic of gun violence continues, she writes, "it's time we listen to them." It's time to look to those closest to the crisis and ask: What are their strategies and goals? How can the rest of us learn from their work?

If you are not ready for any of those actions, a minimum step we all can take is educating ourselves. Understand that gun violence takes a national toll, affects all of us, and impedes America from achieving further greatness. Acknowledge this basic truth: gun violence is not someone else's problem. It is our problem to solve. Elliot Currie writes, "For most people who live outside the most stricken communities, deadly violence exists as part of the background noise of urban America, something that happens in 'bad' neighborhoods—neighborhoods that are not theirs."

It's time to change that way of thinking. The cavitary injury of gun violence affects us all, and we must not look away.

19 | A MOMENT OF SILENCE

The glowing green display on my pager reads: "L1, 17M, GSW chest, traumatic arrest, ETA 6 min." The medical shorthand and acronyms mean that a seventeen-year-old male with a gunshot wound to the chest will arrive in six minutes. His heart has already stopped and, I presume, the first responders have begun CPR. That he will arrive well past midnight on a school night, when most teens should be sound asleep, does not surprise me. The assembly line of bloodied Black bodies needing repair unloads at our trauma center 24/7.

Exiting the call room, I smooth the collar on my white coat and confirm the top three buttons are buttoned. Outside these walls COVID-19 is steamrolling poverty-stricken neighborhoods in Chicago and beyond, inflicting death in record numbers upon the people least able to flee. It is the early months of the pandemic, a time of inadequate PPE for frontline healthcare workers, ventilator shortages for breathless patients, and no vaccine for anyone. In Chicago, Black residents are dying from the coronavirus at nearly six times the rate of white residents.

While infections surge, visitation is restricted. No unnecessary personnel are allowed in the hospital beyond specific quarantined areas. I stay home too, unless I'm working a shift on trauma or in one of the designated COVID intensive care units. Patients are dying alone, and families say goodbye by video or phone calls, if at all. All the while gun violence is breaking records, with more than half of Black teen mortalities, ages fifteen to nineteen, caused by gun violence. By the end of the following year, nearly two years into the pandemic, firearm-related homicides will increase in more than two-thirds of major US cities, breaking previous annual records in at least nine major cities. No matter how hard we who are on the frontlines work, Black people are still dying at rates well within our grasp as a nation to prevent.

I walk to the trauma bay with purpose, the ABCs of trauma cycling in my mind, on my way to join a throng of healthcare heroes. They are fighting to plug a hole in a dam of violence that only society can repair. They prepare to swarm a teenage boy—another gunshot victim, the eleventh since I began this shift nearly twenty-four hours ago. With several hours until the 7 a.m. shift change, I doubt he will be the last. One medic propels the gurney while a second double-times alongside, pumping the sternum of the patient like a steam piston at 100 beats per minute. They park next to the stretcher in a corner bay where a dozen nurses, doctors, and trainees take center stage for a repeat performance at our trauma center.

"Give us report, please," says Dr. Stone, the trauma fellow.

While a flurry of gloved hands transfers the patient to the stretcher, the pushing medic's voice rises above the buzz. "Seventeen-year-old male. Multiple gunshot wounds to the head, chest, and both arms. He was unresponsive when we arrived at the scene." She continues to give us the pre-hospital information needed to save this young man's life as the team goes to work, tossing clothing to the floor, piercing flaccid extremities with intravenous lines, transfusing blood, and slapping EKG leads on his chest. A disorganized rhythm crawls across the heart monitor.

With his cherubic face and short-cut afro with pale-colored streaks along one side, he looks much younger than seventeen. He appears peaceful, lying naked and dependent upon us for survival. A few feet from the foot of the bed, I stand with my hands clasped behind my back, watchful, wordless, and waiting. Dr. Stone, the trauma fellow, is directing the scene.

I've run thousands of trauma activations, but this one is unlike any of those. Dr. Stone is the first Black trauma fellow with whom I've worked. She and I are the two most senior surgeons in the room. Amid the synchronized chaos and her calm directives, I allow this moment to imprint on my memory. This is what Black representation in medicine could mean. Here, still working within the prevailing narrative about gun violence—a narrative where the stories of Black victims and survivors are usually forgotten—is a Black trainee, directing the trauma response. In the last year of her surgical training, Dr. Stone is methodical, calm, and exceedingly competent. I haven't said a word since our patient arrived. This is Dr. Stone's show.

Still, when I backed away from the rolling gurney moments earlier so that she could take charge, I knew exactly how it would end. In some ways, the fact that the trauma fellow herself is Black changes everything, and in other ways it changes nothing. Black people are still dying.

I am not the same person I was when I began my career. Age and experience conjoin to transform us all, I suppose. My own transformation includes moving from assimilation, code switching, and separating myself from the realities of my patients—all in the name of career advancement and acceptance—to now claiming all the ways that my experiences as a Black man connect me to my patients. I've finally learned that while handing over one's dignity for acceptance may clear the path for professional success, it is corrosive to one's selfhood and a barrier to personal growth.

As I have changed, so has the scale of my ambitions. My goal, audacious as it may sound, is to work myself out of my job as a trauma surgeon. To never have to tell another mother she has lost a child to gun violence. To stop the flow of bodies arriving in our emergency rooms and trauma centers because of preventable injuries, treatable diseases, and avoidable death. Treating individual patients occurs within the hospital, but healing entire communities occurs beyond it.

During the coronavirus pandemic, Congress passed more than half a dozen pandemic-related bills, proof that Congress can do big things quickly when needed. Yet none of the bills accounted for race, even though we knew that racial disparities in infections and death defined the pandemic. It's a lesson about the interconnectedness of public policy and healthcare justice we must not forget as we work to heal our nation.

My circumstances have changed, but my motivation has not: to dismantle structural racism, end the epidemic of gun violence, and create health equity. Gun violence is a rolling tragedy that must end, one that exists within the larger ecosystem of healthcare injustice. The solutions are intertwined, and will improve the lives of tens of thousands of gun violence victims and survivors each year. We can have an impact measured not by tens of thousands but by millions by investing in health, not just healthcare.

In the fall of 2021, I moved to Washington, DC, to serve as a Robert Wood Johnson Foundation Health Policy Fellow. Having worked on the frontlines of healthcare and seen the disparities play out in real time against my people, I decided that the center of federal power was where I needed to be: to share my expertise with congressional leaders, contribute to the national conversation on health equity and gun violence, and learn as much as I could about federal policy and legislation.

There is a tremendous amount of bipartisan work occurring on Capitol Hill—more than I anticipated. Many of these bipartisan efforts happen away from the cameras and microphones, and I wish more people could see it in action. As a congressional health policy advisor, I worked on a broad range of federal legislative health issues: gun violence, pandemic response, the opioid crisis, healthcare work-force, mental health reform, reproductive rights, Medicare, Medicaid, and more. The experience of generating a policy idea, meeting with constituents, prepping for hearings, and drafting a bill transformed how I view the legislative process. And C-SPAN is my new guilty pleasure.

Around 9:00 p.m. on June 23, 2022, I sat in the viewing gallery overlooking the Senate chambers with dozens of congressional staffers, gun violence survivors, and gun safety advocates. A parade of senators addressed their colleagues prior to voting, asking them to support the Bipartisan Safer Communities Act. One month prior, almost two years to the day of George Floyd's murder, an eighteen-year-old gunman fatally shot nineteen fourth-grade students and two teachers at Robb Elementary School in Uvalde, Texas. The shooting sparked a wave of political activism that eclipsed that of the mass shooting of Black patrons in a Buffalo, NY, supermarket a week and half earlier. In any event, activists pushed and Congress acted. Some of the provisions included enhanced background checks for buyers under twenty-one, funding for community violence intervention, and expansion of children and family mental health services. The Bipartisan Safer Communities Act became the most significant gun safety legislation passed in nearly three decades.

Working as a health policy advisor, I learned there is hope for making our nation safe from the epidemic of gun violence. I shared tears with survivors and families from the shootings at Sandy Hook, Marjory Stoneman Douglas, Uvalde, and more. I met with staffers, researchers, healthcare workers, policymakers, and an array of gun safety advocates—many of whom were card-carrying members of the NRA. We did not agree on everything. But we did agree that promoting public health and safety was essential, and that to do nothing after the most recent series of tragedies was simply not an option.

Like many of the others, this young man is working to die before our eyes. The foot-long scar bisecting his belly means this is not his first time getting shot. If he survives, there's no guarantee it will be his last. More than half of Black gunshot victims are treated multiple times for gunshot wounds, with their risk of an early death increasing with each subsequent injury.

Being an academic surgeon means I can recite statistics that impress my trainees but are meaningless to my neighbors dodging bullets daily a few blocks from where I work. More than half of gun homicide victims are Black males, and firearms are the leading cause of death for Black children and teens. As of 2020, for the first time in US history, firearms are the leading cause of death for *all* children and teens, regardless of race or ethnicity. The cavitary effect of gun violence impacts us all.

"14-gauge in the right AC, 18 in the left," says a nurse.

"First unit of blood is hanging," says another.

"I see the vocal cords. Hand me the tube."

"I can't feel a pulse."

"Okay, continue CPR," says Dr. Stone.

Less than five minutes after his arrival, our crashing patient is naked, has IV lines in both arms, and a stranger's blood flowing through his veins. He is ready for intubation. On the monitor, the glowing line snaking left to right means the same thing whether you are a civilian or cop, wealthy or poor, and white or Black. It is the last gasps of a dying heart, and there is only one life-saving option.

For the first time, Dr. Stone looks to me for approval and asks, "Should we do a thoracotomy, Sir?"

Before answering, I summarize for the team. "We have a GSW to the head and torso, unresponsive at the scene with greater than fifteen minutes of pre-hospital CPR," I say. "No pulse. No spontaneous breaths. No cardiac activity on sono. Pupils fixed and dilated." Some members of the team were witnessing their first gun-violence death, so I psychologically prepared them for what I knew we would have to do. I've been here enough times to know a thoracotomy is futile. Trainees learning to respect the humanity of the dead is as important as learning to cross-clamp the aorta for maximum resident benefit.

Unclasping my hands, I put on a pair of gloves and examine the patient to confirm what I already know. I confirm the absent pulse, the lack of spontaneous breaths, the unreactive pupils. I trust the team, but the decision to cease life-sustaining treatment is mine.

"No. Call it."

Before moving to Chicago, I heard "Code Yellow" only one time: when Parkland Hospital activated the disaster response to the Dallas police shooting. Code Yellow means different things at different hospitals. At Parkland, Code Yellow set in motion a sequence that mobilized hundreds, including armed police who secured the facility and off-duty personnel who had been relaxing at home.

At the University of Chicago, however, Code Yellow is the routine overhead call in the emergency department for every trauma activation. I hear it multiple times each time I'm on call, and each time my mind flickers back to 7/7. Each Code Yellow I hear is a painfully routine reminder of the worst night of my career. But it is a reminder I will not allow to define me. That night is a historic tragedy that I must integrate into my life. I need to figure out how to use what I learned from it, and the reaction to what I said about it, in order to do maximum good in my fleeting lifetime. To bring unity, not division. To bring light, not heat. To bring love, not hate.

Sometimes I'm still angry, and sometimes I still work overtime not to show it. One of my new colleagues in Chicago, a radiologist who barely knows me, once volunteered, "You seem to have a lot of pent-up rage."

"How do you know that?" I asked.

"It's in your eyes."

He had only known me for a few weeks when he told me this. At the time he knew nothing about 7/7, or Micah Johnson, or the dead Dallas police officers, or anything else about me. Despite all the therapy and inner work, apparently I can't just flip a switch to make the anger go away. And for that I am grateful. Anger is a secondary emotion, beneath which lies feelings of grief, loss, or unmet needs. The challenge is understanding the source of the anger and then channeling that anger into purpose. In response to gun violence, parents, high school students, and doctors have channeled their responses to mass tragedies into purposeful action that is making a difference. But I believe that those with the most experience and knowledge are Black mothers. In their steadfast care for their communities and grassroots activism, they are showing the rest of us how to turn tragedy into purpose.

Anger has become the fuel that propels me on this journey of justice. The best I can do is dial it down and channel that energy in service of the greater good. Anger can be destructive or productive. We can allow it to hold us in a state of inaction, or we can let it inspire us to challenge the injustices around us. I have long identified my anger with shame. No more. Naming it and embracing it has guided me forward. And now I know what triggers my anger most of all: persistent injustice. Anger ignored can consume us, but anger acknowledged can transform us.

I will never forget the three Dallas police officers I treated who died on 7/7: Michael Krol, 40, described as a "big guy with a big heart." Patrick Zamarripa, 32, a Navy veteran who survived three tours in Iraq. Michael Smith, 55, described as "one of the good guys." I even remember the names of those who died at a crosstown trauma center: Brent Thompson, 43; and Lorne Ahrens, 48. I cannot forget, even if I tried, because 7/7 is a part of me.

And then there is Malik. Darrius. Troy. Hassan. I remember some but not all the names of all the gunshot victims I've treated. I tried to save their lives but knew most of them only in death. Their lives mattered too, even in this nation that gave them and their parents and grandparents so much less than they deserved.

It's been said that we live our lives forward but understand them in reverse. I now understand that the countdown timer on my medical career in Dallas began at the moment of the press conference days after 7/7. And although my life and work have unfolded in ways I never anticipated, I am grateful for the redirection and excited for my ongoing journey. I've learned we must all give ourselves the gift of forgiveness. And I'm learning to accept what my wife is teaching me: that everything happens for us, not to us. That we need to walk with a purpose toward our fears. That our job is to become the best version of who we already are. And that seizing the truth is how we begin to heal.

Back in the Chicago ER, the buzz of patient care continues while the frenetic pace of our trauma team slows at the bedside of our latest gunshot victim. Outside, the curtain of night is rising as Chicago awakens to another day. But these temporal cues are meaningless within the trauma bay, with its fluorescent lights and hum of around-the-clock activity. This is a place out of time.

Of the countless deaths I have pronounced before arriving in Chicago, not once did I stop to observe a moment of silence for the victim. The skinhead with a white power tattoo on his forearm: moved on. The drug dealer with teardrop tattoos and Spanish words I didn't understand: kept working. Gang members, drug dealers, cops, women, children, suicide victims, and more: I never stopped. Not once.

But now? Now I do it every single time.

"Everyone, please pause for a moment of silence."

As we stop our work on the body before us, we are silent for a moment. Doctors, nurses, students, medics, and police officers: we all bow our heads. I don't know what my colleagues do during those moments of silence. It's likely some of them pray, and maybe some of them just take deep breaths. Perhaps others feel annoyed.

I often spend that silence imagining the young man now immobile on the stretcher before us as he was in life: maybe with his friends, laughing and shoving and moving from one adventure to the next. I wonder: Was he a better scholar than he was an athlete? A loner or the center of attention? Was he an avid reader or musician? Did he dream of getting married or having kids or serving in the military?

Sometimes in those moments of silence, I think about all these Black men to whom I am bonded, in life and in death. I think of the enslaved men from whom we are descended, the freed men who migrated, the grandfathers and fathers of ours who survived segregation and healthcare injustice and redlining and underfunded schools and violence of all kinds.

This young Black body before me: he is the reason I am here. His life has ended, while mine goes on. So, if only for a moment, I ask my coworkers to unite in silence to honor this stranger. Together we recognize that tomorrow is never promised, and we honor our shared humanity.

At the end of our moment of silence we resume our work. Each member of the team does their part in removing intravenous lines, disconnecting ventilator tubes, and discarding bloodied equipment. Another Black body to be tagged and bagged. Those closest to him will have a funeral, but his death will not receive any national reckoning.

But it's not true that his story will never be told. I am telling it here. It is a partial story, more about his death than his life. But by reading you know he lived. You know he died. You and I: we can't unknow these things.

Having spoken to the medical examiner, I have a final duty to complete: the death note. It's a final version of this young man's life that I must document. In the medicolegal prose required to satisfy the billing specialists, auditors, and attorneys, I type: *17-year-old male arrived at the University of Chicago trauma center as a level 1 activation in traumatic arrest via ground EMS. Sustained multiple gunshot wounds to the head, torso, and bilateral upper extremities. Reportedly unresponsive in the field and 15 minutes of pre-hospital CPR.*

Lacking any information about his life, I only document his violent death. The gunshot wounds. The traumatic arrest. The time of death. How many of these death notes have I written? I wonder. How many more will I have to write?

The disembodied voice overhead breaks into my typing. It blares with a reminder that although this young life has ended, our work has not. "Code yellow, level 1, multiple GSW to chest and abdomen, traumatic arrest, ETA 4 minutes."

The bodies—they just keep coming. We have to make them stop.

RESOURCES

Author's Note: Here are some resources—books, organizations, and websites—that I found helpful in framing the conversation about racism, violence, and medicine. This is not a comprehensive list, but hopefully you'll find it useful in learning more and becoming involved in advocacy and change.

BOOKS

Alexander, Michelle, *The New Jim Crow: Mass Incarceration in the Age of Color-blindness* (New York: The New Press, 2010).

Anderson, Carol, *The Second: Race and Guns in a Fatally Unequal America* (New York: Bloomsbury, 2021).

Blackmon, Douglas A., *Slavery by Another Name: The Re-Enslavement of Black Americans from the Civil War to World War II* (New York: Anchor, 2008).

Currie, Elliott, *A Peculiar Indifference: The Neglected Toll of Violence on Black America* (New York: Metropolitan Books, 2020).

Dawes, Daniel, *The Political Determinants of Health* (Baltimore: Johns Hopkins University Press, 2020).

Garza, Alicia, *The Purpose of Power: How We Come Together When We Fall Apart* (New York: One World, 2020).

McGhee, Heather, *The Sum of Us: What Racism Costs Everyone and How We Can Prosper Together* (New York: One World, 2021).

Roberts, Dorothy, *Killing the Black Body: Race, Reproduction, and the Meaning of Liberty* (New York: Vintage, 1998).

Rothstein, Richard, *The Color of Law: A Forgotten History of How Our Government Segregated America* (New York: Liveright, 2018).

Thompson, Jamie, *Standoff: Race, Policing, and a Deadly Assault That Gripped a Nation* (New York: Henry Holt, 2020).

Tweedy, Damon, *Black Man in a White Coat: A Doctor's Reflections on Race and Medicine* (New York: Picador, 2015).

Villarosa, Linda, *Under the Skin: The Hidden Toll of Racism on American Lives and on the Health of Our Nation* (New York, Doubleday, 2022).

Washington, Harriet A., *Carte Blanche: The Erosion of Medical Consent* (New York: Columbia Global Reports, 2021).

Washington, Harriet A., *Medical Apartheid: The Dark History of Medical Experimentation on Black Americans from Colonial Times to the Present* (New York: Anchor, 2008).

Winkler, Adam, *Gunfight: The Battle Over the Right to Bear Arms in America* (New York: W. W. Norton & Company, 2013).

ORGANIZATIONS

Brady: United Against Gun Violence: One of the nation's oldest gun violence prevention groups, named in honor of James Brady, who served as White House Press Secretary under President Ronald Reagan until he suffered a gunshot wound to the head during an assassination attempt.

Center for Gun Violence Solutions: Associated with the Johns Hopkins Bloomberg School of Public Health, the Center uses "a public health approach to conduct rigorous scientific research to identify a range of innovative solutions to gun violence. Because gun violence disproportionately impacts communities of color, we ground our work in equity and seek insights from those most impacted on appropriate solutions.

Commonwealth Fund: Founded in 1918, the Commonwealth Fund aims to "promote a high-performing, equitable healthcare system that achieves better access, improved quality, and greater efficiency, particularly for society's most vulnerable, including people of color, people with low income, and those who are uninsured."

Everytown for Gun Safety: The largest gun-violence prevention organization in America.

Giffords: A leader in the movement to end gun violence in America. Led by former Congresswoman Gabrielle Giffords, who was critically injured during a mass shooting at a constituent meeting in 2011.

Robert Wood Johnson Foundation: America's leading philanthropic organization solely dedicated to creating a culture of health.

Satcher Leadership Institute: Founded by the sixteenth U.S. Surgeon General, Dr. David Satcher, the institute's mission is to be the leading transformational force for health equity in policy, leadership development, and research.

The Trace: The Trace is an independent nonprofit journalism project devoted to reporting on gun violence, and calls itself the "only newsroom dedicated to covering gun violence." It is my go-to source for daily updates on firearm-related news, policy, advocacy, and research.

ACKNOWLEDGMENTS

This book began as a few hundred stream-of-consciousness words I thumb-typed on my phone after a session with my therapist. Over the ensuing years, the document spent days, weeks, and sometimes months unopened, while morphing into something greater than I planned. I have more people to thank than I can do justice to; however, I must acknowledge a few.

First, my wife and daughter who endured my early mornings writing and late nights editing. Kathianne pulled extra duty as my biggest cheerleader and unapologetic writing critic. Much of this book is her story and not worth reading without her presence, on the page and beyond. Abeni is everything a proud parent could ask for: talented, loving, and full of potential. She has blessed me with a second set of eyes through which to view the world, and the motivation to leave it in better shape for her to inherit.

Omne trium perfectum is Latin for "all good things come in threes," an apropos saying to describe three people, without whom, this book would not exist. First is Bryan Rigg, who became my de facto writing coach while juggling his own projects, wealth management business, and fatherhood. My sincerest thanks for his selflessness, advice, and unvarnished critique. Second is Bonnie Nadell, my literary agent, who took a chance on this first-time author and scrutinized multiple drafts of my proposal while imploring, "It seems like you're holding something back." Her prodding was the key to unlocking the larger story I had to share. Lastly, Valerie Weaver-Zercher, my editor, who saw the potential of this project during its embryonic stages. She understood my vision, worked through several manuscript revisions, and championed this book from proposal to production.

I am also indebted to the team at Broadleaf Books who believed in this project and brought it to life; Isabel Kuh (my agent's daughter), who spent her time during the pandemic shutdown reviewing book proposals, plucked mine from the heap of submissions and enthusiastically passed it along to her mother; and many other supporters whose absent names do not mean the absence of my gratitude.

Finally, to my father, mother, and sister, Trina, who fact-checked my childhood memories of our world-traveling family and whose influences helped mold me into the person I am today.

Onward.

NOTES

CHAPTER 1

"less than 3 percent of doctors," Stacy Weiner, "Black Men Make Up Less Than 3% of Physicians," AAMC, November 23, 2020, https://tinyurl.com/2u6msb7f.

"Fewer than 10 percent of victims," "Gunshot Wound Head Trauma," American Association of Neurological Surgeons, accessed August 7, 2022, https://tinyurl.com/2wa43fmp.

"histories and policies designed to quarantine Black people," To read more about these policies, see Richard Rothstein, *The Color of Law: A Forgotten History of how Our Government Segregated America* (New York: Liveright, 2018); Elliott Currie, *A Peculiar Indifference: The Neglected Toll of Violence on Black America* (New York: Metropolitan Books, 2020); and Whet Moser, "How Redlining Segregated Chicago, and America," *Chicago Magazine*, accessed July 30, 2022, https://tinyurl.com/ytt3dv99.

"37 percent of gun homicides," Dariush Mozaffarian, David Hemenway, and David S. Ludwig, "Curbing Gun Violence: Lessons from Public Health Successes," *JAMA* 309, no. 6 (2013): 551–52.

" 'white-on-white violence' occurs at the same rate," Rachel E. Morgan, "Race and Hispanic Origin of Victims and Offenders, 2012–15," US Department of Justice, Bureau of Justice Statistics, October 2017.

"more people are shot and killed by police," "Police Shootings Database 2015–2022," *Washington Post*, January 22, 2020, https://tinyurl.com/28k6jjz5; Robert VerBruggen, "Fatal Police Shootings and Race," Manhattan Institute, March 9, 2022, https://tinyurl.com/yeecm3mm.

243

"shootings like these predominantly occur in majority-Black neighborhoods," Champe Barton, et al., "Mass Shootings Are Soaring, With Black Neighborhoods Hit Hardest," *The Trace*, September 3, 2020, https://tinyurl.com/3emux3vp.

"Racism lies around like a loaded weapon," Carol Anderson, *The Second: Race and Guns in a Fatally Unequal America* (New York: Bloomsbury, 2021) 159.

CHAPTER 2

"killing Black children at a much higher rate," "Asthma and African Americans," The Office of Minority Health, US Department of Health and Human Services, accessed August 3, 2022, https://tinyurl.com/25vzpnv8.

"environmental injustice is an ever-present companion," Haley M. Lane, et al., "Historical Redlining Is Associated with Present-Day Air Pollution Disparities in U.S. Cities," *Environmental Science & Technology Letters* 9, no. 4 (March 9, 2022): 345–50, https://doi.org/10.1021/acs.estlett.1c01012.

"putative place as a Black person," Elijah Anderson, *The Cosmopolitan Canopy: Race and Civility in Everyday Life* (New York: W.W. Norton & Company, 2011), 253.

"No word comes close," Randall Kennedy, *Nigger: The Strange Career of a Troublesome Word* (New York: Pantheon Books, 2022); see also Mychal Denzel Smith, "Is Using This Word Ever Okay? And Who Has the Power to Decide?" *Washington Post*, February 18, 2022, https://tinyurl.com/bdep9j9.

CHAPTER 3

"Jim Crow and domestic racialized terror," See "The Freedmen's Bureau," National Archives, August 15, 2016, https://tinyurl.com/5n936c7p; W. E. B. Du Bois, "W. E. B. Du Bois on the Freedmen's Bureau," *Atlantic*, March 1, 1901, https://tinyurl.com/bdz9fdbx.

"emergency medical transport services," "Freedom House: Street Saviors," accessed July 30, 2022, http://freedomhousedoc.com/main_page.html; Tanvi Misra, "The Forgotten Story of America's First EMT Services," Bloomberg, March 3, 2015, https://tinyurl.com/3r4abnbz.

"the world's greatest democracy fought the world's greatest racist," Stephen E. Ambrose, *Citizen Soldiers: The US Army from the Normandy Beaches to the Bulge to the Surrender of Germany* (New York: Simon & Schuster, 1998), 304.

"the benefits were denied," Erin Blakemore, "How the GI Bill's Promise Was Denied to a Million Black WWII Veterans," *HISTORY*, June 21, 2019, https://tinyurl.com/5n9ykfjr.

"The racial health gap persists," Kayla Holgash, "Racial and Ethnic Disparities in Medicaid: An Annotated Bibliography," n.d., accessed August 3, 2022.

"white family had eight times the wealth," Neil Bhutta, et al., "Disparities in Wealth by Race and Ethnicity in the 2019 Survey of Consumer Finances," FEDS Notes, September 28, 2020, https://tinyurl.com/53ybu7cd.

"one of the worst racial injustices," Linda J. Bilmes and Cornell William Brooks, "The GI Bill Was One of the Worst Racial Injustices of the 20th Century. Congress Can Fix It," *Boston Globe*, February 23, 2022, https://tinyurl.com/yc4hfuhp.

"death on Black Americans," Andis Robeznieks, "Inequity's Toll for Black Americans: 74,000 More Deaths a Year," American Medical Association, February 22, 2021, https://tinyurl.com/yxybnsy8.

CHAPTER 4

"the AR-15 was the weapon of choice," Jennifer Mascia, "What Is an AR-15 Rifle, Exactly?," *The Trace*, June 7, 2022, https://tinyurl.com/ydfa5srb.

"committed to defending Black people," Kekla Magoon, *Revolution in Our Time: The Black Panther Party's Promise to the People* (Somerville, MA: Candlewick Press, 2021), 44.

"called guns a 'ridiculous way to solve problems,'" Adam Winkler, "The Secret History of Guns," *Atlantic*, September 2011, https://tinyurl.com/yc79289r.

"built on false assumptions and racist tropes," James Forman, Jr., *Locking Up Our Own: Crime and Punishment in Black America* (New York: Farrar, Straus & Giroux, 2017); see also Carroll Bogert and LynNell Hancock, "Analysis: How the Media Created a 'Superpredator' Myth that Harmed a Generation of Black Youth," *NBC News*, November 20, 2020, https://tinyurl.com/r3ssaxe2.

"A riot is a language of the unheard," The Martin Luther King, Jr. Center for Nonviolent Social Change, "MLK: The Other America," Video, YouTube, July 2, 2015, https://tinyurl.com/5h5ey744.

CHAPTER 5

"balancing resident autonomy with patient safety," Miles Moffeit, et al., "UT Southwestern Faculty Let Unsupervised Resident Doctors Operate at Parkland," *Dallas Morning News*, August 1, 2010, https://tinyurl.com/56xbd62t.

"buried beneath the Medical College of Georgia," "Buried Medical School Bodies Give Glimpse of Lost Profession," Associated Press, August 9, 1989, https://tinyurl.com/2s47nact.

"medical students stole the corpses of recently deceased Black people," Allison Meier, "Grave Robbing, Black Cemeteries, and the American Medical School," *JSTOR Daily*, August 24, 2018, https://tinyurl.com/w4vbaujw.

"unregulated industry supplying cadavers," "The Body Trade: Cashing In on the Donated Dead," A Reuters Series, *Reuters*, accessed August 4, 2022, https://tinyurl.com/28nkbnfn.

"bodies are 'traded as raw materials,' " "The Body Trade: Cashing In on the Donated Dead," A Reuters Series, *Reuters*, accessed August 4, 2022, https://tinyurl.com/5y7s5e6x.

"wealthy, white, male physician," Anna Flagg, "The Black Mortality Gap, and a Document Written in 1910," *New York Times*, August 30, 2021, https://tinyurl.com/eekbfrf9.

"discriminated against Black medical schools and doctor-candidates," Abraham Flexner, "Medical Education in the United States and Canada," *Carnegie Foundation for the Advancement of Teaching*, 1910.

"recommending closure of five of the seven Black medical schools," Elizabeth Hlavinka, "Racial Bias in Flexner Report Permeates Medical Education Today," *Medpage Today* (blog), June 18, 2020, https://tinyurl.com/mnb5rjya.

"Fewer Black men entered medical school," See Alicia Gallegos, "AAMC Report Shows Decline of Black Males in Medicine," *AAMC*, December 31, 2018, https://tinyurl.com/4y677p6p; Liz Tung, "3000 by 2000: A History of the Visionary Campaign to Diversify Med Schools, and What Got in Its Way" (National Public Radio, March 12, 2021), https://whyy.org/segments/3000-by-2000/; and Usha Lee McFarling, "After 40 Years, Medical Schools Are Admitting Fewer Black Male or Native American Students," *STAT*, April 28, 2021, https://tinyurl.com/27ervb2k.

"larger-than-life portraits of surgeon-icons," Their photos, along with those of other white male luminaries, were removed in 2018 to place more visible focus on diversity; see Liz Kowalczyk, "In an About-Face, Hospital Will Disperse Portraits of Past White Male Luminaries, Put the Focus on Diversity," *Boston Globe*, June 14, 2018, https://tinyurl.com/5dtyjuw3.

"epithet that generates epithets," Randall Kennedy, *Nigger: The Strange Career of a Troublesome Word* (New York: Pantheon Books, 2022), 59.

"why it was necessary to have a nigger in the first place," James Baldwin, interview with K. Clark, in F. L. Standley and L. H. Pratt, eds., *Conversations with James Baldwin* (Jackson: University Press of Mississippi, 1963), 45; see also Raoul Peck, "I Am Not Your Negro," 2016 documentary.

CHAPTER 6

"160 Black Americans were lynched," "African American Perspectives," The Library of Congress, accessed August 4, 2022, https://tinyurl.com/4nhspy7v.

"formally apologized for its treatment of Black doctors and patients," American Medical Association, "Address to National Medical Association Annual Meeting," July 30, 2008.

"control Black women's reproductive lives," Dorothy E. Roberts, *Killing the Black Body: Race, Reproduction, and the Meaning of Liberty* (New York: Vintage Books, 1999), Kindle Loc 122.

"denied 600 Black men therapeutic penicillin," See "The US Public Health Service Syphilis Study at Tuskegee," CDC, April 22, 2021, https://www.cdc.gov/tuskegee/index.html; and Jean Heller, "AP Exposes the Tuskegee Syphilis Study: The 50th Anniversary," Associated Press, July 25, 2022, https://tinyurl.com/4k3tpban.

"a study of non-therapeutic, whole-body irradiation," "Cold War Radiation Test on Humans To Undergo a Congressional Review," *New York Times*, Apr 11, 1994, https://tinyurl.com/34b8efbn.

"experimentation on Black people," Harriet A. Washington, *Medical Apartheid: The Dark History of Medical Experimentation on Black Americans from Colonial Times to the Present* (New York: Anchor, 2008).

"not accidental but by design," Harriet A. Washington, *Carte Blanche: The Erosion of Medical Consent* (New York: Columbia Global Reports, 2021), 97.

247

William B. Feldman, Spencer Phillips Hey, and Aaron S. Kesselheim, "A Systematic Review of The Food and Drug Administration's 'Exception From Informed Consent' Pathway," *Health Affairs* 37, no. 10 (October 2018): 1605–14, https://doi.org/10.1377/hlthaff.2018.0501.

CHAPTER 7

"our marriage would have been illegal," Evan Andrews, "The Green Book: The Black Travelers' Guide to Jim Crow America," *HISTORY*, February 6, 2017, https://tinyurl.com/nhvjfuza.

"the highway system was a tool of a segregationist agenda," Deborah N. Archer, " 'White Men's Roads through Black Men's Homes': Advancing Racial Equity through Highway Reconstruction," *Vanderbilt Law Review* 73, no. 5 (October 2020).

"gentrification followed the highway," Peter Simek, "The Racist Legacy of America's Inner-City Highways," *D Magazine*, March 18, 2016, https://tinyurl.com/yvtjdsca.

"attempt to pass meaningful federal gun safety legislation," Robert Draper, "Inside the Power of the N.R.A.," *New York Times*, December 12, 2013, https://tinyurl.com/y2a4y8vu.

CHAPTER 11

"State power has only increased their vulnerability," Marc L. Hill, *Nobody: Casualties of America's War on the Vulnerable, from Ferguson to Flint and Beyond* (New York: Atria Books, 2016), XIX.

"streets and neighborhoods as battlefields," Radley Balko, *Rise of the Warrior Cop: The Militarization of America's Police Forces* (PublicAffairs, 2021), Kindle Loc 122.

CHAPTER 12

"used a robot to kill a suspect," For a comprehensive account of the tragedy and aftermath of July 7, 2016, see Jamie Thompson, *Standoff: Race, Policing, and a Deadly Assault That Gripped a Nation* (New York: Henry Holt, 2020).

"Black man who police misidentified as a suspect," For more on what Mark Hughes faced, see Thompson, *Standoff*.

"I want to kill white cops," David O. Brown and Michelle Burford, *Called to Rise: A Life in Faithful Service to the Community That Made Me* (New York: Ballantine Books, 2017), 227.

CHAPTER 13

"Dallas Chief of Police David Brown, and another Black man," Ben Guarino, "Man Falsely Connected to the Shooting by Dallas Police Is Now Getting 'Thousands' of Death Threats," *Washington Post,* July 8, 2016, https://tinyurl.com/2sjtwrbn.

CHAPTER 14

"another live town hall, this time on ABC with President Obama," For more on this whirlwind tour, see Kathianne's 2016 blog series "Accidental Activists" http://nourishcreatebloom.blogspot.com/2016/07/accidental-activists-part-1.html; http://nourishcreatebloom.blogspot.com/2016/07/accidental-activists-part-2_20.html; and http://nourishcreatebloom.blogspot.com/2016/07/unexpected-activists-part-3.html.

"Black physicians who quit or were fired," Pringl Miller, "The Irony of DEI During the Fall of Black Doctors," *MedPageToday*, April 9, 2021, https://tinyurl.com/yy4ntcew.

CHAPTER 15

"human resources avenues to report racism," Quoted in Martha Hostetter and Sarah Klein, "Confronting Racism in Health Care," Commonwealth Fund, October 18, 2021, https://tinyurl.com/mrx8j6se.

CHAPTER 16

"50 percent of the gun violence in Chicago," University of Chicago Crime Lab analysis of City of Chicago Violence Reduction Dashboard data on September, 12, 2022.

"more than 80 percent of the gun homicides," City of Chicago, Office of the Mayor, "Our City, Our Safety: A Comprehensive Plan to Reduce Violence in Chicago," 2020; D. W. Rowlands and Hanna Love, "Mapping Gun

Violence: A Closer Look at the Intersection between Place and Gun Homicides in Four Cities," Brookings Institution, April 21, 2022, https://tinyurl.com/35vzv7xt; and "Gun Crimes Heat Map," Chicago, accessed August 3, 2022, https://tinyurl.com/3t92yxdr.

"thirty-year decrease in life expectancy," "Life Expectancy by ZIP Code: Where You Live Affects How Long You Live," Robert Wood Johnson Foundation, accessed August 29, 2022, https://tinyurl.com/b8aem3dm.

"two miles' distance could mean a twenty-six-year difference in life expectancy," See, for Dallas: Will Maddox, "Two Miles in Dallas Improves Men's Life Expectancy by 26 Years," D Magazine, March 5, 2019, https://tinyurl.com/46t2hnt7; for Atlanta: Andy Miller, "Between Buckhead and Bankhead, Life Expectancy Has a 25-Year Gap," Kaiser Health News, October 6, 2018, https://tinyurl.com/2p8zrxmb; for Boston: Story Hinckley, Hanyang Dong, and Yinglong Chen, "A City Divided in Life and Death," The Margins, Northeastern University, July 30, 2022, https://tinyurl.com/yck7p25r; and for Tampa: American Heart Association Tampa Bay, 2022, https://tinyurl.com/2s4bvhur.

"Your neighborhood shouldn't influence," "Large Life Expectancy Gaps in U.S. Cities Linked to Racial & Ethnic Segregation by Neighborhood," NYU Langone Health, June 5, 2019, https://tinyurl.com/2ym224p4.

"disparities in geographic access to trauma centers," Elizabeth Tung, et al., "Race/Ethnicity and Geographic Access to Urban Trauma Care." *JAMA Network Open* 2, no. 3 (2019): e190138-e190138.

"more likely to be located in a trauma desert," Tung, et al., "Race/Ethnicity."

"hospitals in areas with higher shares of minorities," Yu-Chu Shen, et al., "Understanding the Risk Factors of Trauma Center Closures," *Medical Care* 47, no. 9 (2009): 968–78.

"COVID mortality rate for Black people," Maritza Vasquez Reyes, "The Disproportionate Impact of COVID-19 on African Americans," *Health and Human Rights* 22, no. 2 (December 2020): 299–307.

"two times higher odds of COVID-19 positivity," Elizabeth Tung, et al., "Association of Neighborhood Disadvantage with Racial Disparities In COVID-19 Positivity In Chicago," *Health Affairs* 40, no. 11 (2021): 1784–91.

"firearm homicides eclipse the highest level," Scott R. Kegler, "Vital Signs: Changes in Firearm Homicide," *Morbidity and Mortality Weekly Report* 71 (May 12, 2022).

"record numbers of bullet-ridden bodies," Don Babwin, "Chicago Ends 2020 with 769 Homicides as Gun Violence Surges," Associated Press, April 21, 2021.

"presidents were enslavers," Julie Weil, "Who Owned Slaves in Congress? A List of 1,800 Enslavers in Senate, House History," *Washington Post*, January 10, 2022.

"still ranks near the bottom," See Daniel E. Dawes, *The Political Determinants of Health* (Baltimore: Johns Hopkins University Press, 2020), 9; and "U.S. Health Care from a Global Perspective, 2019: Higher Spending, Worse Outcomes?" Commonwealth Fund, January 30, 2020, https://tinyurl.com/47dzswcv.

"compared to other high-wealth nations," United Health Foundation and American Public Health Association, "International Comparison Annual Report 2020," America's Health Rankings, accessed August 5, 2022.

"tied to where we live, work, learn, worship, and play," Sandro Galea, "The Public Health Spending Mismatch." Public Health Post, December 12, 2016, https://tinyurl.com/3x34drnr.

"The United States ranks last," "Maternal Mortality in the United States: A Primer," Commonwealth Fund, December 16, 2020, https://tinyurl.com/5m8scr32.

"20 percent of our gross domestic product to healthcare," "Defense Spending as a % of Gross Domestic Product (GDP)." n.d. Defense.gov. Accessed October 12, 2022. https://tinyurl.com/534a6rtn.

"still underperform on nearly every metric," Eric C. Schneider, et al., "Mirror, Mirror 2021: Reflecting Poorly." Commonwealth Fund, August 4, 2021, https://tinyurl.com/mrync32u.

"resisted attempts at government-sponsored health insurance," "Medical Care for the American People: The Final Report of the Committee on the Costs of Medical Care," Adopted October 31, 1932. US Department of Health, Education, and Welfare, Public Health Service, Health Services and Mental Health Administration, Community Health Service, 1970.
Also see Clifford Marks, "Inside the American Medical Association's Fight Over Single-Payer Health Care." *New Yorker*, February 22, 2022, https://tinyurl.com/ev5438zz.

"closure of several predominantly Black medical training institutions," See Usha Lee McFarling, "20 Years Ago, a Landmark Report Spotlighted Systemic Racism in Medicine. Why Has so Little Changed?," *STAT*, February 23,

2022; and Anna Flagg, "The Black Mortality Gap, and a Document Written in 1910," *New York Times*, August 30, 2021.

"healthcare prisoners receive is often exceedingly substandard," See https://tinyurl.com/svbypm5n.

"called for a national health service," Minor/Third Party Platforms, Progressive Party Platform of 1912 Online by Gerhard Peters and John T. Woolley, The American Presidency Project, https://www.presidency.ucsb.edu/node/273288.

"the health and vitality of our people," Megan Slack, "From the Archives: President Teddy Roosevelt's New Nationalism Speech," Obama White House Archives, 2011.

"doom the entire plan from the start," Heather McGhee, *The Sum of Us: What Racism Costs Everyone and How We Can Prosper Together* (New York: Random House, 2021), 61.

"Medicaid provides coverage," To learn more about Medicare, visit medpac.gov. For information about Medicaid, visit macpac.gov.

"the single most important piece of healthcare legislation in American history," David Blumenthal and James Morone. *The Heart of Power: Health and Politics in the Oval Office* (Berkeley: University of California Press, 2010), 163.

"Johnson's signing of the Medicare and Medicaid Act of 1965," "Racial and Ethnic Disparities in Medicaid: An Annotated Bibliography," Medicaid and CHIP Payment and Access Commission, 2021.

"States establish their own eligibility standards," Medicaid and CHIP Payment and Access Commission. n.d. "Medicaid 101." MACPAC, https://www.macpac.gov/medicaid-101/.

"81.9 million people across the United States," "May 2022 Medicaid and CHIP Enrollment Trends Snapshot," Centers for Medicaid and Medicare Services, https://tinyurl.com/ycxxw8t7.

"President Biden signed the Inflation Reduction Act," "Congressional Budget Office Cost Estimate," 2022. Estimated Budgetary Effects of Public Law 117-169. Congressional Budget Office Cost Estimate, https://tinyurl.com/57uzhvcf.

"effort to repeal failed," For more on the evolution of US healthcare reform see Blumenthal and Morone, *The Heart of Power*, Michael E. Porter and Elizabeth O. Teisberg, *Redefining Health Care: Creating Value-based Competition on Results* (Cambridge, MA: Harvard Business School Press, 2006).

"access to affordable, high-quality healthcare varies widely," Adina Marx "Health and Racial Justice: Untangling Why It Is So Difficult to Make Progress," Families USA, February 15, 2022, https://tinyurl.com/t8ywvrsb.

"race and ethnicity remain significant predictors," Institute of Medicine, "Unequal Treatment: Confronting Racial and Ethnic Disparities in Health Care," The National Academies Press, n.d.

"reviewing patient safety according to eleven different indicators," Anuj Gangopadhyaya, "Do Black and White Patients Experience Similar Rates of Adverse Safety Events at the Same Hospital?" Urban Institute, July 20, 2021.

CHAPTER 17

"many of them actually unfold gradually," Raghavendra L Girijala and Ruth L Bush, "Review of Socioeconomic Disparities in Lower Extremity Amputations: A Continuing Healthcare Problem in the United States," *Cureus*, October 5, 2018, https://doi.org/10.7759/cureus.3418.

"If a patient cannot afford insulin," Hamlet Gasoyan, et al., "Disparities In Diabetes-Related Lower Extremity Amputations in The United States: A Systematic Review," *Health Affairs* 41, no. 7 (2022): 985–93.

"technologies underperform in Black and Brown people," Itai Bavli and David S. Jones. "Race Correction and the X-Ray Machine—The Controversy over Increased Radiation Doses for Black Americans in 1968." *New England Journal of Medicine* 387, no. 10 (2022): 947–52.

"understanding the factors, systems, or structures (laws and policies)," Dawes, *The Political Determinants of Health*, 13.

"Structural racism is a form of violence," Johan Galtung, "Violence, Peace, and Peace Research," *Journal of Peace Research* 6, no. 3 (September 1969): 167–91.

"racism contributes to worse mental and physical health," Y Paradies, et al., "Racism as a Determinant of Health: A Systematic Review and Meta-Analysis," *PLoS One* September 23;10(9);

Christine Vestal, "Racism Is a Public Health Crisis, Say Cities and Counties." The Pew Charitable Trusts, June 15, 2020, https://tinyurl.com/3y2sfkse.

"color-coded maps of every metropolitan area," Rothstein, *The Color of Law*, 51.

"unhidden public policy that explicitly segregated," Rothstein, *The Color of Law*.

"formerly redlined neighborhoods remain impoverished," Bruce Mitchell and Juan Franco, "HOLC 'Redlining' Maps: The Persistent Structure of

Segregation and Economic Inequality," National Community Reinvestment Coalition, 2018.

"health disparities that continue to this day," Rothstein, *The Color of Law.*

"over half of their income on housing," Matthew Desmond, *Evicted: Poverty and Profit in the American City* (New York: Crown, 2017), 4.

"eliminating opportunity gaps," Diane Ravitch, *Reign of Error: The Hoax of the Privatization Movement and the Danger to America's Public Schools* (New York: Alfred A. Knopf, 2013).

"five social determinants of health," For more social determinants of health, see this helpful site: "Social Determinants of Health: Healthy People 2030," Office of Disease Prevention and Health Promotion. Accessed August 16, 2022.

"Neighborhood, education, and economic stability," "About Social Determinants of Health (SDOH)." n.d. Centers for Disease Control and Prevention. Accessed October 2, 2022. https://www.cdc.gov/socialdeterminants/about.html.

"racial and gender disparities for Black men and women," W. E. B. Du Bois, *The Philadelphia Negro: A Social Study* (Philadelphia: University of Pennsylvania, 1899).

"important role non-clinicians could play," David R. Williams and Michelle Sternthal, "Understanding Racial-Ethnic Disparities in Health: Sociological Contributions," *Journal of Health and Social Behavior* 51, no. 1_suppl (March 2010): S15–27.

"human suffering has been viewed with such peculiar indifference," Du Bois, *The Philadelphia Negro.*

"the power of such narratives," Carol E. Anderson, *White Rage: The Unspoken Truth of Our Racial Divide* (New York: Bloomsbury, 2016), 4.

"communities of opportunity," See Ai-jen Poo Aditi Vaidya, "Why Community Power Is Fundamental to Advancing Racial and Health Equity—National Academy of Medicine," *NAM Perspectives*, June 13, 2022; Paul Speer Manuel Pastor, "Community Power and Health Equity: Closing the Gap between Scholarship and Practice—National Academy of Medicine," *NAM Perspectives*, June 13, 2022; and Lili Farhang and Xavier Morales, "Building Community Power to Achieve Health and Racial Equity: Principles to Guide Transformative Partnerships with Local Communities—National Academy of Medicine," *NAM Perspectives*, June 13, 2022.

"reduce the burden of endemic violence," Currie, *A Peculiar Indifference*, 180.

"racism as a public health threat," Centers for Disease Control and Prevention. 2022. "MMWR, Provisional COVID-19 Age-Adjusted Death Rates, by Race and Ethnicity—United States, 2020–2021." CDC. https://tinyurl.com/mrwkjze. Rose Wong, "Why Are More Black Americans Dying of COVID-19?" Commonwealth Fund, June 26, 2020, https://tinyurl.com/92www8bw.

"the AMA created a Center for Health Equity," To learn more about the work of the AMA and AAMC to promote racial justice and create health equity, visit: American Medical Association. "AMA Center for Health Equity," American Medical Association. Accessed September 22, 2022. https://tinyurl.com/2xdyt3zs.

"racism a public health crisis," "Racism declarations pass new milestone." July 25, 2022, Public Health Newswire, https://tinyurl.com/2p8juu52.

"whole-of-government equity agenda," "Executive Order On Advancing Racial Equity and Support for Underserved Communities Through the Federal Government." 2021. The White House, https://tinyurl.com/3vnwpr96.

"state-by-state racial and economic disparities in healthcare," "Left Out: Barriers to Health Equity for Rural and Underserved Communities." House Ways and Means Committee, 2020.

"challenges to overturn President Obama's Affordable Care Act," "Supreme Court Rejects ACA Challenge; Law Remains Fully Intact," Health Affairs Blog, June 17, 2021.

"record lows in the number of children living in poverty," "Income, Poverty and Health Insurance Coverage in the United States: 2021," US Census Bureau, 2022, https://tinyurl.com/bddzud2e.

"highest level of health for all people," "CMS Framework for Health Equity 2022–2032." n.d. CMS. Accessed August 16, 2022.

CHAPTER 18

"greater bodily damage," Vincent DiMaio, *Gunshot Wounds: Practical Aspects of Firearms, Ballistics, and Forensic Techniques*, Third Edition (Boca Raton, FL: CRC Press, 2021).

"the damage done by a bullet," David V. Feliciano, Kenneth L. Mattox, and Ernest E. Moore, *Trauma*, Ninth Edition (New York: McGraw Hill Professional, 2020).

"weapon of choice for mass shooters," Scott Pelley, "What Makes the AR-15 Style Rifle the Weapon of Choice for Mass Shooters?" 60 Minutes, *CBS News*, June 13, 2021.

"victims unidentifiable without analyzing DNA," Gina Kolata and C. J. Chivers, "Wounds From Military-Style Rifles? 'A Ghastly Thing to See,'" *New York Times*, March 4, 2018. William Cummings and Bart Jansen, "Why the AR-15 Keeps Appearing at America's Deadliest Mass Shootings," *USA TODAY*, February 15, 2018.

"more guns than people," "There are now more guns than people in America," *Vox*, July 27, 2016, https://tinyurl.com/2n63xz2u.

"The psychological trauma," "Introducing 'Aftershocks,' a Series About Surviving Gun Violence in Chicago," *The Trace*, July 7, 2021.

"survivors suffer from post-traumatic stress," "Nonfatal Gun Violence," The Educational Fund to Stop Gun Violence, https://tinyurl.com/47rhx7e8.

"effects can traumatize neighborhoods," Christina Caron, "What Gun Violence Does to Our Mental Health," *New York Times*, June 3, 2022, https://tinyurl.com/4tkpb3x3.

"annual economic toll of gun violence," Senate Joint Economic Committee, 2022, The Economic Toll of Gun Violence, https://tinyurl.com/5av2mvhb.

"We must view the gun debate through the prism of race," Brandon Hunter-Pazzara, "The Possessive Investment in Guns: Towards a Material, Social, and Racial Analysis of Guns," *Palgrave Communications* 6, no. 1 (May 4, 2020): 1–10; "Episode 181: Race, Stand Your Ground Laws, and Gun Violence," Brady, April 22, 2022; and *Examining the Race Effects of Stand Your Ground Laws and Related Issues*. The United States Commission on Civil Rights. February 2020, https://tinyurl.com/5n6m24wb.

"most gun-owners are white," Kim Parker, et al., "The Demographics of Gun Ownership," Pew Research Center, June 22, 2017, https://tinyurl.com/yzs359r3.

"motivated by the need for self-protection," See Travis Mitchell, "The Demographics of Gun Ownership," *Pew Research Center's Social & Demographic Trends Project*, June 22, 2017; and Deborah Azrael Miller, Lisa Hepburn, David Hemenway, Matthew, "The Stock and Flow of U.S. Firearms: Results from the 2015 National Firearms Survey," n.d., accessed August 5, 2022.

"the most significant terror-related threat," "DHS Draft Document: White Supremacists Are Greatest Terror Threat," *POLITICO*, accessed August 6, 2022.

"archetypes of independent, brave men," Amy Cooter, "Citizen Militias in the U.S. Are Moving toward More Violent Extremism," *Scientific American* 326, vol. 1 (January 1, 2022): 34–41.

"typical media narrative about white shooters," Anthea Butler, "Shooters of Color Are Called 'Terrorists' and 'Thugs.' Why Are White Shooters Called 'Mentally Ill'?" *Washington Post,* June 18, 2015, https://tinyurl.com/5b3vspyp.

"majority of armed demonstrations were driven by far-right activists," Roudabeh Kishi, "Armed Assembly: Guns, Demonstrations, and Political Violence in America," Armed Conflict Location & Event Data Project and Everytown for Gun Safety, August 23, 2021, https://tinyurl.com/8846f9um.

"Domestic Terrorism Prevention Act of 2021," "Text - H.R.350 - 117th Congress (2021–2022): Domestic Terrorism Prevention Act of 2022," n.d. Congress.gov. Accessed August 7, 2022.

"account for nearly two-thirds of firearm homicides in the United States," "The Type of Gun Used in Most US Homicides Is Not an AR-15," *ABC News,* accessed July 30, 2022. "FBI — 2019 Crime in the United States." Uniform Crime Reporting Program. Accessed August 16, 2022.

"lived in fear of their children becoming victims," "One-Third of US Adults Say Fear of Mass Shootings Prevents Them from Going to Certain Places or Events," American Psychological Association, August 15, 2019, https://tinyurl.com/mt72mfst.

"modern stand-your-ground laws," "Stand Your Ground Laws Increase Gun Violence and Perpetuate Racial Disparities," April 2021, https://tinyurl.com/y6f4ahpj.

"Public Safety and Recreational Firearms Use Protection Act of 1994," "Impacts of the 1994 Assault Weapons Ban: 1994–96 (Research in Brief)." Office of Justice Programs, US Department of Justice, 1999. "The Effects of Bans on the Sale of Assault Weapons and High-Capacity Magazines," 2018, RAND Corporation.

"most mass shootings are done with handguns," "Mass Shootings in America," Everytown for Gun Safety Support Fund, November 21, 2020. "Guns Used in Mass Shootings U.S. 2022," Statista.

"this policy, which is responsible for more deaths," Michelle Degli Esposti et al., "Analysis of 'Stand Your Ground' Self-Defense Laws and Statewide Rates of Homicides and Firearm Homicides," *JAMA Network Open* 5, no. 2 (February 21, 2022): e220077, https://doi.org/10.1001/jamanetworkopen.2022.0077.

"Stand Your Ground laws have *increased* deaths," Sarah Childress, "Is There Racial Bias in 'Stand Your Ground' Laws?," *Frontline PBS*, July 31, 2012; "Repeal Stand Your Ground Laws," Everytown for Gun Safety, accessed July 30, 2022, https://tinyurl.com/393bttbr.

"deemed 'justified' by judges and juries five times more often," John Roman, "Race, Justifiable Homicide, and Stand Your Ground Laws," August 2013.

"two times more likely to be convicted," "Race, Justifiable Homicide, and Stand Your Ground Laws," 2013, Urban Institute, https://tinyurl.com/37m8hhmu. "What are "Stand Your Ground Laws?" Brady Campaign. Accessed October 4, 2022, https://tinyurl.com/3r3xay3n.

"Stand Your Ground laws are so protective of white men," "Stand Your Ground Laws Increase Gun Violence and Perpetuate Racial Disparities," 2021, The Educational Fund to Stop Gun Violence, https://tinyurl.com/5fbt6v3k, Page 11.

"Second Amendment does not apply to Black Americans," David A. Graham, "Philando Castile, Alton Sterling, and Why Blacks Are the Second Amendment's Second-Class Citizens," *Atlantic*, July 7, 2016.

"woman purchased the murder weapon," "Gun That Killed Trayvon Martin 'Makes $250,000 for Zimmerman,' " *BBC News*, May 22, 2016.

"Black youth who die during their teenage years," Arionne Nettles, "Black Mothers Are the Real Experts of The Toll of Gun Violence," *New York Times*, May 6, 2021.

"who relive this trauma repeatedly," "Community Violence Intervention," COPS OFFICE, accessed August 4, 2022.

"80 percent of homicides are due to firearms," "Leading Causes of Death – Males – Non-Hispanic Black – United States, 2018," Minority Health, Centers for Disease Control and Prevention. Accessed October 4, 2022, https://tinyurl.com/3abd6e5x.
"Leading Causes of Death – Males – Non-Hispanic White – United States, 2018," Minority Health, Centers for Disease Control and Prevention. Accessed October 4, 2022, https://tinyurl.com/yrut9psj. John Gramlich, "Gun Deaths in the U.S.: 10 Key Questions Answered," Pew Research Center, https://tinyurl.com/yc3re25z.

"idea of 'Black-on-Black crime,'" "Impact of Gun Violence on Black Americans," Everytown for Gun Safety, Accessed August 16, 2022.

"gun violence, is a byproduct of proximity," D. W. Rowlands and Hanna Love, "Mapping Gun Violence: A Closer Look at the Intersection between Place and Gun Homicides in Four Cities," *Brookings*, April 21, 2022.

"twice as likely to commit violent crimes," "Household Poverty and Nonfatal Violent Victimization, 2008–2012," Bureau of Justice Statistics, 2014.

"why some groups of Americans are more affected," Tyler Weingart, "How Social Factors Shape Health: Violence, Social Disadvantage and Health," Robert Wood Johnson Foundation, May 2011.

"Black people are less likely to be armed," Fallis, David, and Danielle Rindler. n.d., "Police shootings database 2015–2022." *Washington Post*, Accessed October 12, 2022, https://tinyurl.com/bdzwh4sb.

"More people are shot and killed by police," Marisa Iati, Steven Rich, and Jennifer Jenkins, "Fatal Police Shootings in 2021 Set Record since The Post Began Tracking, despite Public Outcry," *Washington Post*, February 9, 2022; and 2022. Mapping Police Violence.

"gun violence will require a multilevel effort," Aliza Aufrichtig et al., "Want to Fix Gun Violence in America? Go Local," *Guardian*, January 9, 2017.

"interviewed Black mothers about gun violence," See Arionne Nettles, "Black Mothers Are the Real Experts on the Toll of Gun Violence," *New York Times*, May 6, 2021, https://tinyurl.com/4tuuwr7z.

"the background noise of urban America," Currie, *A Peculiar Indifference*, 6.

CHAPTER 19

"Black residents are dying from the coronavirus," Cecilia Reyes et al., "Chicago's Coronavirus Disparity: Black Chicagoans Are Dying at Nearly Six Times the Rate of White Residents, Data Show," *Chicago Tribune*, April 6, 2020.

"gun violence is breaking records," Ari Davis, et al., "A Year in Review: 2020 Gun Deaths in the U.S." The Johns Hopkins Center for Gun Violence Solutions, April 28, 2022, https://tinyurl.com/8ur7swyw.

"firearm-related homicides will increase," Priya Krishnakumar, "Murders Rose Sharply in 2020 but Data Is Lacking across Much of the Country," *CNN*, September 27, 2021, https://tinyurl.com/y278nvem.

"Black gunshot victims are treated multiple times," "Black Gunshot Survivors Face 'Trauma Recidivism,' " *The Crime Report*, May 2, 2022.

"firearms are the leading cause of death for *all* children and teens," Jason E. Goldstick, Rebecca M. Cunningham, and Patrick M. Carter, "Current Causes of Death in Children and Adolescents in the United States," *New England Journal of Medicine* 386, no. 20 (May 19, 2022): 1955–56.

"big guy with a big heart," Terrence McCoy, " 'It Doesn't Seem Real': Family of Slain Dallas Officer Mourns 'Big Guy' with 'Big Heart,' " *Washington Post,* July 8, 2016.

"survived three tours in Iraq," John Woodrow Cox, "Officer Patrick Zamarripa Survived Three Tours in Iraq before Being Killed in Dallas," *Washington Post,* July 8, 2016.

"one of the good guys," " 'One of the Good Guys': Michael Smith Had Been a Dallas Police Officer for 25 Years," *Washington Post,* accessed July 30, 2022.